FOREIGN RELATIONS

AMERICA IN THE WORLD

SERIES EDITORS

Sven Beckert and Jeremi Suri

ALSO IN THE SERIES

FOREIGN RELATIONS

American Immigration in Global Perspective

Donna R. Gabaccia

PRINCETON UNIVERSITY PRESS

PRINCETON AND OXFORD

Copyright © 2012 by Princeton University Press

Published by Princeton University Press, 41 William Street, Princeton, New Jersey 08540

In the United Kingdom: Princeton University Press, 6 Oxford Street, Woodstock, Oxfordshire OX20 1TW

press.princeton.edu

Jacket Photograph: *Ellis Island Immigrants,* circa 1907. © Bain News Service/Gary Lucken. Courtesy of fotoLibra.

ISBN 978-0-691-13419-2

Library of Congress Cataloging-in-Publication Data

Gabaccia, Donna R., 1949–
    Foreign relations : American immigration in global perspective / Donna R. Gabaccia.
        p. cm. — (America in the world)
    Includes bibliographical references and index.
    ISBN 978-0-691-13419-2 (hardcover : alk. paper)
    1. United States—Emigration and immigration—History.
    2. Globalization—United States—History.   I. Title.
    JV6450.G22   2012
    304.8'73—dc23
                                                                    2011035173

British Library Cataloging-in-Publication Data is available

This book has been composed in
Adobe Caslon Pro with Trade Gothic Display

Printed on acid-free paper. ∞

Printed in the United States of America

1 3 5 7 9 10 8 6 4 2

In memory of
Julie Marie Gabaccia McKenna,
April 24, 1951–November 2, 2007

CONTENTS

PREFACE

As a resident fellow participating in the 2000–2001 "Global America" Seminar at Harvard University's Warren Center, I first began to acknowledge the conceptual ground shared by diplomatic historians and historians of U.S. immigration. Both groups were responding to the same end-of-a-millennium challenges posed by globalization theory and global studies of various kinds. During that wonderful year in Cambridge, I also began to imagine a U.S. history viewed from the territory these two groups of historians share.

Sven Beckert, editor of the series America in the World, worked hard to convince me to make these imaginings concrete and to write a short book—an extended interpretative essay, really—aimed at students and general readers and covering the long term of U.S. history, from the days of the early American republic to the present. My goal was not to provide a synthesis, but instead to nurture an emerging field of scholarly inquiry with provocative new perspectives.

By 2006, when Sven first contacted me, I knew what a difficult task it would be to bring diplomatic and immigration histories together. Diplomatic historians had been deeply engaged for fifteen years in developing a new field called international history, which focuses on the international relations created by both state and nongovernmental actors, while immigration historians had for a decade increasingly imagined themselves writing transnational histories, which focus on how migrants conduct lives in two or more countries. While both international and transnational histories produce global perspectives, the two do not share a common intellectual agenda. In the first, governments remain key agents of change, while in the second, nation states sometimes fade completely from view. Social, cultural, and demographic histories of immigration and of the making of an American nation, even when written from a transnational perspective, rarely devote much attention to international relations or diplomacy. Historians who focus on international relations often completely ignore migration. Both too easily dismiss immigration policy as a domestic matter. While historians who view U.S. history from global perspectives—notably Thomas Bender, Carl Guarneri, David Thelen, and Ian Tyrell—recognize immigration and diplomacy as linkages between the United States and the world, none ponders, as I do, how immigrants' transnational lives intersect with the international relations pursued by the American government.

As my enthusiasm for tackling the challenge of this short book for general readers grew, I also entered what became the saddest years of my life. I made progress with the writing of this book only with considerable and excellent assistance from Minnesota Ph.D. students Erika Cardenas-Busse, Nate Holdren, Johanna Leinonen, Lisong Liu, and Elizabeth Zanoni. I can now also thank two anonymous readers and my patient Princeton University Press editor, Brigitta van Rheinberg. I especially appreciate the collegiality and generosity of Nando Fasce, Torsten Feys, Dirk Hoerder, Drew Keeling, Erika Lee, Adam McKeown, and Pierre-Yves Saunier, who shared unpublished work or read early drafts. I am happy, too, that Angelina Strambi Welk described again the Gabaccia family's history of relations to other countries.

And how lucky I was to receive invitations from John Gillis and Carl Guarneri to talk about the book just as I began in all earnestness to write it! An equally welcome invitation, from the Society for Historians of Foreign Relations (SHAFR) program co-chairs Naoka Shibusawa and Anne Foster, arrived just as I was starting the first round of revisions. I thank the participants in the 2007 NEH Summer Institute, "Rethinking America in Global Perspective" and in the 2010 SHAFR program, "Crossing Boundaries: Foreign Relations and Transborder Histories," for their probing and often difficult questions.

Finally, I am indebted beyond measure to wise neighbors. Long walks with Jeffrey Pilcher around Minneapolis's Lake of the Isles helped me to accept the hard choices of my sister, Julie, to whom this book is dedicated with feelings, still, of unspeakable sorrow and loss.

FOREIGN RELATIONS

INTRODUCTION

Policy debates in the United States today treat immigration almost exclusively as a domestic problem that must be solved, somehow, with the passage by Congress of better laws. Americans repeatedly debate what those laws should be. Yet laws that treat immigration as a purely domestic problem are likely to fail. Why? Because immigration is an important, continuous, and contentious relationship between the United States and rest of the world. With this book, I suggest that immigration policies might better be debated from a global rather than a domestic perspective.

Of course, immigration is just one of many connections between the United States and the world, and over the past two decades historians have enthusiastically written transnational, international, and global histories to explore those connections. Unlike many historians who write about the United States from a global perspective, I will not try to analyze or to assess the entire tangle of economic, social, and cultural connections that constitute a global America. I will focus steadfastly on the intersection of transnational linkages created "from below" by immigrants—I will call these "immigrant foreign relations"—and American international or foreign policies, created "from above" by the federal government. Immigrants, much like diplomats and State Department officials in Washington, are deeply concerned with the world beyond U.S. borders. Their interest in their own foreign relations finds expression in the memoirs they write; such accounts most often suggest that the global perspectives of immigrants differ from, conflict with, and diverge from those of both diplomats and other Americans. Studies of official American foreign relations, by contrast, occasionally point to moments when the global perspectives of immigrants and of the executive branch encourage them to become political allies in domestic struggles with Congress or with coalitions of American voters over the implementation and direction of the official foreign policies of the United States.

Immigrant foreign relations originate in the reality that almost all immigrants remain connected to the people and places they supposedly left behind when emigrating. Initially, their connections may be limited to private, social networks of family, kin, and friends. Immigrants are often, quite literally, the foreign relatives of Americans: many—and at times even the majority—of immigrants have migrated to the United States in order to join friends or members of their own families. Once arrived, the newcomers encourage others to join them, thus continuing a practice that scholars have long labeled "chain migration" or "family unification." Chain migration creates a unique and changing geography of foreign places and foreign peoples connected to the United States; this geography has become more extensive and global over time. Nevertheless, scholars more often label immigration as transnational rather than international. In the early 1990s transnational theorists imagined that the migrants' social relations revealed the declining power of nation states in a globalizing world; some predicted that proliferating transnational relations were undermining the importance of national governments and nation states, rendering them irrelevant. I demonstrate instead that no one understands better than immigrants the continuing power of national governments to draw borders and to set rules for crossing them. Immigrants experience the power of nation states in an extremely intimate fashion, sometimes on a daily basis.

Because humans typically form deep, sentimental attachments to the places where they and their ancestors were born—immigrants are not different in this regard from other Americans—immigrants' personal ties to people in foreign lands have often persisted over several generations. Their lives thus challenge sociological theories of swift or straightline assimilation that measure Americanization as the progressive abandonment of social and cultural connections to foreign lands.

Because they are deeply felt, immigrant foreign relations can also at times extend into the public arena as political mobilizations, whether in the United States or transnationally. Immigrants' power to mobilize varies with their gender, race, and class, but even poor, female, and racially stigmatized immigrants have at times collaborated across borders, for example in attempts to influence the politics and governance of their homelands. Immigrants have also repeatedly mobilized as residents and as naturalized citizen voters in the United States. Their goals in mobilizing are not always domestic. On the contrary, immigrants often seek to influence American policy toward their countries of origin or to influence the immigration policies that inevitably shape the lives, decisions, and transnational moves of their friends and relatives.

In the United States, the intersection of immigrant foreign relations with the far-better-known history of American diplomacy becomes most visible in domestic political struggles over some of the main themes of global history—that is, in the areas of foreign trade and investment, empire-building, warfare, and geopolitics. Collectively these struggles illustrate a central tension historians have observed between Americans' desire for isolation from a world that they perceive as somehow dangerous and the obvious global activism of the U.S. government, particularly in the twentieth century. Domestic debates about global matters can and have transformed immigrants and their foreign relations from welcome friends and allies into dangerous enemy aliens. A focus on the intersection of immigrant foreign relations and American international relations reveals clearly that immigration has never been a purely domestic matter. Global perspectives on American immigration provide the foundation for pondering why efforts to control immigration through domestic legislation are likely to fail.

DOMESTIC AND GLOBAL HISTORIES OF U.S. IMMIGRATION

Figure 1 and table 1 serve to introduce readers to the time-worn outlines of U.S. immigration history. In data like this, historians have found evidence of the purportedly unique racial and ethnic challenges of nation-building in the United States, a country with a long history of quite diverse immigration. That the history of immigration, as traced here, is in fact not so very exceptional—similar figures and tables could easily describe Argentina, France, Canada, Israel, or Singapore as "nations of immigrants"—is a point worth making, even though I offer only fitful comparisons of the United States to other countries in the chapters that follow. Here,

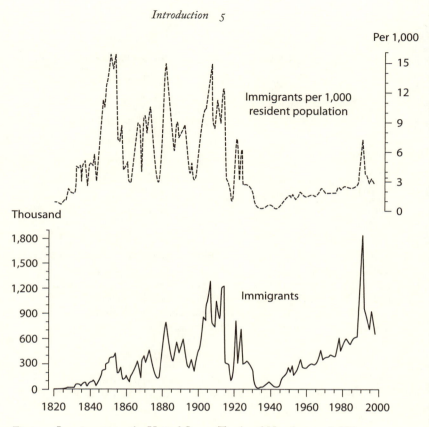

Figure 1. Immigrants to the United States, Total and Number per 1,000 in Resident Population: 1820–1998. Adapted from *Historical Statistics of the United States, Millennial Edition* (Cambridge: Cambridge University Press, 2006).

figure 1 and table 1 are included mainly to tease out the global perspectives buried in their data.

The immigration graphed in figure 1 meant that, between 1850 and 1950 and again after 1980, foreign-born residents of the United States constituted between 10 and 15 percent of the American population. (Chapter 1 will suggest

Table 1. Immigrants, by Continent of Last Residence, 1820–1997

	1820–1849	1850–1924	1924–1965	1966–1997
Europe	90%	87%	52%	15%
Americas	4%	10%	43%	49%
Asia/Pacific	—	3%	5%	33%
Africa-origin				
Caribbean	5%*			
Africa			—	2%
TOTAL	99%	100%	100%	100%

Note: My calculations, based on Susan B Carter, et al., eds., *Historical Statistics of the United States, Millennial Edition* (Cambridge: Cambridge University Press, 2006), Table Ad90-97.

*Immigrants of unknown origin have been excluded from this table, with one exception. To acknowledge the forced mobility of slaves during the antebellum years, I have added an estimated figure for slaves illegally smuggled into the United States after 1808. As with most illegal—and in this case, illegally forced—entries, the exact origins cannot be known. Most, however, including those possibly born in Africa, had been smuggled into the southern states from the nearby Caribbean Islands by slave traders.

that migratory linkages to the rest of the world were just as significant in the late eighteenth century.) In addition, the children of the foreign-born typically constitute an equivalent or somewhat larger segment of the American population. During peak periods of immigration, voluntary immigrants (together, in the past, with a sizable population of enslaved or recently emancipated Americans of African origin) truly built America. But the same numbers suggest that there were many times when 20 to 30 percent of the American population was potentially engaged in immigrant foreign relations. Since a third or more of the white foreign-born, along with all of their children, have throughout American history been citizens and since, over time, naturalization and birth-right citizenship has increasingly empowered foreigners of all backgrounds to participate in American politics, immigrants have also intermittently become very important influences on American politics.

Immigrants built an America that changed in its racial and ethnic composition over time. After the abolition of the slave trade in 1808, migrations from Europe facilitated the building of a white nation. Nineteenth-century immigrants promised to submerge the demographic legacies of the country's colonial origins—represented racially to most Americans by its enslaved African American and conquered indigenous populations—in a sea of new settlers from northern and western Europe. Demands for immigration restriction rose in the second half of the century as an effort to exclude immigrant workers from Asia, initiating what would become a long period of immigration restriction that figure 1 also documents. Even after racial barriers to entry and national belonging were eliminated by civil rights legislation in the mid-1960s, immigrants from Asia, Latin America, and Africa have continued to experience special difficulties in becoming American. This is why domestic accounts of immigration, race, and ethnicity, and of exclusionary and inclusionary nation-building will likely remain important well into the future. Such a history provides a useable past for a nation still confronting issues of racial bias.

An American history written from a global perspective, drawing on exactly the same data as figure 1 and table 1, raises different but equally important questions. Many of these questions are about the dynamics that define relationships between U.S. immigration and foreign trade, the formation of a global economy, American and European empire-building, anti-imperial movements, international warfare, and American geopolitical strategies as they have shifted, collectively, "from isolation to global hegemony."[1] Viewed from a global perspective, the United States comes into focus as an empire builder that created its own empire in the North American West with immigrant settlers and as an independent nation still almost completely embedded— through its immigrants and its foreign trade—in the imperial and Atlantic trading and labor market circuits of its former ruler, Great Britain. As chapter 1 will argue, the United States was independent; but it was not isolated from the global economy and empires of the early nineteenth century. The subsequent expansion of American merchants, investors, and missionaries into Asia and the Americas— accomplished through "dollar diplomacy," through the building of a strong and globally engaged navy and army, and through the acquisition of foreign territories—accompanied the vast international migrations of the late nineteenth and early twentieth centuries. Chapter 2 will argue that the rise of the United States to global leadership rested on expanding industries that in turn depended on the employment of millions of newly arrived immigrant workers, many of them from disintegrating foreign empires on the peripheries of Europe and East Asia. Both American immigration and U.S. empire-building helped to forge an increasingly interconnected global economy, linking closely the Atlantic to the Pacific, already in the years around 1900.

A global interpretation of U.S. immigration also calls attention to the fact that American campaigns for immigration restriction, and the sharp drop in U.S. immigration that followed (as figure 1 shows), unfolded against a backdrop of domestic political struggles over the global role of the United States. The United States built its empire of trade and influence—at first ambivalently and then briefly embracing a more active global role—in the years preceding World War I. After the war, immigration restriction triumphed in the United States as part of a powerful and isolationist congressional backlash against the internationalism of President Woodrow Wilson and his promise to make the world safe for democracy. Emerging from a global depression in the 1930s, American international activism carried a heavy price in the form of recurring and expensive military engagements and foreign wars, a development that chapter 3 portrays as feeding continuing demands by worried American voters for protection, including protection from the threat supposedly posed by immigrant foreigners.

Also visible in figure 1 is the temporary dampening effect on immigration of almost every American war fought prior to 1945. After World War II, by contrast, scattered but often long-term American military engagements—many of them undeclared regional wars—did not prevent the rise of immigration numbers. To understand the changing role of global warfare in shaping American immigration dynamics and policies requires that we pay close attention to the nature of American global leadership. For example, after World War II increasing proportions of the immigrants tracked in figure 1 were either refugees who fled from areas of U.S. military engagement or foreign brides of American soldiers. Table 1 also clearly demonstrates that by the last decades of the twentieth century, the origins of the newest immigrants were in Asia and in Latin America; immigrants, in other words, had come to mirror the geography of an American global empire built through trade, military intervention, and international investment.

Global perspectives raise new questions about the timing, geography, and significance of American immigration. Overall, a history of American immigration written from a global perspective cannot sustain hoary domestic myths of either an isolated United States or independent immigrants easily detached from their origins. It points toward the impact of changing U.S. geopolitics on foreign places, foreigners, and America's borders and toward the transformation of immigration from a foreign to a domestic policy, a story told in chapter 3. It suggests that American global leadership and immigration restriction have linked histories that both draw on rising xenophobia and fears of threats that originate beyond the borders of the United States.

Where did that fear originate? Although the existence of immigrant foreign relations can be documented continuously from the colonial era down to our own times, Americans' awareness of and attitudes toward immigrants and their foreign relations changed dramatically with America's role in the world. Chapter 2 demonstrates that the same theories of "scientific" racism that encouraged American empire-building also fostered hostility toward immigrant foreigners, and especially toward those whose foreign relations connected the United States to countries outside the small circle of the powerful empire-building nations of northern and western Europe. Hostility toward Asian and southern and eastern European immigrants emerged from a complex cocktail of both xenophobia and racism. Xenophobia is arguably a constitutive element of all human societies—since all necessarily distinguish between insiders and outsiders—but

American xenophobia intensified as the United States abandoned its ideological commitment to remaining isolated from the international system of diplomacy and foreign wars that Europe had created in the eighteenth century. Not surprisingly, immigration restriction and hostility to immigrants' transnational political mobilizations became persistent and populist features of American political life as the country's leaders, including Republican Theodore Roosevelt and Democrat Woodrow Wilson, embraced internationalism and American global leadership. By recognizing the importance of xenophobia, this book encourages readers to ponder a late-twentieth-century paradox—that popular hostility to immigrants has outlived the racism that is understood to have motivated immigration restriction.

The persistence of xenophobia in a twenty-first-century world led, if not completely dominated, by a powerful United States, also raises a final troubling question. If, indeed, it was a deeply rooted desire for isolation and protection from a suspect world that exacerbated American hostility to immigrants through the middle years of the twentieth century, why did the United States, as leader of the capitalist free world during the Cold War, again move toward allowing increasing numbers of foreigners—many of them from Asia and Latin America—to enter the country, as both figure 1 and table 1 document? Had Americans finally become so comfortable with their country's global activism that they no longer feared the world beyond its borders? Had immigrants' own political mobilizations played a role in this change? This key question about U.S. immigration policy, provoked by global perspectives, deserves an answer, and chapter 4 will provide one.

AMERICAN FOREIGN POLICY AND IMMIGRANT FOREIGN RELATIONS

Fortunately, there is no need to resort to abstractions in order to answer questions like these, for stories of individual migrants nicely illustrate the complex intersection of immigrant foreign relations and U.S. foreign policies in rich, human detail. Take the case of just one immigrant from China, Yitang Chang, and his family. Historian Haiming Liu has teased the Chang family story from a series of family letters and oral histories covering more than seven decades.[2] Throughout that time, the Chang family sustained their ties to China while responding to, and often also challenging, the official international policies of the United States.

Yitang Chang was a trader in medicinal herbs who departed Hong Kong on the British steamer Strathgyle and arrived in San Diego in July 1900. He disembarked carrying several bolts of silk and perhaps also the thousand dollars that he would soon invest in a Los Angeles business. Rules and practices put in place by the U.S. State Department (the government agency charged with the conduct of foreign affairs) governed Chang's first contacts with the United States. As he entered the offices of Customs Collector William Wallace Bowers, Chang handed the Chinese inspector a folded paper written in two languages; it included his photo (figure 2). Called a "Section Six Certificate" and named after the section of a bilateral treaty that made this certificate a requirement for immigrant merchants, it had been issued to Chang by a diplomat, the U.S. consul in Hong Kong. The purpose of the document was to certify Chang's identity as a merchant.

Hidden and sometimes completely missing from domestic histories of U.S. immigration is a curious detail that nevertheless determined every detail of Chang's entry into the United States. For much of the nineteenth century, it was bilateral commercial treaties negotiated by diplomats to encourage foreign trade that kept U.S. ports open to merchants, their cargo, and their foreign passengers. When Pacific migrations began—soon after the signing of a U.S. trade treaty with China in 1844—angry white Californians, among them many recent immigrants from Ireland, demanded protection from the foreign threat of a "yellow peril" supposedly posed by the racially disparaged Chinese. Western legislatures listened to angry voters, but the U.S. Supreme Court overturned most of the restrictions imposed by state law on the immigrant Chinese. Such laws violated not only the treaties the United States had negotiated with China, but also the constitutional empowerment of Congress, and Congress alone, to regulate foreign trade. Only when Congress—under pressure from western voters—forced President Rutherford Hayes in 1880 to send his diplomat James G. Angell to negotiate a new treaty specifically allowing Congress temporarily to exclude Chinese laborers did Congress begin to insist that immigration was a domestic matter. And even then tensions between Congress and the executive branch simmered for decades, because this treaty with China continued to guarantee reciprocal liberty of movement and residence to Chinese and American merchants, including Yitang Chang.

In the years after 1900, as American dollar diplomacy flourished in Asia under the leadership of presidents and their State Departments, Congress consolidated its control over immigration, wresting it from bilateral treaties and

"Section   it is hereby amended so as to read as follows:—

"SEC. 6.   to the faithful execution of the provisions of this Act, every Chinese person, other than a laborer, who   said Treaty or this Act to come within the United States, and who shall be about to come to the Unite   obtain the permission of and be identified as so entitled b   e Chinese Government, or of such other forei   of which at the time such Chinese person shall be a subject, in each case to be evidenced by a Certificate iss   a Government, which Certificate shall be in the English language, and shall show such permission, with the name of   permitted person in his or her proper signature, and which Certificate shall state the individual family and tribal name in full, title or official rank, if any, the age, height and all physical peculiarities, former and present occupation or profession, when and where and how long pursued, and place of residence of the person to whom the Certificate is issued, and that such person is entitled by this Act to come within the United States. If the person so applying for a Certificate shall be a merchant, said Certificate shall, in addition to above requirements, state the nature, character and estimated value of the business carried on by him prior to and at the time of his application as aforesaid: *Provided*, That nothing in this Act nor in said Treaty shall be construed as c   acing within the meaning of the word 'merchant,' hucksters, peddlers, or those engaged in taking, drying or otherwise preserving shell or other fish for home consumption or exportation. If the Certificate be sought for the purpose of travel for curiosity, it shall also state whether the applicant intends to pass through or travel within the United States, together with his financial standing in the country from which such Certificate is desired. The Certificate provided for in this Act, and the identity of the person named therein, shall, before such person goes on board any vessel to proceed to the United States, be viséd by the indorsement of the diplomatic representatives of United States in the foreign country from which such Certificate issues, or of the Consular representative of the United States at the port or place from which the person named in the Certificate is about to depart; and such diplomatic representative or Consular representative whose indorsement is so required is hereby empowered, and it shall be his duty, before indorsing such Certificate as aforesaid, to examine into the truth of the statements set forth in said Certificate, and if he shall find upon examination that said or any of the statements therein contained are untrue it shall be his duty to refuse to indorse the same. Such Certificate viséd as aforesaid shall be *prima facie* evidence of the facts set forth therein, and shall be produced to the Collector of Customs of the port in the district in the United States at which the person named therein shall arrive, and afterward produced to the proper authorities of the United States whenever lawfully demanded, and shall be the sole evidence permissible on the part of the person so producing the same to establish a right of entry into the United States; but said Certificate may be controverted and the facts therein stated disproved by the United States authorities."

Article 3, of the Treaty between the Government of the United States and the Government of China, proclaimed by the President of the United States on the 8th day of December, 1894, reads as follows:—

The provisions of this Convention shall not affect the right at present enjoyed of Chinese subjects, being officials, teachers, students, merchants or travellers for curiosity or pleasure, but not laborers, of coming to the United States and residing therein. To entitle such Chinese subjects as are above described to admission into the United States, they may produce a Certificate from their Government or the Government where they last resided viséd by the Diplomatic or Consular representative of the United States in the country or port whence they depart.

It is also agreed that Chinese laborers shall continue to enjoy the privilege of transit across the territory of the United States in the course of their journey to or from other countries, subject to such regulations by the Government of the United States as may be necessary to prevent said privilege of transit from being abused.

CHINESE ADMITTED AS MERCHANTS CANNOT BECOME LABORERS.

(Extract of Opinion, U. S. v. Yong Yew, respondent.)

ADAMS, District Judge: * * * "Construing all the legislation on this subject in the light of our internal policy as already stated, I am disposed to hold that the law, properly and effectually construed, contemplates that a "merchant" of China may enter this country and remain here as a merchant only. He may not under guise and pretence of being a merchant, secure entry as such, intending immediately to become and continue a laborer. * * * his (the respondent's) conduct in proceeding immediately to work as a laborer and continuing to do so continuously up to the time of his arrest, belies his pretensions as a merchant. The *prima facie* case made by his certificate is overcome by the facts."

CHINESE TRADERS AND CLERKS NOT ADMITTED.

" It may be stated comprehensively that the result of the above both of these laws and decisions thereon is to determine that the true theory is not that all Chinese persons may enter this country who are not forbidden, but that only those are entitled to enter who are *expressly* allowed."

July 15th, 1898.   (Signed) JOHN W. GRIGGS, *Attorney General.*

" You are, therefore, directed to hereafter refuse admission to all Chinese persons whose occupation or station does not clearly indicate that they are members of the exempt class of Chinese as defined by law, and applicants for admission as persons described as salesmen, clerks, buyers, bookkeepers, accountants, managers, store-keepers, apprentices, agents, cashiers, physicians, proprietors of restaurants, barbers, laundrymen, etc., should be absolutely rejected by you."

July 20th, 1898.   (Signed) W. B. HOWELL, *Asst. Sec. of Treasury.*

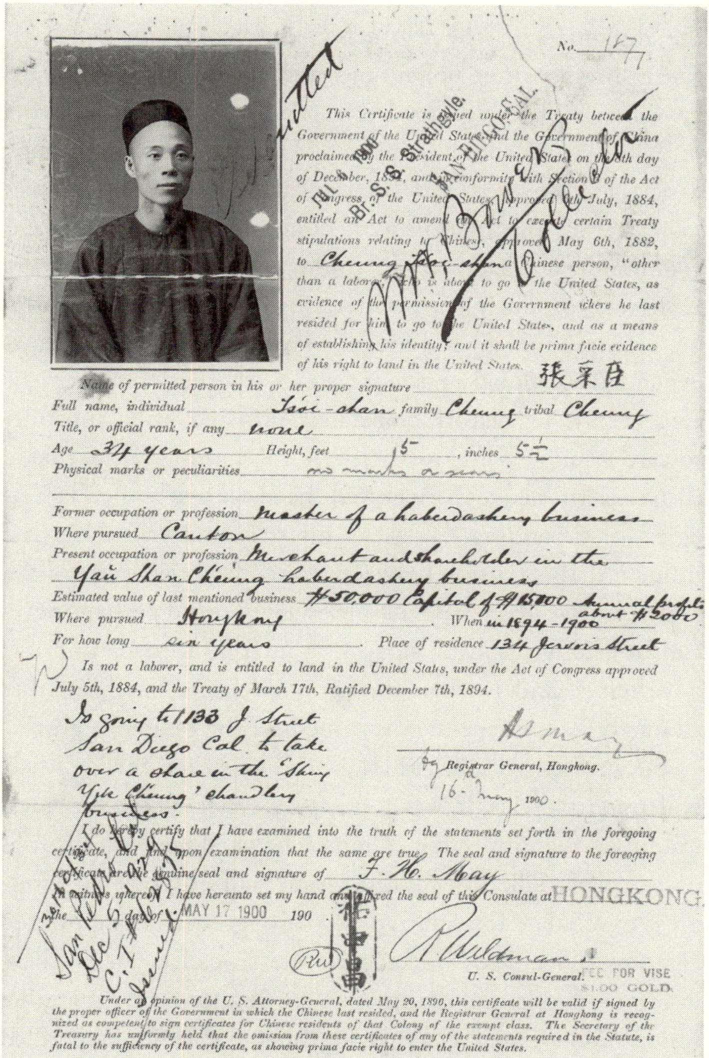
No. 187

This Certificate is issued under the Treaty between the Government of the United States and the Government of China proclaimed by the President of the United States on the 8th day of December, 1894, and in conformity with Section 6 of the Act of Congress of the United States approved 5th July, 1884, entitled an Act to amend an Act to execute certain Treaty stipulations relating to Chinese, approved May 6th, 1882, to Cheung Tsoi-shan *a Chinese person, "other than a laborer," who is about to go to the United States, as evidence of the permission of the Government where he last resided for him to go to the United States, and as a means of establishing his identity; and it shall be prima facie evidence of his right to land in the United States.*

Name of permitted person in his or her proper signature 張采臣

Full name, individual Tsói-shan *family* Cheung *tribal* Cheung

Title, or official rank, if any none

Age 34 years *Height, feet* 5 *, inches* 5½

Physical marks or peculiarities no marks or scars

Former occupation or profession master of a haberdashery business

Where pursued Canton

Present occupation or profession Merchant and shareholder in the Yau Shan Cheung haberdashery business

Estimated value of last mentioned business $50,000 Capital of $15,000 Annual profits about $2000

Where pursued Hongkong *When* in 1894–1900

For how long six years *Place of residence* 134 Jervois Street

Is not a laborer, and is entitled to land in the United States, under the Act of Congress approved July 5th, 1884, and the Treaty of March 17th, Ratified December 7th, 1894.

Is going to 133 J. Street San Diego Cal. to take over a share in the 'Shing Yik Cheung' chandlery business.

Registrar General, Hongkong.

16 – May 1900.

I do hereby certify that I have examined into the truth of the statements set forth in the foregoing certificate, and find upon examination that the same are true. The seal and signature to the foregoing certificate are the genuine seal and signature of F. H. May

In witness whereof I have hereunto set my hand and affixed the seal of this Consulate at HONGKONG

the day of MAY 17 1900 *190*

R. Wildman

U. S. Consul-General. FEE FOR VISE $1.00 GOLD

Under an opinion of the U. S. Attorney-General, dated May 20, 1896, this certificate will be valid if signed by the proper officer of the Government in which the Chinese last resided, and the Registrar General at Hongkong is recognized as competent to sign certificates for Chinese residents of that Colony of the exempt class. The Secretary of the Treasury has uniformly held that the omission from these certificates of any of the statements required in the Statute, is fatal to the sufficiency of the certificate, as showing prima facie right to enter the United States.

Figure 2. Title Six Certificate of Yitang Chang (front and back). Courtesy of the National Archives at Riverside.

the diplomats of the executive branch, thereby domesticating immigration policy, and making it—along with the governance of foreign territories, and of U.S. citizens living in Asia—a unilateral exercise of U.S. sovereignty through a newly discovered and Supreme Court–sanctioned "plenary power." In a nation with universal manhood suffrage, xenophobic and racist voters could now continue to pressure Congress, producing a proliferating catalog of restrictions on immigration during the years when the United States expanded its global presence and its international activism. Repeatedly, legislators translated growing voter hostility toward foreigners into restrictive immigration policies that in turn undermined and frustrated the executive branch's strategies for expanding American international leadership and influence. This tension between democratic electoral politics and executive geopolitics has never been—and perhaps never can be—fully resolved, since it is integral to constitutional governance and to the famous "checks and balances" that characterize the federal government of the United States.

Because migration had long been governed through federal trade policies, it was a customs collector who in 1900 examined the immigrant, Yitang Chang, along with his rolls of imported silk. The Constitution had empowered Congress to regulate foreign trade and Congress had empowered customs officers to collect both the so-called "head taxes" it imposed on immigrants (which financed an expanding immigration bureaucracy) and the tariff fees (also called "customs" or "duties") it imposed on imported goods (which provided most of the revenue needed by the federal government). As Yitang Chang entered the United States, Congress was debating the benefits of higher vs. lower tariffs with a fervor devoted more often today to debates over immigration policy.

As Yitang Chang waited patiently for Customs Collector William Bowers to review his papers and rolls of silk, however, change was underway in the governance of foreign trade as well. American presidents, hoping to expand foreign trade by lowering U.S. tariffs, regularly encountered resistance from members of Congress whose elections as "high tariff" candidates encouraged them to represent their constituents' fear of foreign economic competition. Presidential successes in wresting tariff policies from the hands of Congress came only after 1912, as income taxes began to replace tariffs as the most important source of federal revenue, and as voters came to see immigration restriction as a better protection than high tariffs against foreign threats. Thereafter, tariffs were increasingly set through bilateral and multilateral executive-branch diplomacy rather than through congressional legislation. Only today's Immigration and Customs Enforcement (ICE) Agency, which polices smuggling and other border violations involving both imports and immigrants, remains as a reminder of immigration policy's origins in the governance of foreign trade.

Smuggling was very much on the mind of Customs Collector William Bowers in San Diego when he encountered the Chinese merchant Chang in 1900. Surprisingly, his concerns actually worked to Yitang Chang's advantage. Well known as an anti-Chinese zealot, Bowers had for some time worried over the possibility that Chinese laborers were entering the country illegally across San Diego's largely unguarded land boundary with nearby Mexico.[3] Focused on this possibility, Bowers chose not to challenge Chang's right to enter the United States, as he had other merchants from China. Yitang Chang exited the San Diego Customs House as an immigrant resident alien. Unlike many other Chinese merchants, he was not detained for further questioning.

In becoming an American immigrant, Yitang Chang did not cut his ties with China. On the contrary, the lives of the Chang family unfolded across borders and across the Pacific Ocean for over seventy years. Theirs was a transnational family for many decades. Chang had journeyed to San Diego because distant relatives of his wife lived there: he slept that night on a bed improvised from a table in their business office. When he relocated to Los Angeles, his first business partners shared his lineage name and were also probably relatives. Because his wife had remained in South China with their children, Chang returned to China in 1904. When he again boarded a ship for America, his youngest son, Elbert, accompanied him. This chain migration of family members continued to grow. For years afterward, Chang sent money (called "remittances") to his relatives in China. Historian Haiming Liu describes China as remaining the family's "cultural home" for many years.[4]

The Chang family and their white neighbors undoubtedly viewed chain migration very differently. Under anti-Chinese laws, merchants could bring their wives and children to the United States, just as American merchants could bring theirs to China. Racist westerners hated this acquiescence to diplomatic reciprocity. And they hated how merchants like Yitang Chang made this provision into a loophole through which restrictive congressional laws could be bypassed. After his wife in China died, Chang sponsored entry to the United States not only for his own son, Sam, a policeman, but also for several nephews, by claiming that they too were his sons. Since the nephews were not merchants, they had no other way to enter the United States. Chang sent coaching papers to prepare the nephews for their entry interviews; those papers replicated false information about his children that Chang had given years before in order to prepare the way for the nephews' migration. Chang's goal was a mundane and humane one—he wanted to assist the nephews he already supported—but Americans instead saw his "paper sons" as criminals who disobeyed American laws and who thereby threatened their own security.

The Chang family's ties to China raised even greater suspicions as relations between the United States and China soured. Under the racially discriminatory naturalization laws that were in effect before 1943, Chang and his China-born children could not become citizens. Even Chang's American-born, citizen children found it difficult to acquire higher education and professional opportunities in California. Thus, during the same years when Chang's paper and biological sons settled into American life, two of Sam's children and their uncle Elbert returned to China. After studying in China in the 1920s, Chang's grand-daughter Constance escaped her war-torn homeland and immigrated to New York, where she eventually married a young Chinese-American war veteran. Then, in 1949, after the successful communist revolution in China, the United States ended trade and diplomatic relations with "Red China," and FBI director J. Edgar Hoover declared the Chinatown laborers' organization employing Constance's husband to be communist-influenced. Terrified, the young couple fled with their newborn, American-citizen daughter to the People's Republic of China. Many years later, in 1972, that same daughter, Nancy, served as translator for President Richard Nixon when he traveled to China to thaw the Cold War between communism and the "free world" and to reestablish diplomatic and trade ties with China. According to Sam Chang, "The U.S. president was impressed by Nancy's American accent."[5] Official relationships between China and the United States had had direct, intensely personal consequences for the Chang family for over seventy years.

With many foreign kin, the Chang family understandably maintained a lively interest in politics in both China and the United States. In South China, Sam Chang had supported the 1911 republican revolution and was an advocate of modernization and Chinese self-rule. While there is no evidence that Sam or Yitang Chang joined the California Chinese associations that supported warring political factions in China during the 1920s and 1930s, their sense of political engagement with China (which scholars label as "diaspora" or "long-distance" nationalism) certainly made them opponents of the corrupt warlords who fought for control of much of southern China. The Chang children who returned to China quickly became critics of European and American imperialism, of Western economic domination of China's coastal cities, and of the Japanese imperial aggression that sparked World War II in Asia. Prior to 1949, no one in the Chang family had expressed much enthusiasm for Mao Zedong's communist movement. Whether Constance accommodated to the new communist regime after 1949, as the appointment of Nancy as Nixon's official translator suggests, or suffered from the intense xenophobia and suspicion of Chinese with foreign connections that marred both China's "Great Leap Forward" (in the 1950s) and its 1960s "Cultural Revolution" is not known.

In the United States, the Chang family undoubtedly resembled many other immigrant families in becoming more interested over time in American electoral politics. As citizens and voters, Chinese-Americans supported laws that allowed naturalization by the China-born, created visas for refugees from Asia, and provided access to scarce visas for close family members. Undoubtedly, too, in the 1950s, the Chang family hotly debated whether the family's paper sons should confess to their status (in order to gain legal permanent residency) or whether they should remain silent for fear that such confessions might exacerbate suspicions of their loyalty (as citizens of a communist country) and possibly provoke deportation or harassment. By 1972, members of the Chang family almost certainly hoped that the revival of diplomatic ties between the United States and China would allow them again to visit, study, and send money to China and to welcome visits or even to initiate a renewed chain migration.

The Chang family's story belies domestic histories of immigration that frequently portray immigrants exclusively as Americans-in-the-making. What we see instead is a chronicle of transnational connections involving economic assistance, return migration, and political mobilization that sustained immigrant foreign relations over several generations. The Chang family viewed China differently from both American voters and American officials in the State Department. For the immigrant family, China was a familiar but also very complex place. American voters more often viewed China simplistically, with a combination of awe, anger, or fear. And American officials perceived China mainly as a potential ally, enemy, or trading partner within their larger geopolitical strategies.

Americans' ambivalence toward China, toward the world, and toward their country's exercise of global power are central themes in a history of American immigration written from a global perspective. Today's debates about immigration are a product of that history. The exact threats Americans have perceived as coming from abroad have changed over time— from entangling alliances and foreign wars, to imported, foreign-manufactured goods, or immigrants themselves. Strategies for protecting Americans from foreign threats also have changed, from military isolation and economic protection by means of high tariffs to immigration restriction. The tension between electoral politics focused on the protection of citizens from foreign threats and American foreign policies of economic expansion and international activism and leadership have all worked to transform the United States from an immigrant nation secure in its supposed isolation into a militarily and economically powerful advocate of free trade that restricts immigration but uncomfortably tolerates high rates of illegal residence by foreigners. Completely lost in this transformation was popular support for the liberty to move and to travel internationally, a liberty that had been created through commercial diplomacy and then eliminated by democratic, legislative politics.

To explain such a dramatic shift requires readers to pay attention both to American foreign policy and to the global concerns and political mobilizations of native and foreign-born citizen voters. As political actors, immigrants most often sought advantage for their homelands and unification with their relatives. Rightly or wrongly, Americans have desired protection from threats they perceive as coming from abroad. Periods of international warfare have almost always heightened xenophobia and demands for protection from immigrant threats. Until Americans better understand how their country became an international power and how the exercise of global power has nurtured xenophobic fear of immigrants and immigrants' foreign relations, they are unlikely to resolve the political impasse over immigration legislation that characterizes our own times.

1

ISOLATED OR INDEPENDENT?

American Immigration before 1850

Why do immigrants' foreign attachments so often seem invisible to Americans? Consider the scene captured in 1907 by famed photographer (and child of German Jewish immigrants) Alfred Stieglitz, in the photo entitled *Steerage*. Students see in *Steerage* the deeply familiar image of European immigrants arriving at Ellis Island during the mass migrations of the late nineteenth century. So do careless scholars. They have used Stieglitz's photograph to illustrate accounts of peasants fleeing poverty in Italy and of Jews fleeing pogroms in Russia.[1] The publishers even put this photo on the cover of the third edition of *The Heath Anthology of American Literature*.

But *Steerage,* unlike the jacket illustration of this book, does not depict Emma Lazarus's much-romanticized "wretched refuse"[2] about to find an American welcome. These are indeed steerage passengers dressed in their old-world clothes, but they were not approaching Ellis Island and a new life in the United States. They, along with Stieglitz and the other first-class passengers standing on the upper deck, were en route to Europe. They had, in fact, already been steaming eastward from New York for three days. Some would disembark in Southampton, in England; more would end their voyage in German port cities and disperse by railroad to destinations on Europe's eastern peripheries. *Steerage*, one specialist concludes with delicious irony, depicts the unimaginable: it is an image of immigrants "leaving the Promised Land."[3] It is with this almost unimaginable image that my analysis of immigrant foreign relations begins.

IMMIGRANTS AND AMERICAN NATION-BUILDING

Americans misunderstand Stieglitz's photo because they have almost all absorbed from childhood a domestic tale of immigration and American nation-building. Beginning in primary school, American students learn about how immigrants built America and about how they settled the American West, worked in American industry, and populated American cities. The typical high-school history of the American nation describes immigrant lives that begin at Castle Garden or Ellis Island in the nineteenth century and then goes on to tell of their difficult cultural adjustments and of natives' hostility toward the newcomers. The story generally ends with the immigrants either incorporating into the white American mainstream or joining America's racialized minorities, which together constitute a multicultural or culturally plural American nation. Scholarly histories of immigration, race, and ethnicity offer far more complex stories than this, but they too consistently analyze immigration as a metaphor for American nation-building as embodied in the motto of the Great Seal of the American nation—"out of many, one" (*E pluribus unum*).

So powerful is Americans' image of the United States as a unique nation of immigrants that it renders literally invisible key dimensions of immigrant life, including the connections to the world that immigrants build and maintain. Yes, there have been emigrants who joyfully abandoned their former homes or who happily distanced themselves from personal, economic, or political conflicts and hardships in their countries of origin. But these were the exceptions. Historians now estimate that, depending upon the group, between 10 and 80 percent of nineteenth-century immigrants returned one or more times to their countries of birth. Most immigrants experienced separation from their previous homes and from their social relations as hardships; most invested time, energy, and resources in staying in touch across the distance they had traveled.

Americans' conviction that immigrants must necessarily separate from their pasts and from their former, foreign homes is a powerful myth in part because it is an expression of the equally powerful, nation-building myth of the United States as a country that was isolated from the rest of the world until at least 1898 (when the United States became involved in a foreign war, with Spain) or until 1917 and its entrance into World War I. It is extremely easy for readers today to imagine the eighteenth- and nineteenth-century world, with its technologies of communication and transportation that seem impossibly primitive to modern eyes, as composed of largely isolated nations. But this was not in fact the case. Scholars now trace the consolidation of a global economy and of an international system connecting the major countries of the world through trade and diplomacy to the years between 1500 and 1800. Intermittently—for warfare and revolution did repeatedly disentangle the linkages that trade, diplomacy, conquest, and empire constructed—global networks existed even before the new American nation was created.

Throughout the nineteenth century, the myth of immigrants' isolation from their homelands persisted, in part because of its powerful resonance with Americans' under-standing of their new nation as isolated. Even a century and a half after its independence, and after almost a century of intensifying economic globalization, most of the scholars writing within the Chicago School of Sociology still focused their attention almost exclusively on immigrant adaptation, integration, and assimilation as distinctive American pro-cesses, taking place exclusively within the boundaries of the United States. For the Chicago School, too, immigration was a maker of the American nation, and immigrants' lives were dominated by the quest to become American. Their origins and their former social attachments mattered little in such analysis. Today, too, many Americans believe that the first step a foreigner takes toward becoming an American is relin-quishing her foreign connections. That is why some become angry when they hear immigrants speaking their mother tongues. The use of languages other than English suggests that immigrants have not abandoned their ties to foreign lands and thus may not be good Americans.

Americans have had no word for immigrants' ongoing relationships to foreign places; I have invented the term "immigrant foreign relations" in order to describe it. This difficulty in seeing and naming immigrant foreign rela-tions is especially important for understanding the new American nation in the years before 1850, because it points toward a central paradox in American nation-building. Many Americans paradoxically believed their country to be safely insulated from the negative and corrupting influences of Europe—formerly the country's colonial master—even as millions upon millions of Europeans entered the United States as immigrants. By ignoring their ongoing connections to Europe, Americans idealistically transformed immigrants into symbols of the new nation's independence. And they did so at a time when that independence was still extremely fragile. The invisibility of immigrant foreign relations made a new and still weak nation appear safely isolated from a dangerous world. Like its immigrants, however, the United States was not isolated from either the global economy or the system of international relations between governments created by the imperial and expanding "great powers" of Europe.

No one did more to popularize the image of immigrants detached from their foreign birthplaces than the immigrant J. Hector St. Jean de Crèvecoeur. In his *Letters from an American Farmer*, first published in 1782, Crèvecoeur wrote with great insight but also with characteristic blindness:

> What then is the American, this new man? He is either an European, or the descendant of an European, hence that strange mixture of blood, which you will find in no other country. . . . *He* is an American, who leaving behind him all his ancient prejudices and manners, receives new ones from the new mode of life he has embraced, the new government he obeys, and the new rank he holds.[4]

In this oft-cited passage, Crèvecoeur brilliantly sketched a portrait of both immigrants and a new nation. He pointed toward the future of the United States as a melting pot of peoples from many European nations while at the same time acknowledging and accepting the fundamentally racist assumptions that would long exclude non-European immigrants from naturalization and membership in the nation.

Crèvecoeur became the first of many subsequent writers who described immigrants—much like the new country—as having left behind all foreign (and therefore "ancient" or former) habits and having broken all connections to Europe. In his view, immigrants were scarcely foreigners at all; their separation from Europe was in itself enough to make them Americans. This helps to explain, perhaps, why the word "foreigner" resonates in such negative ways for American English–speakers, who have always preferred to speak of "emigrants" or "immigrants" rather than of "foreigners," a term commonly used in other nations and in other languages for the same mobile people Americans call "immigrants." One finds no foundation for xenophobia or for fear of foreigners in Crèvecoeur's description of the new Americans. Their former rulers in Europe may have been both powerful and corrupt, requiring the United States to demand and defend its independence through isolation, but Europeans themselves posed no threat to the new nation.

In the aftermath of the American Revolution, many in the United States, including most of its political elite, fervently believed that the new nation had separated itself from its past as a colonized territory of Britain and from Europe's "ancient ways." By the early twentieth century, such assertions of U.S. separation from the world came to be called "isolationism." Diplomatic historians long insisted that before war in 1898 delivered Puerto Rico, Cuba, and the Philippines into American hands as colonies, the United States had been "isolationist" in its orientation to the world.[5] Only in 1960 did a British historiographer finally object to these linked tropes for immigration history and histories of American foreign relations. Frank Thistlethwaite noted with a touch of sarcasm that no "salt-water curtain"[6]—comparable, in other words, to the "iron curtain" that divided the communist Warsaw Pact nations from the "free world" in the 1950s—had ever sundered the Atlantic into two unconnected halves. Thistlethwaite aimed his critique mainly at those U.S. students of immigration who ignored immigrants' origins and their ongoing relations with their homelands. But his observation applied equally well to students of American isolation. By most measures, Thistlethwaite suggested, the United States had never "turned its back on Europe," as diplomatic historians sometimes insisted.[7] Neither had the immigrants whom Stieglitz captured in 1907 with his camera.

MAKING IMMIGRANT FOREIGN RELATIONS VISIBLE

And neither had the immigrants who settled British North America or, after 1776, the new United States. True, the colonial ligaments that connected the Americas to Europe in the early modern era of European empire-building did begin to unravel as the United States and other nations in the Americas achieved independence between 1776 and 1824. But they did not thereby succeed in destroying the global network constructed since 1500. Europe's early modern empires had already connected Asia, the Americas, and Europe in the 1600s, as the globe was circumnavigated. Within a century, the price of silver bullion in the Americas shaped the politics of both Spain and imperial China. The demand for the labor that could make American colonies profitable for European rulers drew Africa, too, into global circuits and an emerging early modern Atlantic labor market. While economic historians have described these circuits of trade and empire, it is the life stories of individual immigrants that provide the best lens for viewing immigrant foreign relations during this earlier era of globalization.

The United States emerged in 1776 as an independent nation on the North American territories that had been conquered and colonized between 1500 and 1750. First Spain and then France, England, and the Netherlands had wrested control of land and resources from the North American natives, even as they quarreled repeatedly with each other over Atlantic trade, resources, and religion, and over possession of particular European and American territories. European empire-building ushered in an era of far-reaching demographic change in the Americas, first in the form of tragic mass death among the conquered indigenous Americans, then through an equally massive import of enslaved African laborers, shipped like living freight to new world plantations, and finally through imperially sanctioned and sometimes forced transfers of Europeans as missionaries, soldiers, prisoners, merchants, and workers and farmers. Travel and communication, trade and migration, and imperial administration were considerably more difficult in the eighteenth century than they would later be, but the movement of large numbers of people was nevertheless possible, especially when profits and power served as incentives to imperial rulers, eager investors, and ruthless merchant shippers.

It is still impossible to assess accurately the demographic and economic importance of the colonial Atlantic relative to other commercially vibrant, mobile, older, and economically more developed economies that had formed much earlier around the China Seas and the Indian Ocean. We can be sure however that transpacific migrations were much, much smaller than transatlantic migrations. Twelve million Africans forced across the Atlantic between 1500 and 1800 outnumbered European transatlantic migrants during the same centuries by at least a factor of four. Even without firm estimates of Indian Ocean and China Seas migrations, the figure for the Atlantic migrations alone suggest that the world's population in 1750 was only slightly less mobile than it is in our own times. Migrants traveled under very different, and far more coercive, circumstances than in later times, but their numbers were scarcely trivial.

North America occupied a rather marginal place in the Atlantic trade and migration circuits of Europe's empires. As the largest migration of the colonial era, the slave trade sent only two hundred to three hundred thousand Africans to North America before 1800. North America was of greater importance for Europe's migrants and for Britain's rulers, of course. Unlike its imperial competitors, Britain actively encouraged settlement of its colonies, which as a result grew more rapidly than New Spain and New France. The most marginal British subjects—English religious minorities, prisoners forced to Georgia, and indentured Scottish or Scotch-Irish artisans and laborers, along with foreigners (especially from Germany)—were prominent among the emigrants headed toward British North America. Many desperately poor Europeans traveled under contract ("indenture") and then suffered seven years of servitude in order to pay off the debt they incurred for transportation. Collectively the early modern migration guaranteed that creating new nations out of Europe's Atlantic empires would be no simple task. The new nations of the Americas, including the United States, could not claim cultural homogeneity as their foundation;

instead, the writings of men like Crèvecoeur pointed to new routes to national unity.

The earliest Atlantic migrations of people—they were almost never called "immigrants" by their contemporaries— and the conditions under which they had traveled and worked influenced Americans' understandings of immigrant foreign relations long before Crèvecoeur wrote his influential treatise on the new American nation. Many of the migrants of the colonial Atlantic had little hope of ever returning to, or even communicating with, loved ones in their countries of birth. Enslaved Africans had been torn from their home-lands and forced to a new world and a new way of life that allowed for very limited hopes of connection, no communi-cation, and no return. This means that most slaves probably did, in a very real sense, pass through the kind of salt-water curtain whose existence Thistlethwaite questioned. Nev-ertheless, the famous, if controversial, life story of a single slave, Olaudah Equiano, who later wrote in support of aboli-tion and told his life story while doing so, documented how hope of reconnection to loved ones—in Equiano's case to his sister—flourished even against great odds.[8] Prisoners may have had no desire to return to England, while indentured servants could scarcely entertain such hopes until they had completed their seven-year period of servitude.[9] Well into the 1830s, their relatives in Europe nevertheless purchased space in North American newspapers requesting contact addresses "should the notice meet the eye of" the departed servants to whom they still felt connected.[10] Americans' early insistence that transatlantic passengers separated irrevocably from Europe thus almost certainly drew on the memory and language of the most coerced migrations of the colonial-era

Atlantic. With eighteenth-century Atlantic fares equal to half the yearly income of poorer residents of Britain and to a full year's income for many in Germany, return to Europe was in fact uncommon in the eighteenth century.

But it was not unknown, neither among the most prosperous migrants nor among the poorest, who included Atlantic sailors such as Equiano. Crèvecoeur's own life, for example, completely belied the myth of the new American that he helped to create. When he wrote *Letters from an American Farmer*, he was neither an American nor a farmer. He was a British subject living by his wits, and his pen, in London. (In this he much resembled Israel Zangwill, the playwright who would later popularize the "melting pot" metaphor for American society: Zangwill, too, lived in London, where he had been born to Latvian-Polish Jewish immigrant parents.[11]) Born in France, Crèvecoeur knew England well; he had learned to speak English there as a young student, and it was from England that he had first set sail, alone, for French Canada in 1755. Prior to departure, he had quarreled with his father over marriage prospects. As a young man he may have dreamed of severing familial ties to achieve independence, but by the time he wrote his book—a work of fiction, and not a memoir as many readers assumed—he was back in London, planning a reunion with his father in France.[12]

Crèvecoeur's loyalties shifted constantly as he traveled. After joining the French imperial army, he left French Canada once war again broke out between France and Britain. Relocating from Canada to New York in 1759, he quickly swore allegiance to the British king and became a British subject. Ten years later, when he married an American-born

Protestant woman, his short life as an American farmer began. Within a decade that life too ended. When the American Revolution began in 1776, Crèvecoeur's wife and her family remained loyal to Britain. Crèvecoeur proclaimed his own neutrality, whereupon his relations with both his wife and his more patriotic neighbors became strained; in 1779 he fled his farm, along with his eldest son. Because France, his birth country, had allied itself with the American patriots against Britain, the British soldiers occupying the port of New York City initially detained Crèvecoeur as a spy. Able to prove himself a British subject, however, he sailed with his son to England, where the publication of *Letters from an American Farmer* generated revenues for further travel to France, where his book was also soon published.

Both ties of kinship and changing relations between the United States and Europe influenced Crèvecoeur's shifting decisions for the next decade. By the Revolution's end in 1783, his American wife had died, and Crèvecoeur had lost both his American farm and contact with his two younger children. Renouncing his British citizenship, Crèvecoeur again declared his loyalty to the king of France, which enabled him to travel to New York as a French consul and thereby to locate and to reunite with his children. In 1787— just before the failure of the shipping company he operated while working as consul—he adopted U.S. citizenship. Once again finding himself without a dependable income, however, Crèvecoeur returned to France, arriving on the eve of yet another revolution that would threaten his livelihood. In the midst of this latest uncertainty, Crèvecoeur nevertheless called for his three children to join him and he again became a farmer—this time in Normandy, on his father's lands.

In 1813, the creator of a nearly unshakeable myth about migrants' isolation from Europe died in France, where his three American-born children also lived. Crèvecoeur's life made visible the kinds of connections immigrants regularly maintained to foreign lands—connections that his *Letters from an American Farmer* has worked so successfully to erase over the intervening centuries.

While family ties were surely the most central motivation for his choices, Crèvecoeur's commitments also ranged across the international relations and politics of several empires and nations. His political loyalties are hard to fathom, seemingly changing to keep step with his familial and personal needs. Here was a man who first fought against the British in French Canada and soon thereafter acquired British citizenship; unable either to share his wife's loyalty to Britain or to commit fully to the American patriots, he returned to England only to leave promptly for France and to become again first a French subject and then an American citizen. His *Letters from an American Farmer* celebrated the simple virtues of American republicans, but his personal connections in France were almost exclusively with the minor aristocracy and intelligentsia. Crèvecoeur did not hesitate to serve as consul for a French monarch, although he had also sought American employment, unsuccessfully, with the U.S. Minister to France.

After 1776, there were more than a few men like Crèvecoeur in the newly independent United States, men whose connections to Europe regularly extended beyond the familial realm, challenging American notions of loyalty to a single nation. Approximately 400,000 persons arrived in the United States from across the Atlantic between 1776 and 1820, almost all of them subjects of America's former imperial ruler and continuing international adversary, Great Britain. Refugee aristocrats, slave-owners, and conservatives also fled to the United States in small numbers from the turmoil of the French, Haitian, and Spanish-American revolutions. Men who took inspiration from the American Revolution and from republicanism were numerous among these immigrants, and their political activism regularly threatened to embroil the United States in international intrigues. Among this group was, for example, the Spaniard Francisco Javier Mina who launched an invasion of Mexico from New Orleans in 1817.[13]

By far the most numerous of the immigrants maintaining an active interest in the politics of their former homelands were the Irish republicans who celebrated the American Revolution and who bitterly opposed the continued British rule of England's first colony, Ireland. In the United States, anti-imperialist Americans of Irish origin and descent loudly objected to the 1794 Jay Treaty (which temporarily strengthened U.S. commercial ties to Britain). They burned John Jay in effigy and stoned Secretary of State (and Jay Treaty supporter) Alexander Hamilton, himself a foreign-born Federalist, on the streets of New York City. Americans may have largely ignored immigrants' continuing concerns with the politics of their countries of birth, but these concerns nevertheless found vivid, public expression in the early American republic.

Well known among Irish supporters of republican, anti-imperial revolution was William Sampson, an Irish Protestant with relatives in North Carolina, whom he had visited briefly in the 1790s. Imprisoned and then exiled by Britain after his return to Ireland—a result of his role in the 1798 Irish rebellion—Sampson first sought refuge in Portugal,

France, and Germany, before traveling again to the United States in 1807. Once arrived, he published a memoir defending his life and political commitments and excoriating Britain's continued rule over Ireland and its other colonies.[14] Once naturalized, men such as Sampson often aspired to public office and influence in the United States, as well; their long lives as activists had prepared them for this course.

Of the millions of immigrants who entered the United States after 1820, many more resembled Crèvecoeur and Sampson than they did either Crèvecoeur's "new man"—his imaginary, isolated and independent American farmer—or the indentured servants and coerced slaves of the earlier Atlantic economy. The resources that Europe drew from its American colonies fostered the development of European industries and commercial agricultural enterprises that undermined the livelihood of millions of European peasants and artisans. Not wishing to sink into the dependency and insecurity of wage-workers, many affected by the disruptions of economic development in Europe ventured abroad in hopes of continuing more familiar ways of life.

Typical of these immigrants were the intermarried artisans, domestic servants, and farmers of the Stille and Krumme families, originally from Tecklenburg in the Westphalia region of Germany. International migration was nothing new to this family. An uncle had married and moved from Germany to Holland already in 1820. In 1833, Wilhelm Stille became the first of the family to travel to the United States. Together with a group of fellow villagers who accompanied the wife of their previously emigrated Protestant pastor to southern Ohio—all of them without passports—Stille boarded an American-owned sailing ship in Bremen. For three weeks he undoubtedly complained, as did others, of seasickness, crowded sleeping bunks, and poor and scanty food.

After his long-distance travels, via New York City, Wilhelm Stille felt uncertain about the social impact of emigration on those he had left behind. He tentatively began a first letter home to his "dear parents, brothers and sisters, If I can still call you that. . . ."[15] Once assured of their continued interest in him, Stille began a long-term campaign to reunite the family by urging kin to join him in the United States. He assisted the migration of a nephew in 1836 and a sister, along with her fiancé, Wilhelm Krumme, in 1837. Nine more Stilles and eleven additional Krummes followed over the next ten years, creating an extensive chain migration that connected Westphalia to the American Midwest.

Even during the age of sailing ships and even in the absence of international postal conventions, the Stilles and Krummes managed to continue their transatlantic communication and travel. Contact with kin satisfied fundamental material and familial emotional needs as love, gossip, and even hurt feelings crossed the Atlantic in both directions. Most of the letter writers in the Stille and Krumme family were men, but for immigrant women, too, the act of writing eased homesickness. Take the case of Henrietta Jessen, a Norwegian woman living in Milwaukee in 1850. She ostensibly took up her pen that year to thank her sister in Norway for sending a small butter tub. But most of her letter simply sent "a thousand greetings to you, Norea, with your husband and children, and you Dorea, with your husband and children, from me, my husband and children." Henrietta assured her sisters that her "greatest pleasure" was "talking with the children about their grandmother and aunts and uncles in Norway; that is our daily talk, and what pleases me so specially is from the smallest to the largest they answer me with a happy smile as soon as I begin to talk about home in Norway, about grandmother and aunts."[16] In Ohio, Caroline Schulte Krumme, upset by a dispute unfolding over a family inheritance in Westphalia, wrote sarcastically to Europe that "yes, dear brother-in-law I know that I have a sinful soul and only a short time to live that's why I will take care not to soil my soul with a few worldly goods that are not mine."[17] Distance could not easily diminish the emotional importance or liveliness of immigrants' relationships to Europe.

Exchanges of information and goods further reinforced emotional ties. Early letters from the Stille family to Germany provided rich and detailed information for prospective migrants. Prepaid tickets for passage followed. Once in the United States, the Stilles and Krummes quickly missed familiar items from Europe; one wrote home to request that a neighbor produce and send a coat "like rich folks in Lengerich wear."[18] Other migrants requested seeds, cloth, or books. They received gifts for American-born children and they sent back gifts and, after 1840, daguerreotype photographs. Cash, too, flowed in both directions. (Surprisingly, letters written by Germans, including the Stille family, contained many more requests for cash, loans, and inheritances from Germany than they did notices of resources sent to Europe.[19])

While difficult and time-consuming, transatlantic visits no longer seemed impossible by the 1830s. Only one member of the Stille family may have returned to Westphalia during this family's forty-year chain migration, but evidence of returns and visits are readily found in other family accounts. The physician husband of Jette Bruns, for example, first journeyed to

Missouri from Westphalia to locate a place for settlement (a town that would soon also be named Westphalia); he then returned to Germany to accompany his wife to the United States in 1836. In 1856, Jette Bruns journeyed to Germany for a two-month visit; she made a second trip later, by steamship. Bruns posted a final letter to relatives from Jefferson City, Missouri, fifty-two years after her arrival.[20] By then, members of her family had crossed the Atlantic seven times.

If the American neighbors of the Bruns, Stilles, Krummes, or Jessens ever perceived their comings and goings as threatening, none of the letter writers called attention to the problem. Even immigrants who named midwestern towns after their birthplaces in Europe—which certainly hinted at their intentions of reproducing familiar, if foreign, ways of life—roused little concern among Americans before 1850. Except in a few exceptional cases, addressed below, Americans' occasional recognition of immigrants' connections to Europe failed to inspire widespread xenophobia. And even those occasional moments of xenophobia—usually during wartime—failed to produce significant or long-lasting restrictions on immigration. Largely oblivious to immigrants' foreign relations, Americans seemed satisfied that their nation's isolation provided sufficient protection from the evils of the old world.

HOW ISOLATED FROM THE WORLD WAS THE UNITED STATES?

Viewed from the vantage point of the early twenty-first century, it is hard to understand how a country with so many immigrants from Europe could imagine itself as isolated or completely separate from Europe. It is true that voluntary migrations from Europe had diminished after 1750 and that immigration remained low from 1776 until the end of the Napoleonic wars in 1815. Still, by 1820, indentured migration had almost disappeared and the slave trade had been driven into illegality, reducing the significance of the salt-water curtain through which coerced migrants had indeed crossed. As the United States began to count immigrants and as their numbers began to increase—from 128,502 in the 1820s to over half a million in the 1830s and 1.4 million in the 1840s—official American statistics surely made visible the fact that half of those arriving as immigrants to the newly independent United States still originated in Great Britain, the country's former imperial ruler. By 1850, when 2.2 million immigrants from Europe lived in the United States, persons from Britain (1.3 million) formed the largest group, along with migrants from other British colonies—the Irish (961,719) and the Canadians (147,711)—far outnumbering Germans (583,774) and slaves of African birth (somewhat more than 100,000). Fully a quarter of the exceedingly rapid population growth of the United States—the population stood at 24 million in 1850—was attributable to immigration. Yet the United States still believed itself safely isolated from Europe.

Early assertions of American isolation and independence— "our separation from England,"[21] Jefferson called it—sound both vigorous and a bit anxious to the modern ear. The most cursory attention to the foreign affairs of the new country suggests why: the isolation of the United States rested largely on a single, if key, principle—and that was the proclaimed intention of the country to reject all bilateral and multilateral military alliances that might draw it into European or other foreign wars. On this point, two Founding Fathers whose ideas otherwise diverged—the patrician George Washington and the democrat Jefferson, both of them slaveholders— were of one mind. It was Washington in 1796 who first asked, "Why . . . entangle our peace and prosperity in the toils of European ambition, rivalship, interest, humor or caprice?" and concluded, "It is our true policy to steer clear of permanent alliances with any portion of the foreign world."[22] This rejection of bilateral and multilateral military and defensive alliances constituted an impressive critique of the existing system of international relations, which rested still, to a considerable degree, on precisely such alliances among a few great European powers.

However, even Washington and Jefferson did not insist that the United States reject all international relations, but only such entangling alliances as might lead to war. Fears of Europe and its political intrigues did not prevent the United States from actively pursuing, through war and diplomacy, territorial expansion in the North American West—where Jefferson talked of creating an "empire of liberty" for yeoman farmers[23]—or from seeking global trading opportunities through an active program of commercial diplomacy. Official strategies like these helped to guarantee that immigrants kept the United States rather closely connected to Europe for its first century of independence.

The building of a western empire—whether imagined as a Jeffersonian "empire of liberty" or merely as an impatiently executed, piecemeal conquest of the indigenous peoples living there—required both diplomacy and military mobilization. James Monroe had laid the groundwork for the purchase of the vast Louisiana territories from France in 1804;

later negotiations resulted in the joint occupation with Britain of Oregon in 1818, the acquisition of East Florida from Spain in 1819, and the compromise settlement of Oregon boundary issues with Britain in 1846. War against the Indians (regarded at the time as independent and sovereign—but not foreign—nations) opened the western empire, where European immigrants such as the Stilles and Krummes subsequently settled. Military campaigns against Indians in the Old Northwest Territories (1790–94) and six major wars with Creeks, Seminoles, and other Indian nations preceded the expulsion of most of the remaining Native Americans from the southeastern states in 1834. The rejection of foreign military alliances and the isolation Americans celebrated scarcely dampened enthusiasm for what President James Polk, with considerable hyperbole, proclaimed to be the "rapid and brilliant successes of our arms" in the American invasion of Mexico (which, again, was not considered a foreign war) in 1848.[24] If, as German military strategist Clausewitz insisted, war was simply the continuation of international relations, or in his words, "political commerce, a carrying out of the same by other means," then the United States remained entangled in international affairs even as it avoided entangling alliances. In fact, official commitment to isolation constituted little more than a preference for unilateralism in the conduct of American foreign affairs.[25]

But even that observation exaggerates American isolation, because it ignores the active and bilateral diplomacy the United States pursued in order to encourage global trade and commerce. As much as westward expansion, the United States glorified commerce and saw the promotion of trade between nations as a mutually reciprocal and beneficial undertaking. Trade, not warfare, would be the basis for the country's international ties and geopolitics. That, at least, is how many of the country's political elite saw it in the aftermath of the American Revolution. The new country's trade policies had such long-term significance for the development and governance of American immigration that they are well worth exploring in some detail.

In warning against the dangers of alliances with Europe in 1801, Jefferson had in the same breath insisted upon "Peace, Commerce, and honest friendship with all nations—entangling alliances with none."[26] Delaware congressman Louis McLane made a similar point when speaking in 1826 against American participation in an early Pan-American congress, called in Panama by the republican revolutionaries of the new, Spanish-speaking American nations. "In extending our commercial relations" with these new American nations, he declared, "we should have with them as little political connection as possible."[27] This enthusiasm for commercial bilateralism, even as the country rejected military alliances, had its origins in the complaints American patriots raised against Britain in 1776.

Like the other global imperial powers of the early modern era, colonial administrators in London had tried to control colonial trade in order to benefit the development of the mother country; their policies would later be labeled "mercantilist." Britain for example barred imports from other empires into its North American colonies by enforcing embargoes against them; it forbade foreign merchants from entering colonial territories and it prohibited British North Americans from trading at home or abroad with foreign powers. Yet even within these imperial limits, export trade became the bedrock of the colonial American economy. Not surprisingly, the patriots of 1776 envisioned the expansion of foreign trade as the foundation for the country's independence, and not a violation of its isolation.

Writing that year in *Common Sense*, patriot journalist Tom Paine humorously (if again somewhat anxiously) claimed that Europe would remain dependent on trade with America so long as "eating remained the custom there." Paine advocated a revival of trade and hoped to succeed because, he asserted, "It is the interest of all Europe to have America a free port." Like other patriots, Paine saw Europe and, even then, also China as potential markets. Like Jefferson, Paine thought commerce required the United States to "steer clear of European contentions." "Europe," Paine wrote, "is too thickly planted with Kingdoms to be long at peace, and whenever a war breaks out between England and any foreign power, the trade of America goes to ruin."

The American war of independence provided an unfortunate illustration of this point; after 1776, the volume of foreign trade with the United States declined by between 10 and 15 percent. American patriots quickly sought to rectify the decline by concluding their first bilateral commercial treaty with France during the same year in which Paine wrote *Common Sense*.[28] Thereafter, American presidents frequently appointed merchants to serve as consuls abroad in order to seek commercial "friendship" agreements with foreign nations. It was a difficult task for the consuls, especially when Europe again collapsed into war after the French Revolution. Still, by the time the United States signed the Treaty of Ghent, ending its own 1812 war with Great Britain, U.S. consuls had secured eight additional commercial treaties with France, Great Britain, Prussia, the Netherlands, Sweden, Morocco, and Tunis. After 1812, American commercial diplomacy gradually and almost imperceptibly began what would become a long-term geopolitical shift in trade policies away from Europe and toward the Americas and the Pacific. Between 1815 and 1848, the United States signed thirty-two additional bilateral commercial treaties—fourteen with governments in Europe; eight in the Americas; four in Asia; two in Africa.

For good reason (see table 2), citizens and political leaders of the new American nation made a consistent and positive association between foreign trade and immigration. Both still mirrored closely the early modern circuits of the Atlantic: Britain remained the United States's most important trading partner as well as the homeland of its largest groups of immigrants. To a considerable degree, immigration to the United States followed the flags of American merchant

Table 2. The Geography of U.S. Commerce, 1821–1848

		Imports	Exports
Europe		66%	70%
	U.K.	39%	43%
	France	15%	14%
	Germany	3%	4%
Americas		24%	27%
Asia		9%	2%
TOTALS		2790*	2641*

Note: My calculations, based on Susan B. Carter, et al., eds., *Historical Statistics of the United States, Millennial Edition* (Cambridge: Cambridge University Press, 2006), Series Ad106-120.

*Dollar value in millions.

shippers trading with Great Britain. Migrating people typically traveled on the same vessels that hauled trade goods. Upon arrival in Europe, ships carrying American exports refitted their holds (creating what later came to be known as steerage accommodations), thus allowing merchant shippers to earn profits on both legs of their Atlantic journeys and causing immigration to mirror, at least roughly, the geographies of trade and of commercial diplomacy.

Coordination between immigration and trade was not perfect of course. While the United States traded extensively with France, very few French men and women immigrated to the United States; and the French constituted less than 1 percent of all immigrants before 1850. (Falling French birth rates may explain this paucity of emigration.) Bilateral treaties signed with North African countries generated little trade or immigration (nor, as we will see later, were they intended to), while immigration from Germany grew to impressive levels—25 percent of all immigrants— without any increased volume in Germany's trade with the United States. Economic historians suggest it was declining passenger fares that drove increases in German emigration. Fares to New York dropped from twelve pounds in 1816 to only three pounds in 1836, in part because merchant shippers carrying American exports to Britain had high incentives to fill their empty holds in nearby German ports. (Shipping routes connected the United States to English and German ports well before Alfred Stieglitz traveled as a passenger on a similar route, and on a far grander ship, in 1907.) American merchant shippers could deposit exports in Liverpool and then easily embark passengers in Hamburg or Bremen. Chain migrations sparked by immigrant foreign relations then helped to support the costs of further migration, guaranteeing that migration continued to escalate even after fares stabilized and temporarily rose again. Until the American Civil War, American merchant shippers almost completely dominated what contemporaries called the Atlantic passenger trade, carrying passengers to the United States; and they made enormous profits doing so.

U.S. commercial diplomacy and trade with British North America (Canada) and with Asia also had some impact on immigration patterns. Migrants from the very thinly populated territory of British Canada constituted only 5 percent of American immigrants before 1850, although this was probably an under-count since most land crossings escaped enumeration. Migration from China began soon after the United States initiated commercial diplomacy and sought business in the Chinese port cities opened forcibly by the British in the still-wealthy but politically declining Chinese empire. But because the United States imported so much more from China than it could export (there was no Chinese market for American raw materials such as timber or hides), Pacific shipping merchants faced a different calculus than their Atlantic counterparts. Their ships loaded wares, not people, in China. The challenge for the Pacific shippers was to find American products the Chinese might want to purchase. Even after the ratification of an 1844 trade treaty between the two countries, migration from China remained small in volume until the discovery of gold in California.

References to the close and positive relationship between trade and immigration littered the speeches of congressmen and other government officials during the first half of the nineteenth century. For example, in 1849, Supreme

Court Justice John McLean observed that "the transportation of passengers had always given profitable employment to American ships and in the past few years had required an amount of tonnage nearly equal to that of imported merchandise."[29] When members of Congress discussed foreigners arriving on U.S. shores, they, too, rarely spoke of "immigrants" but rather, like McLean, pointed to rising numbers of "passengers." Southerners like Jefferson had always referred to shipments of migrants, much like those of colonial era slaves, as "importations"; westerners adopted this southern perspective, and they continued to write about their hopes for "importations" or "transportations" of "emigrants" to settle their regions. Some Americans even referred to passengers arriving on merchant traders' ships as "living freight."[30] McLean, as his quotation makes clear, did not hesitate to equate tons of people with tons of imported goods. That equation jars modern sensibilities—so closely does it echo the language of the coerced trade in slaves (importations) and transportations of prisoners and of indentured servants—but it also illustrates the close association of trade and immigration in the minds of many Americans in the early nineteenth century. (Today, this association of coerced and unfree migrations with commerce survives mainly in the stigmatizing term "trafficking.")

With Americans commonly conflating trade goods with passengers, it is scarcely surprising that the earliest American responses to global threats other than European warfare focused as much on imports as on immigrants. As this suggests, in the eyes of many early Americans, the governance of migration was no domestic matter. On the contrary, it was largely an adjunct of policies governing foreign trade.

FOREIGN POLICY:
GOVERNING AMERICAN IMMIGRATION

Popular opinion and much scholarly work points to the important role of white Americans' racism in keeping the doors of the United States open to immigrants until the Chinese began to arrive in California in the late 1840s. White Europeans were perceived as would-be Americans: why should their migration be restricted? While accurately highlighting racism as a central feature of American nation-building, this view mistakes the absence of legislated restrictions based on race, class, or ethnicity for evidence that the United States had no need or desire to govern immigration so long as immigrants arrived exclusively from Europe. But while Congress's role in the governance of immigration was more limited before 1850 than it would become in later years, the United States did govern immigration during these years. This governance occurred largely within a constitutional framework and through administrative mechanisms created to foster and to regulate foreign trade, in part by Congress and in part by the executive branch and the State Department.

Key American ideas about the governance of immigration had originated with rebellious patriots' objections to Britain's mercantilist imperial policies. Among the "train of abuses and usurpations" which patriots protested in their Declaration of Independence were complaints about Britain's interference with migration and naturalization. Britain had initially encouraged colonial migration by permitting foreigners such as Crèvecoeur to become British subjects through naturalization, but that encouragement faltered during Britain's seven-year war with France (1756–1763). In the Declaration of Independence, patriots accused Britain of having thereby "endeavoured to prevent the population of these States; for that purpose obstructing the Laws for Naturalization of Foreigners; refusing to pass others to encourage their migrations hither, and raising the conditions of new Appropriations of Lands." While the signers seemed with this language to support active governmental encouragement of migration, easy naturalization, and an end to prohibitions against white settlement of western Indian territories, the Declaration of Independence itself listed none of these among the specified powers (which included "full Power to levy War, conclude Peace, contract Alliances, establish Commerce") of the new, independent government it created. In 1787, Jefferson again asserted: "The present desire of America is to produce rapid population by as great importations of foreigners as possible."[31] But after a few early efforts by private speculators to recruit European land purchasers—which all ended in failure—neither Congress nor any of the individual states before 1850 offered any incentives beyond printed propaganda to lure migrants to their "empire of liberty." In the end, the absence of formal recruitment schemes did not matter much, for chain migrations encouraged immigration more effectively than official policy.

Nor did the Constitution of 1789 say much about immigration or its governance: the word "immigrant" appears nowhere in the document. Still, it is clear that xenophobia and a fear of foreign political influence did affect the drafters of the document. Charles Pinckney of South Carolina, for example, worried over the impropriety of opening Congress's door "to those who have foreign attachments."[32] Fearing the political loyalties of foreign-born monarchists and self-interested cosmopolitans such as Crèvecoeur, the drafters of the Constitution reserved the highest executive office, the presidency, to natural-born citizens, and it imposed long residency requirements on naturalized candidates for higher legislative office. Despite these constitutional limits, the proportion of foreign-born men serving in Congress was actually higher between 1789 and 1820 than it would ever be again, another reminder of the highly mobile world in which the United States emerged as an independent nation.[33] The Constitution also either buried the divisive issue of slavery (in a line forbidding Congress from prohibiting the importation of "certain persons," that is, slaves, before 1808) or—read from a slightly different perspective—it sanctioned congressional prohibition of the slave trade in 1808. From these few, meager textual references the earliest presidents and Congresses constructed a system to govern immigration within constitutional provisions for the conduct of the official foreign affairs of the United States.

First, and of greatest importance for the governance of immigration, the Constitution made foreign affairs an exclusively federal matter, shared by the executive and legislative branches. Individual states could not keep "Troops, or Ships of War in time of Peace" or enter into "any Agreement or Compact with another State, or with a foreign Power." Within the executive branch, furthermore, a department of Foreign Affairs (quickly renamed the State Department) assisted the president in managing relations between the United States and foreign countries. To prevent executive despotism, the president, under the Constitution, had to seek the advice and receive the consent of two-thirds of the senators in Congress in order to ratify treaties negotiated by State Department officials. To Congress, the Constitution also granted the power to create rules for the naturalization of foreigners, and, through its Commerce Clause, to regulate commerce with foreign nations and to raise revenues to pay the costs of government. Each of these constitutional provisions contributed to the governance of immigration prior to 1850.

The bilateral trade treaties negotiated to renew or expand trade between the United States, Europe, the Americas, Africa, and Asia determined many of the main features of U.S. governance of international migration. Most treaties with Europe outlined a reciprocal liberty for persons seeking to enter or to trade in either country, along with their goods. Until the 1830s, Americans labeled this treaty-defined liberty to move about and to trade as "free trade." Free trade thus carried a very different meaning in the early nineteenth century than it does in our own times, when it has come to mean instead the removal of tariffs or duties on internationally traded goods. Under the nineteenth-century system of bilateral treaties, almost all governments, including that of the United States, taxed imported goods in order to finance governmental activities; thus in the United States it was Congress, with its responsibility for raising revenues, that set the rates for tariffs on foreign imports. A first tariff act passed by Congress in 1789 produced $3 million in revenues—about 12.5 percent of the value of the taxed goods.[34] No one at the time saw tariffs as a violation of free trade; their focus was instead on the liberty to move trade goods about, freed from the constraints of mercantilism. Free trade in this sense created Europeans' liberty to relocate to the United States.

Typical of commercial diplomacy's governance of immigration was an American trade treaty with Prussia, signed in 1786. It allowed subjects of the Prussian king, along with U.S. citizens, not only to "frequent the coasts" of the other country but also to "reside and trade there."[35] An 1827 treaty governing commerce and navigation between the United States and the Kingdom of Sweden and Norway used more explicit language, stating, "The citizens and subjects of each of the . . . contracting parties may, with all security of their persons, vessels, and cargoes, freely enter the ports, places and rivers, of the territories of the other, wherever foreign commerce is permitted" (which was to say, anywhere in the United States).[36] Another guaranteed the "liberty to sojourn and reside in all parts" to all citizens and subjects of the cosigning nations.[37] Treaties like these with European nations assured the liberty to travel and reside not merely to merchants but to all subjects or citizens of the cosignatories.

Treaties signed with African and Asian countries had considerably narrower provisions. Race mattered internationally, as well as domestically, and U.S. diplomats shared the prejudices of Europe in perceiving Africa, in particular, as a barbarian, uncivilized, and unsafe place. Thus an 1826 treaty with Tunis established that "vessels belonging to the citizens and inhabitants of the United States" or to the "subjects and inhabitants of the Kingdom of Tunis" could enter the ports of the other country, but it failed to include a liberty for either group to reside where they traded.[38] Commercial diplomacy allowed for free migration to the United States from Europe and the Americas while guaranteeing only toleration of the entry, not the residence of merchants from Africa and Asia, who were thereby forced into transiency or temporary sojourns.

It is important to emphasize that such treaties held the power of law within the United States. A ruling by John Marshall's Supreme Court in 1829 established that Senate ratification of commercial treaties made them binding on every local and state court in the United States. This meant that trade treaties as instruments of immigration governance existed almost completely beyond the reach of electoral democratic politics. The senators who first advised the president and then consented to executive-branch commercial treaties were not elected officials, but rather appointees of state legislatures. Generally, in fact, elected representatives and American voters had only limited influence over any dimension of American foreign affairs: the drafters of the Constitution had worried that local and regional interests and biases might too easily undermine national unity, weakening the country in its relations with foreign states.

Congress did have a role in the governance of immigration, however. First, as the Constitution stipulated, it alone defined rules for naturalization. Congress acted quickly to create a white nation through this power; the Naturalization Act of 1789 limited citizenship to free, white aliens—no African, Asian, or European immigrant servant still under indenture could apply. By requiring free, adult white men to wait only five years after entry before swearing an oath of allegiance to the Constitution, this naturalization policy reflected the American belief that Europeans quickly and easily put their ancient ways behind them, just as Crèvecoeur had argued.

Congress's subsequent prohibition of the slave trade in 1808 (again in keeping with constitutional provisions) is now regarded by some scholars as the first legislated American restriction on international migration and thus as the precedent for all the restrictive immigration laws that democratic electoral politics would later produce. Prior to abolishing the slave trade, however, the House of Representatives had also considered alternative strategies, including the possibility that a high tariff, or "a tax or duty of ten dollars per head" on "all slaves hereafter imported into any of the United States"[39] might be sufficient to end the trade without resort to restrictions. Given their habitual conflation of imported property and importations of population, southern slave-owners vehemently objected to the prohibition of the slave trade as an embargo and a constraint on trade as hateful as Britain's earlier mercantilist prohibitions against foreign imports. Southern merchants also responded to this new embargo in much the same way they had to Britain's earlier embargoes: faced with restrictions on their liberty to trade, merchant shippers became smugglers who ignored the federal law abolishing the slave trade.

As this suggests, American voters and democratic electoral politics could influence the governance of immigration only through Congress's right to regulate trade and to tax imports. Within ten years of the abolition of the slave trade—and again following both British precedent and the Constitution's Commerce Clause—federal legislators moved to regulate the Atlantic passenger trade. Congress's 1819 Act Respecting Passenger Ships and Vessels (sometimes called the Steerage Act) limited the numbers of migrants traveling on any ship to two persons for every five tons of regular freight—thus creating an equation of commodities and living freight, with the added refinement of a measurable ratio.

The act required ship captains to collect basic information about arriving foreigners, thus marking the beginning of U.S. efforts to count immigrants. Customs officials collected and compiled the information, along with any tariffs or "customs" on trade goods, including passengers' luggage, for the Treasury Department. In 1847, a second Passenger Act changed the ratio with the intent of expanding the steerage space required for each passenger. In the face of powerful market forces and changing shipping technologies, which doubled and redoubled volumes of traded goods during these decades, neither congressional restrictions on shipping nor Congress's imposition of customs duties on imports had much impact on the numbers of passengers traveling the Atlantic.

As the executive and legislative branches of the federal government patched together rules for the governance of foreign trade, evidence of popular, electoral discontent with Washington's policies also occasionally surfaced. At times, voters' unease demonstrated an awareness that immigrants had not cut their ties to Europe; more often, it reflected their belief that poor foreigners, like foreign trade goods, could threaten at least some Americans' jobs and pocketbooks. Perhaps, this discontent suggested, the avoidance of entangling alliances alone did not sufficiently isolate Americans from the dangers of the world. Certainly the regulation of immigration through commercial diplomacy and the Commerce Clause had not diminished the numbers of immigrants or imports arriving in the United States. To their dismay, discontented voters would repeatedly discover how little influence their mobilizations had over the conduct of foreign affairs, even in their supposedly democratic republic.

PROTECTING VOTERS FROM FOREIGN THREATS

After 1789, whenever foreign wars interrupted Americans' sense of safe isolation from Europe, levels of xenophobia and hostility to foreigners rose, and citizens' elected representatives in Congress took action to protect them from foreign threats. In times of peace, by contrast, voters' identification of foreign threats and their demands for protection had less influence, especially in Washington. Local and state governments were more likely to respond to voter pressure. Increasingly they sought to restrict the entry of trade goods or of immigrants, and they sought to recover— whether from shipping companies or from immigrants—the costs that imports and immigrants supposedly imposed on Americans (largely unemployment or the provision of charity aid to impoverished or sick foreigners). None of these local efforts at restriction survived for long. Both Congress and the Supreme Court seemed determined to limit local meddling in the conduct of foreign affairs, just as the Constitution specified.

The best illustration of how foreign wars threatened Americans' sense of security through isolation, intensifying fears of foreigners from Europe, comes from the years between the French Revolution in 1789 and the defeat of Napoleon in 1815, when republicans, refugees, and exiles from failed revolutions and fallen governments in Europe and the Americas numbered prominently among the diminished ranks of newcomers entering the United States. At the time of the American Revolution, some American patriots, such as Tom Paine, had expressed their hope that the United States would serve as "the asylum for the persecuted lovers of civil and religious liberty from every part of Europe."[40] But when war between the United States and France seemed imminent in 1798, and when vicious foreign policy conflicts between the pro-British Federalists and the pro-French Democrats threatened to tear Congress apart, the result was not an open welcome to exiles but rather the passage of four Alien and Sedition Acts, which aimed to suppress any expression in the United States of immigrants' ideological attachments to their countries of origin. One of these acts required aliens to wait fourteen years prior to naturalization. A second authorized the American president to deport any alien deemed dangerous to the peace and safety of the United States, even if his origin was in a friendly country. A third permitted the wartime arrest, imprisonment, and deportation of subjects or citizens of countries with which the United States was at war. Hotly debated, the Alien and Sedition Acts suggested how deeply foreign affairs could roil domestic politics, especially when political factions, parties, or sections of the country espoused differing geopolitical strategies or foreign trade policies, as they frequently did between 1815 and the onset of the Civil War.

The long-term impact of the Alien and Sedition Acts nevertheless proved to be quite limited. Already in 1800, a Congress newly controlled by the Jeffersonian Democrats quickly reduced again the period that immigrants had to wait prior to naturalization. Shortly thereafter, the Supreme Court also overturned the act permitting deportation of aliens from friendly nations. But the same Court also let stand—down to the present day—limitations on the wartime rights of resident aliens from enemy nations. (Japanese immigrants during World War II would particularly suffer under this provision.)

Strange as it may seem today, the next major congressional battles over the governance of international relations and the protection of Americans from foreign threats broke out not over the competition to Americans posed by recently arrived, desperate, or poor immigrant job-seekers but rather over the impact on American jobs of cheap foreign imports produced abroad by cheap labor. This legislative battle between advocates of high (protective) tariffs and those who favored low tariffs ("free trade," in the modern sense of the term) began in the 1820s and continued for a century. Southerners and westerners interested in exporting agricultural goods generally desired low tariffs on imports so that their exports would not face reciprocal high tariffs abroad. As a Congress in need of revenue nevertheless raised tariffs after 1816, southerners claimed the right of any state to reject such federally determined tariffs, and in 1832, the angriest voters in South Carolina threatened to secede in protest against a high protective tariff they termed a "bill of abominations."[41] (President Jackson denounced the Carolinians' mobilization as treason, dispatched troops to Charleston, and gained permission from Congress to use soldiers to collect tariffs, if needed, while Congressman Henry Clay instead arranged for the passage of a compromise tariff bill to assuage the disgruntled southerners.)

By contrast, northeastern industrialists and their wage-earning employees believed that high tariffs were necessary to protect newly emerging American industries and workers from the competition of cheap imports. Already in 1820, the American political economist Daniel Raymond had argued: "It is the duty of the legislator to find employment for all the people. . . . He is not to permit one half of the nation" (meaning the North) "to remain idle and hungry, in order that the other half"—and here he meant the South and West—might "buy goods where they may be had the cheapest."[42] Even more explicit on this issue was a pro-tariff resolution sent to Congress in 1842 from Rhode Island, asserting it was as much "the duty of Congress to protect the labor of the country from a competition"—the competition of foreign imports—as it is was "to defend the soil from foreign aggression."[43] In this view, imports were as powerful as invading armies, and the desire for protection transformed inanimate trade goods into the weapons of aggressive foreign nations. In 1860 Justin Morrill claimed that advocates of free trade regarded "the labor of our own people with no more favor than that of the barbarian on the Danube or the coolie on the Ganges."[44] Those who later demanded congressional restrictions on immigration would borrow many of the arguments first developed by advocates of protective tariffs, along with their racialized language.

But heated debates about the governance of immigration before 1850 usually focused less on racialized immigrant barbarians from the Danube or coolies from the Ganges than on the so-called paupers arriving from Europe. Fear of foreign paupers first emerged in the 1820s in East Coast port cities as the United States began to count immigrants for the first time. Typical in seeing the intrigues of hostile foreign states as responsible for the "export" of so many poor immigrants, one xenophobe writing in the *Princeton Review* in 1840 insisted: "Our country has been made the Botany Bay and the Poor House of other nations," thereby connecting immigrants in his city to Britain's creation of a penal colony in far-off Australia. European governments, this writer insisted, shoveled out their paupers by sending to the United States "the *canaille* of their streets—hospitals and prisons." With this reference to the disreputable and revolutionary Parisian "rabble," the author hinted that only political chaos could follow. Concluding with a flourish, he warned of the disastrous results of immigration for natives: "The number of imported thieves, highway robbers, counterfeiters, and murderers, is terrific." The same writer approvingly quoted a fellow Philadelphian who had contrasted the earlier, and desirable, German migrants to the "ignorant, besotted, destitute" immigrants who were now "begging, pilfering, and even forcing their way" into good citizens' houses.[45] He viewed the influx of paupers as a hostile invasion organized by European governments unwilling to bear the costs of supporting their own poor. No longer traveling under indenture, poor immigrants struck this writer as out of control and dangerous. In passages like these, we encounter for the first time the xenophobic rhetoric portraying immigrants as criminals or invaders that will feature in many future efforts to curb immigration.

This angry white, Philadelphia writer was, of course, also a male voter; and as a voter he believed he should use his democratic rights and the electoral process in an effort to restrict the numbers of paupers allowed to enter the United States. Unlike some of his northeastern contemporaries, he apparently did not believe protective tariffs guarded him sufficiently from foreign competition. In this quotation, at least, he seems unconcerned with Americans' jobs, nor does he focus on the issue of whether or how completely paupers abandoned their ancient habits. For him, the driving issue was the cost to taxpayers of supporting the poor and the threat to natives' property and lives posed by criminal paupers. English poor law—which made indigent persons the responsibility of their home or birth community and not of any destination to which they might wander—seemed to provide a powerful precedent for excluding foreign paupers. So did international law, which quite literally obligated governments to protect their citizens from harm; Swiss diplomat and philosopher Emer de Vattel had specifically established already in the mid-eighteenth century that "every Nation has the right to refuse to admit an alien into its territory when to do so would expose it to evident danger or cause it serious trouble."[46] A government's interest in protecting its citizens would even be upheld in an 1837 Supreme Court case on locally mandated immigration restrictions.[47]

As the 1837 Supreme Court case suggests, state and local elected officials rather quickly responded to the demands of disgruntled voters like the Philadelphian. Beginning in 1820, New York required the physical examination of all newcomers and the quarantine of any arriving passengers who appeared to be ill. Subsequent laws required ship owners to pay "hospital money" to cover these services. In 1824, New York began to require arriving passengers to themselves pay a hospital fee, and in the 1830s it required ships' captains to post bonds for passengers, insisting that indigent aliens would otherwise overwhelm municipal poor houses and native taxpayers. Boston followed suit. Shipping merchants could pass along such costs to their customers in the form of higher ticket prices, but they nevertheless chafed under such regulations as an inconvenience that raised their costs of business and recordkeeping.

Immigrants chafed, too. Forced to pay a head tax in order to enter a U.S. port, even poor immigrants expected services in return. When Richard Weston arrived in 1833 and paid his "five shillings," he learned to his annoyance that he would nevertheless have to "bivouack under the canopy of heaven" in a pouring rain. He responded by writing a book that advised prospective migrants to travel instead to Canada.[48] Nor was he alone in his awareness of competition for passengers' business: New York and Boston hesitated to raise taxes or fees on migrants or shippers too high, fearing that Baltimore or New Haven would capture a greater proportion of the lucrative Atlantic passenger trade. Hoping to do just that, other port cities imposed no head taxes at all.

Merchant shippers involved in the Atlantic passenger trade repeatedly took state and local governments to court in hopes of overturning the restrictive laws passed by local legislatures and assemblies. This strategy ultimately proved successful, because local restrictions on immigration violated key elements in the constitutional governance of international relations generally and of foreign commerce in particular. In hearing the 1849 Passenger Cases, for example, the Supreme Court ruled that Congress, and Congress alone, could regulate foreign commerce by imposing duties or head taxes on imports and passengers. The Court's decision was anything but decisive, since the justices not only divided fairly evenly (5–4) but eight of the nine, including all four dissenters, wrote separately to explain their decisions, providing fuel for renewed assaults on the majority judgment.[49] This rich array of opinions on the governance of trade and immigration pointed to the seriousness of the constitutional issues raised, some of which would soon provoke armed combat and Civil War between the northern and southern states. Sharp domestic political disagreements about the relative power of federal and state governments and about the location of American sovereignty and citizenship figured centrally in antebellum discussions not only of slavery and tariffs, but of immigration, too.

In 1849, supporters of New York's and Boston's head taxes on immigrant passengers, like the South Carolina tariff rebels before them, insisted before the Supreme Court that individual states were sovereign and therefore empowered by international law to protect their citizens from foreign threats. In a classic statement of states' rights, dissenting chief justice Roger Taney (who eight years later would redefine congressional regulation of interstate travel, allowing slave-owners to transport their human property even to free states, as part of the infamous Dred Scott decision) added a new interpretive twist to this argument. Taney insisted that passengers were free people who should not be governed like trade goods under the Commerce Clause, because to do so wrongly equated free men with slaves. (Taney and the other dissenters failed to note that Supreme Court Chief Justice John Marshall in 1824 had already ruled against the exclusion of the passenger trade from Congress's regulation of commerce on the grounds that "the transportation of passengers is as much a portion of the American marine as one employed in the transportation of a cargo."[50]) All the dissenters also observed—rightly, on this point at least—that taxes on passengers violated no existing commercial treaties, for those treaties did not prohibit the imposition of taxes on trade goods or passengers.

The majority justices simply pointed to the Constitution's empowerment of Congress to end the slave trade, to regulate foreign commerce, and to write laws governing naturalization. And with that they rested their case. For them, sovereignty and citizenship rested not with the individual states but in the federal union, and the Constitution that created that union clearly stated that only Congress could regulate foreign commerce. Their straightforward reading of the Constitution frustrated one of the New York attorneys who had brought the case to Washington; he demanded that the justices explain to him how states might actually "exercise our police powers by protective and preventive measures." "When, how, and where" if not through taxation and a head tax, the attorney wondered, might a state counter "the moral pestilence of pauperism?"[51] Even this advocate of immigration restriction could not imagine imposing an embargo against free immigrants as, in his view, Congress had done in prohibiting the slave trade. Commercial diplomacy's assurances of the liberty to trade, to profit from trade, and to travel drew on values shared even by those who hoped to turn paupers away.

With the 1849 Passenger Cases, the Supreme Court established that even voters and legislators seeking protection from foreign threats would have to respect the Commerce Clause. Only Congress could impose a head tax or declare an embargo against incoming immigration. For this reason, supporters of states' rights, who were loathe to accept congressional authority on many matters, also had no stomach to pursue immigration restriction through legislation at the federal level. Only after the Civil War and Reconstruction had eliminated slavery, clarified the location of sovereignty and of citizenship (at the federal level), and changed the balance of power between states and federal government would voters begin to demand protection and security from the threat of immigration from Congress. And only then would Congress put itself on the collision course with executive-branch commercial diplomacy that made Yitang Chang's entry into San Diego in 1900 such an anxious one.

Already in 1850, then, immigration had been defined as a political issue that, in the much later words of political scientist Daniel Tichenor, seemed "insulated from anti-foreign sentiment and organized restrictionist groups." Even in a democracy, where voters could regularly express their interest in restriction through electoral politics, foreign affairs remained distant from their influence.[52] Immigration, in short, remained insulated from voters in large part because it was still understood to be an international, rather than a domestic, matter.

The mechanisms devised by the United States to govern its foreign affairs helped to guarantee American independence, territorial expansion, and economic growth. But among the foreign threats perceived by voters during the early years of the American republic, immigrants' continuing relations to their foreign countries of birth surfaced only occasionally, and then most often during periods of foreign wars or intense domestic political strife, for example, between Federalists and Jeffersonians, and between the supporters and opponents of states' rights. Not all immigrants could maintain their transnational kinship networks—slaves and indentured servants faced overwhelming obstacles in doing so—but by the 1850s most European immigrants remained in touch with family and friends, and many remained concerned about the politics not just of the United States but of their original homelands as well.

For much of the nineteenth century, foreigners enjoyed easy entry into the United States not simply because Americans celebrated them as whites and as fellow builders of an American empire in western North America or because Americans saw them as having passed through a salt-water curtain, but also because many powerful Americans valued their own liberty to trade and viewed the expansion of trade as the foundation for their country's independence and prosperity. The State Department and its diplomats remained relatively remote from the turmoil of electoral politics—indeed, that is how the Founding Fathers and the Constitution appeared to have wanted it—and supporters of states' rights were loath to seek federal immigration restriction from the federal government in the halls of Congress. As the American "empire of liberty" for white citizens expanded to the Pacific and as a new era of intensifying globalization of labor, financial, and industrial markets dawned, a major reassessment of the dangers that threatened from outside the United States and of the mechanisms for governing immigration had only just begun.

2

||||||||||||||||||||||||||||||||||||||||||||||||||||||||||||||||||||||

EMPIRE AND THE DISCOVERY OF IMMIGRANT FOREIGN RELATIONS, 1850–1924

Rooted as they are in powerful and almost universal human emotions, the relations between immigrants and their places of origin do not alter dramatically as the origins of immigrants shift. But the world around immigrants and their social networks *is* apt to change, and to change dramatically. The global economy, with its markets for goods, labor, and capital, alters as connections between various parts of the world thicken, tighten, diminish, or are broken. New transportation and communication technologies transform the global circuits through which ideas are exchanged and information and people travel. Empires and nations are built or collapse. Revolutions and wars relocate borders, altering world maps, geopolitics, and the loyalties of peoples. Historically, each era of globalization has worked to transform the decidedly local places from which migrants depart and toward which they travel. Over the course of the nineteenth century, peasants and artisans most often experienced the impact of globalization on villages in Europe and Asia in the form of growing populations, shrinking access to land, growing demands for taxes and military service, and a shift in agricultural and artisanal production from dispersed, small-scale workshops and farms toward centralized, urban factories and vast commercial enterprises. As a result, whole generations of young men and women in many parts of the world faced drastically altered options for earning their living, making families, and creating homes. Immigrants in the United States shifted their focus as well. They were no longer drawn to western frontier lands, small towns seeking white farmers and set-tlers, and urban households in need of servants, but rather to urban factories, western mines, and scattered construction sites where the need was largely for male workers.

By the end of the nineteenth century, Americans' aware-ness of their country's changing place in the world also had far-reaching repercussions for the newest of immigrants. Their ongoing connections to the foreign places where their friends and relatives lived became more visible and began also to seem more threatening to Americans. Immigrants them-selves began to appear more foreign. This was not because their behavior had changed. Rather, the myth of American isolation that had rendered immigrants' foreign connections invisible was becoming more difficult to sustain as the United States expanded its international influence and activism.

Replacing the myth of isolation were new and purport-edly scientific notions of race that justified empire-building by the industrializing powers of the world by differentiat-ing supposedly modern and civilized nations from inferior and less-civilized peoples. With Atlantic and eventually also Pacific sea-lanes increasingly connected by railroad to con-tinental hinterlands, immigrants now arrived in the United States from unfamiliar and less economically powerful parts of Europe, the Americas, and Asia. Technological innova-tions such as the steamship and the telegraph improved options for international travel and communication, both for immigrants and for Americans who now also traveled the world more often to invest, trade, or spread their religious faith. It may appear paradoxical, but it was no accident that the immigrants Americans deemed least desirable by century's end came from those places in the world—for example Mexico and China—where investors, merchants, missionaries, and diplomats worked to expand American influence.

As such people traveled the world, the myth of American isolation waned, and natives in the United States began to question their old assumption about immigrants' easy abandonment of their ancient habits. As a result, more immigrants began to share some of the experiences of Yitang Chang and his family. The United States, like other countries around the world, now forced migrants to acquire growing piles of official papers permitting them to travel across borders; more immigrants experienced difficulties in finding work and making a home in the United States; more also now anticipated short sojourns and returned to their birthplaces. The liberty to travel, still guaranteed by bilateral commercial diplomacy, came under sharp attack.

RACE AND GLOBAL CHANGE IN ONE IMMIGRANT'S LIFE

Compare, for example, the life of Baldassare D'Anna to the story of Yitang Chang and his family. In 1898, when he steamed out of Palermo on an Italian ship loaded with lemons and bound for New Orleans, D'Anna also initiated a chain migration that would continue for seventy years.[1] He was an illiterate peasant born in Sambuca, an agricultural town of 10,000, located in southwest Sicily. Work was scarce in Sambuca during the 1890s, and D'Anna had no land of his own: he worked as many days a year as possible, often for daily wages, cultivating or harvesting wheat fields owned by wealthier people. When he left for the United States at age twenty-four, he was undoubtedly excited about the week-long voyage, for the father of the woman he would marry in New Orleans had promised to help him find work there. His prospective father-in-law had been one of 150 male peasants who had left Sambuca to harvest cane on sugar plantations in southern Louisiana during the previous decade. A fellow villager, listed in Sambuca's records as an emigration sub-agent, had recruited the men, loaned them money to purchase the steamship tickets he sold, and directed them to a friend in New Orleans, who then arranged for their work, in temporary harvest gangs, on nearby plantations. The lucky ones repaid their debts in a season and then worked several additional seasons, either remitting their wages to Sambuca or saving money in anticipation of a return to their homeland.

Most of the men returned to Sambuca, where locals teased them—calling them "veterans," and suggesting they had been drafted into wage-earning in America in the same way they had been drafted as young men into the Italian army. In a town where few of the poor attended school, their frequent transatlantic travels did not call for new resources such as telegraphy, postal services, and international banking, and eventually even the *padrone*'s loans became unnecessary. Village news, gossip, American cash, and pre-paid steamship tickets traveled with the men themselves.

D'Anna's father-in-law had been among the lucky; not only had he settled year-round in New Orleans where he operated a small business, but he had paid for his wife and youngest daughter to join him. Some of his fellow villagers had found seasonal work as trackmen on U.S. rail lines and journeyed onward to urban labor markets in Chicago and Rockford, Illinois, where year-round work in furniture and machinery factories beckoned. Others departed instead for Ybor City, near Tampa, Florida, where they became cigar workers alongside Cuban and Spanish immigrants. (In this context, many would later also become enthusiastic supporters of Cuban independence and critics of U.S. military intervention in the Caribbean.) For unknown reasons, D'Anna's father-in-law, by contrast, returned to Sambuca shortly after his daughter's marriage to D'Anna.

As they traveled, both Baldassare D'Anna and his father-in-law, like Yitang Chang and his nephews, violated new laws that were being passed to regulate migration. D'Anna, for example, left Italy without having obtained a *nulla osta*, a document required by Italian law in which mayors testified that no legal impediment, such as outstanding military service or debt, precluded a man's departure. D'Anna's father-in-law had instead violated the American Foran Act; passed in 1885, it forbade entry to laborers under contract. Both men discovered New Orleans immigration inspectors to be uninterested in enforcing such laws, especially when working-age male immigrants arrived—as they often did—just prior to the Louisiana cane harvest when heightened demand for labor threatened to push wages higher. With slavery abolished, and many of Louisiana's African-Americans departed for other states, local employers wanted immigrant labor, and federal law still meant little either to local employers or to the southerners charged with enforcing federal laws that many despised.

In the twentieth century, however, the requirement to show "papers" during migration increasingly constrained the

D'Anna family's choices. Unemployed after the completion of his first harvest, D'Anna returned to New Orleans and sent from there a copy of his marriage certificate to Sambuca's municipal office. Over the next ten years, he mailed off birth certificates for each of his four children, born in different Louisiana sugar parishes: this transatlantic flow of papers documented both D'Anna's temporary and seasonally changing workplaces in Louisiana and his intention—fulfilled in 1910—to return home again. (Rates of return migration to Italy were high—at least 50 percent—but they did not match return rates to Asia and Mexico, which reached 80 to 90 percent.)

What was it that lured the D'Annas back to Sicily? It would seem that D'Anna's father-in-law had died, leaving a small house as inheritance to D'Anna's wife. Financially more stable than in 1898, D'Anna became a sharecropper, working on a yearly contract, although he still plowed, harvested, and gleaned the far-away wheat fields that belonged to wealthier neighbors. He walked miles to the fields each week, leaving his wife and still-growing family to occupy their tiny home in Sambuca's poorest quarter. By 1924, when the United States began to demand both passports and scarce visas (only three thousand were allotted to Italians annually), Baldassare D'Anna had died in a work-related accident. Suddenly, the local copies of his eldest children's Louisiana birth certificates became extremely valuable. D'Anna's eldest daughter presented hers and received an Italian passport from a fascist government official otherwise disinclined to grant permission to depart. Together with her husband, another *americano* (as residents of Sambuca called those born in or returned from the United States), D'Anna's daughter relocated to Rockford, Illinois, while her youngest Sicilian-born sister took responsibility for caring for D'Anna's widow and never married. In Sambuca, the remaining D'Anna siblings maintained contact with their emigrated sister, and also with a maternal uncle and several cousins in Chicago and Rockford. The siblings lost hope of returning to the United States once depression reduced the availability of U.S. visas still further and World War II made international travel dangerous if not impossible. The youngest son of the D'Anna family sought change at home and became a proponent of communist revolution in the early 1920s. He remained under government surveillance throughout the fascist era.

Clearly, the D'Anna family faced tougher obstacles to migrating and to nurturing migration chains than had the Stille and Krumme families in the first half of the nineteenth century. But they were also not excluded outright from the United States, as Yitang Chang's relatives would be after 1924. Most histories of U.S. immigration attribute the problems faced by the families of Yitang Chang and Baldassare D'Anna to American racism. Such prejudices were in fact very real. Blatant racism played as central a role in the history of immigration restriction as it did in the construction of vast new global empires in the second half of the nineteenth century. But the scramble for foreign territories and power by European nations and the United States did more than awaken white Americans' deeply rooted racial prejudices. Fear of foreign things and fear of immigrants as foreigners—in a word, xenophobia—also intensified in the second half of the nineteenth century as Americans became more aware of the world, built a global empire in the Americas and Asia, and in the process abandoned the myth of isolation that had made them oblivious to immigrants' attachment to the lands they had left behind.

THE AMERICAN EMPIRE OF TRADE IN AN ERA OF MASS MIGRATIONS

Unlike the stable and emotionally unchanging foundation for immigrants' ties to foreign lands, American involvement with the world continued to increase during the nineteenth century. Nor was the United States alone in becoming better connected to other parts of the globe after 1850. Scholars now compare the years between 1850 and 1914 to our own times, seeing in these years an era of industrial globalization. By 1914, empire, trade, and migration connected every corner of the earth, including the supposedly still-isolated United States. To understand how globalization enabled Americans to discover and to learn to fear immigrant foreign relations, one must attend both to a well-studied theme—the country's abandonment of isolation as it built an empire of trade and acquired foreign territories—and to the less-well-understood lives of the mobile Americans who built the American empire of trade. Those emigrant empire-builders are almost as invisible as immigrants' foreign relations in histories of American nation-building. But there would have been no American empire had Americans been a sedentary people.

Empire-building, the gradual abolition of slavery, and the capitalist development of mines, industries, and plantations on a global scale so exacerbated the gap between richer and poorer regions worldwide in the nineteenth century that migration—a response to perceived inequalities in world history—became a particularly prominent feature of the era of industrial globalization. To date, scholars have focused most of their attention on the so-called proletarian mass migrations of the nineteenth century.[2] Certainly, these were enormous in scope: one scholar estimates that at least 161 million workers (10 percent of the 1.6 billion people living on Earth in 1900) moved from one continent to another between 1830 and 1940. More than 30 million traveled toward the frontiers of Siberia and Manchuria in Asia; an equal number journeyed toward the mines, plantations, and industries of southeastern Asia. Such migrations approached in volume the much better known international migrations that headed for the frontiers and industries of the Americas. (In all likelihood, equivalent or even greater numbers of people also moved about *within* each continent.)

Residents of the United States have understandably focused their studies on the arrival in their country of over thirty-two million new immigrants. But they have rarely noted that these immigrants constituted only about 20 percent of the total numbers worldwide. Statisticians have documented that by 1910 almost 15 percent of American residents were born outside the country, but few Americans know that the same was true of Switzerland, a country that few view as a nation of immigrants. Even more impressive is the fact that in 1910 one out of three Argentine residents was an immigrant: the demographic impact of immigration on the United States, in other words, was only half its impact on Argentina.

Focused on immigration, the American government did not even count people leaving the country during most of the years of mass immigration. Among those departing, however, were not only foreigners like Baldassare D'Anna, but also the almost invisible builders of the American empire of trade and investment. Few thought of themselves as empire-builders, of course. By 1900 large parts of Europe, and most of Africa and Asia were governed by a few great imperial European powers; they ruled through vast administrative and military bureaucracies designed to facilitate the transfer of economic resources to the industries and consumers of Britain, France, Germany, Belgium, and Russia. This is how Americans viewed empire, but the United States did not build its empire in quite this way or in quite this form. The American empire developed as investors, businessmen, and missionaries—much like the immigrants to the United States—traveled abroad in pursuit of private agendas and interests. As nongovernmental actors, these American emigrants otherwise much resembled European colonizers, however; they clung to their own languages and religions, transplanting their corporate and civic cultures, exercising considerable economic and cultural power, and—a crucial similarity—expecting protection from their national governments when faced with hostility from natives. Although the United States did not directly govern huge, colonized territories, America's foreign policies, its consular representatives, the State Department, and even the president of the United States responded with increasing frequency to the needs, fears, and demands of traveling Americans who were pursuing business and missionary agendas abroad.

The mobile American empire-builders were not much like the immigrants traveling to work in the United States. They did not view themselves as immigrating to foreign nations, and the natives of the lands where the Americans lived and worked did not consider them immigrants either. On the contrary, they viewed Americans as imperialists.

Americans who went abroad most definitely did not pass through any salt-water curtain or abandon their ancient habits as they migrated.

Because "empire-builder" may seem a harsh and pejorative label to readers who may never have thought of mobile Americans in quite this way, the story of Rosalie Caden, an eighteen-year-old American girl who moved with her family to Mexico in 1896, will serve us as a sympathetic introduction to the lives of Americans traveling and settling outside the United States.[3] Like the Stille family, the Caden family was no stranger to migration. Rosalie's father, Thomas Caden, was an immigrant from Ireland to the United States; after marrying an American woman in New Orleans, Caden relocated his wife and their daughters to Galveston, Texas, where he became an importer of animal hides from Mexico, a country he visited often before transferring his business offices there. Puebla, the Caden family's new home, was an important commercial and transportation center in the highlands of central Mexico. In Puebla, the Cadens became part of what they and the Mexicans both called the "foreign colony." It was a lively and cosmopolitan group of businessmen, ranchers, investors, and professionals from the United States, Britain, Spain, France, Germany, and Italy. In 1898, Rosalie Caden married Harry Evans, manager of the Puebla branch of a London-based bank. Like all American women who married foreigners—Harry was British—she lost her American citizenship. When Evans purchased a large ranch in nearby San Pedro Coxtocan, the young couple settled—permanently, they hoped—into a comfortable, quiet life of horseback excursions through their wheat fields, winter sojourns in Puebla and Mexico City, and summer trips to Europe and the United States. Rosalie Evans often sojourned in the United States with her sister and brother-in-law, a naval officer who lived and worked on some of the newest American warships, built in part to protect the lives and business interests of Americans doing business abroad.

Like this young couple, most of Puebla's foreign colony invested or worked in foreign-owned railroads, banks, businesses, and textile factories. They were in Mexico because Porfirio Díaz, the long-ruling and autocratic Mexican president, hoped foreign capital and expertise would modernize his country. Few Mexicans were as enthusiastic about the foreign colonies as Díaz was, however. In 1910, Rosalie and Harry Evans fled Puebla in panic, forewarned by friends of the approach of Mexican peasant revolutionaries intent on seizing, occupying, and cultivating the lands foreigners owned. Soon after their hasty departure, the revolutionaries sacked the Evans's rural home, and Porfirio Díaz fled to Paris. The Mexican revolution continued for three more tumultuous decades. When Harry Evans died unexpectedly after returning to Mexico to check on conditions on his estate a few years later, Rosalie Evans realized that the lands near Puebla constituted her only source of income. In her moment of desperation she also learned that Mexico had enacted a law requiring all aliens to relinquish their lands. Rosalie Evans returned to Mexico City to bury her husband and to try to seek remedy through the Mexican courts and in meetings with local Puebla political bosses. She appealed to the local American and British consuls, but there was little they could do. Mexico expected foreigners and aliens to obey its laws, just as the United States did. Evans and the other Americans in Mexico did not enjoy the privileges of businessmen in China, where for example the British lived under British law in China's port cities.

In the summer of 1923, Rosalie Evans began patrolling the boundaries of her estate, using the force of her considerable personality—and the gun she carried—to chase off peasants seeking to cultivate her lands. On August 3, 1924—the same year in which the United States closed its gates to so many immigrants—Evans was ambushed and killed. What one contemporary termed an "unnecessary" human tragedy enacted over "a small tract of only about twenty-seven hundred acres" horrified American investors, including Guy Stevens, director of the Association of Producers of Petroleum in Mexico.[4] Stevens's worst fears were realized later, in 1938, when the Mexican government seized foreign-owned oil fields as well.

Such possibilities had probably not even entered the mind of future secretary of state William H. Seward when, in 1853, he expressed the very old hope, reaching back to the American patriots of 1776, that U.S. foreign policy would focus on "the commerce of the world, which is the empire of the world." Seward, like Jefferson and Patrick Henry before him, assumed commerce would produce peace and understanding among nations. In his view, building an American empire through commerce was not a hostile act. Looking well beyond North America and the Jeffersonian empire of liberty in the continental West, Seward imagined a global American empire of trade expanding into the "Pacific Ocean and its islands and continents" and throughout the American hemisphere.[5] As secretary of state, Seward pursued that dream. In 1867, he purchased his infamous "icebox"—Alaska. The following year he approved a new Treaty of Peace, Amity, and Commerce with China. Known popularly as the Burlingame Treaty, the agreement precipitated decades of intense conflict between the executive and legislative branches of the federal government over the governance of immigration (a topic for chapter 3).

In building its empire of trade, the United States finally succeeded in turning its back on Europe. Between 1850 and 1887, the country signed only four new commercial treaties in Europe while completing five in Africa, fifteen in the Americas, and seventeen in Asia and the Pacific. As in the past, trade treaties opened the door for Americans to work, live, invest, reside, and trade abroad. The influence and power of these American emigrants far exceeded their numbers, although the numbers themselves were by no means trivial.

In 1910, 10,000 American citizens like the Cadens constituted 2 percent of the population of Mexico City; another 11,000 lived outside the capital city, making Americans the third largest group of foreigners (after Spaniards and Guatemalans) in Mexico. More significantly, foreign investors like Thomas Caden and Harry Evans controlled three-quarters of Mexico's largest businesses. In 1902, Americans operated over a thousand such companies and owned 18 percent of Mexico's lands; by 1910, they owned more than a quarter of Mexico's acreage. To the north in Canada, in 1911, there lived an even more astonishing 303,680 persons born in the United States: they constituted 4 percent of the population. The largest groups of Americans in Canada were ordinary, hardworking midwestern farmers or the descendants of escaped African-American slaves. (Some were undoubtedly also the children of Canadians who had relocated temporarily to the United States before returning to Canada.) But wealthier American entrepreneurs exercised extensive economic power in Canada, too. They owned and operated at least two hundred factories around the Great Lakes and St. Lawrence River Valley and also numbered among the developers of Canada's western railroads.

Elsewhere, too, Americans established a small but powerful presence. About 2,500 American merchants, investors, and missionaries lived in China in 1900. In 1898, the 3,000 American merchants, labor recruiters, and planters of Hawaii constituted 3 percent of the population. Two hundred Americans lived on the island of Cuba, and the largest Cuban landowner was an American, Edwin Atkins, the son of a Boston sugar trader who had arrived in Cuba already in 1869.[6] Between 1890 and 1895 alone, the *New York Times* reported on news from "American colonies" of investors, businessmen, and missionaries in Algeria, Mexico, Chile, France, Germany, Italy, Great Britain, Brazil, China, Japan, Hawaii, Liberia, Argentina, Canada, and Nicaragua. Because European powers had already carved out concessions (colonial territories under their direct rule) in Chinese port cities, the U.S. State Department after 1898 instead sought an Open Door Policy that would allow American merchants to trade in China on the same basis as the Europeans. (Their desire for free trade—in the older sense of the term—would open the door for Chinese to enter the United States, and would keep the door open to merchants such as Yitang Chang.)

U.S. foreign trade now also began to conform more closely to the geography of commercial diplomacy with its new emphasis on Asia and the countries of the Americas. Whereas in 1848 half of all imports into the United States had come from Europe and only 26 percent from the Americas and 7 percent from Asia, by 1913 almost half of all imports came from the Americas and Asia. Exports to Europe also declined relative to exports to the Americas and Asia, especially as manufactured goods and western farm wheat replaced cotton as major exports. After 1860, an especially dramatic consequence of growing U.S. interests in the Pacific and Americas was the exit of U.S. shipping merchants from the once-lucrative Atlantic passenger trade. In 1850, most immigrants had arrived in the United States on American ships. By 1900, over half of the European passengers disembarking in New York traveled with one of four large and still growing British- and German-owned lines. Alfred Mahan, at the time the most outspoken advocate for building a strong U.S. navy, looked at this dismal Atlantic commercial record and feared the United States was still not "fitted to develop a great seapower."[7]

Mahan should not have worried. The Caribbean and the Pacific, not the Atlantic, would constitute the heart of the American empire. American naval power, however limited at first, delivered military successes in the Spanish-American war in 1898, giving to the United States Cuba (temporarily), Guam, Puerto Rico, and the Philippines as colonial territories, and provoking U.S. investment in the building of the Panama Canal as a means to connect the nation's Caribbean and Pacific possessions and trade empire.

Unfortunately, neither the rising number of Americans going abroad nor the rising volume of foreign trade fostered peace in the way Seward had anticipated. On the contrary, almost everywhere they emigrated, American missionaries, businessmen, investors, and even ordinary employees of American-owned businesses found themselves greeted as colonizers, foreigners, and oppressors. Even in nearby,

English-speaking western Canada, the president of the Canadian Pacific Railway, Sir William Van Horne (himself born in the United States) felt the need to calm Canadians' fear of an "American invasion." Unfortunately he did so by arguing that "all of Canada is more or less Americanised already."[8] Neither in Asia, on the islands of the Caribbean and Pacific, nor in Latin America, did natives view Americans as immigrants eager to abandon their ancient habits in order to fit into and promote the development of native societies and economies. On the contrary, American foreign investments, as much as conquest and direct imperial European-style rule, disrupted local societies in ways natives found objectionable but lacked the power to stop.

Feeling themselves under attack by hostile natives, American citizens like Rosalie Evans expected to have, and often succeeded in gaining, protection from the U.S. government, thus destroying yet another basis for the American myth of isolation. Protection for Americans living abroad took many forms. Consuls had long assisted Americans in foreign lands, and it was to the British and American consuls in Mexico that Rosalie Evans turned in 1923. As she discovered, however, the power of consuls to protect Americans citizens abroad rested on the same bilateral commercial treaties that facilitated Americans' trade and travel. In Asia and Africa, the United States had, since the late eighteenth century, negotiated what scholars call unequal treaties; these guaranteed certain privileges and liberties, notably extraterritoriality, to Americans but not to the citizens and subjects of the treaty cosigners. In Africa and Asia, extraterritoriality meant that Americans lived under U.S., not local, law. (When, for example, the Ottoman Empire in 1893 accused returned, naturalized American citizens, originally immigrants from Armenia, of fomenting rebellion on its territories, President Grover Cleveland decried the migrants' revolutionary motives but nevertheless instructed his minister in Constantinople to protect them as American citizens from "harshness of treatment" under Ottoman law.[9]) Wherever they lived in Asia, Americans lived within their own settlements, governed by U.S. law.

Rosalie Evans did not enjoy the privileges of extraterritoriality as she tried to hold onto ownership of land in Puebla. In hopes of building American hemispheric influence, and even of assuming leadership of the nations of the new world, the United States had signed with all Latin American countries the same kinds of reciprocal commercial treaties as it had signed with European nations. Treaty provisions typically included reciprocal guarantees of the liberty to trade, reside, and sojourn for citizens of both countries but also required both groups to live under the laws of the country where they resided. In Latin America and in Europe, only American diplomats enjoyed extraterritoriality (just as Latin American and European diplomats did in the United States) Rosalie Evans thus fought for and lost her lands under the terms of Mexican law. The 1868 Burlingame Treaty, signed during Seward's term as secretary of state, would become controversial at least in part because it put China and its subjects, along with Americans in China, on an equal footing, promising both the "inherent and inalienable right of man to change his home and allegiance."[10]

Convinced of the racial inferiority of the foreign peoples among whom they resided, many emigrated Americans around the world resembled Rosalie Evans in disdaining the laws of the countries where they lived and did business. This meant, in the mild words of an international lawyer writing in 1914, that the same "movements of men, money and commodities" that created advantageous "bonds of mutual dependency" internationally—a clear reference to the consolidating global economy of his era—could also "create occasional friction."[11] That "occasional friction" generated dozens of interventions by a small but growing U.S. military; under executive order, the U.S. Marines and the growing U.S. Navy responded frequently to the complaints of Americans living and working abroad. Political intrigue, rebellion, and demands for military assistance by Americans in Hawaii produced first a failed, and then, in 1898, a successful annexation treaty. That same year, the U.S.S. Maine steamed to Cuba to protect American property during an anti-imperial Cuban rebellion against the tottering empire of Spain. When the Maine exploded in Havana's harbor under mysterious (and still unresolved) circumstances, it was an American sugar planter, Edwin Atkins, who advised President McKinley as to the appropriate response. So began the Spanish-American War—the event that for many observers best symbolized the end of American isolation. Two years later, a popular rebellion aimed at "foreign devils" (including Americans) living in China resulted in the United States entering into a truly entangling alliance with eight European nations to provide for the mutual defense of their citizens and subjects in China and to pursue reparations for their losses from the Chinese empress. In short, isolation could scarcely survive American empire-building, although isolation's defenders in the United States remained numerous and vociferous. Increasingly during these years, proponents of isolation began to notice, and to complain of, the threats posed by immigrants. Isolationists in Congress would also play important roles in legislating immigration restriction for the next thirty years.

Few American presidents advocated isolation, however. In 1903, Theodore Roosevelt proclaimed a further new role for the United States in the Americas with his Corollary to the Monroe Doctrine. The Roosevelt Corollary asserted the right of the United States to intervene militarily and unilaterally in order to guarantee financial stability, largely for American investors, anywhere in the hemisphere. Between 1850 and 1914, without ever declaring war, U.S. presidents sent troops to Cuba, Haiti, Nicaragua, China, Korea, Mexico, Panama, Samoa, Honduras, and the Dominican Republic. Roosevelt described this foreign policy as "speaking softly but carrying a big stick." "Speaking softly" was probably a reference to his hopes to negotiate a new, multilateral Pan-American alliance of republics, but the "big stick" of which he wrote was instead the "thoroughly efficient navy," that Mahan and Roosevelt himself had desired—built and "kept at the pitch of the highest training."[12] By 1914 American ships could sail through the Panama Canal, finally completed by the Army Corps of Engineers, to connect and protect an empire of Americans trading, investing, and working around two oceans and three continents.

Demanding protection for themselves and their property, emigrated U.S. empire-builders like Rosalie Caden began to transform more sedentary Americans' understanding of the dangers of the world by demonstrating, among other things, that foreigners often did not much like Americans, their money, their religion, or their social and cultural influence. Each U.S. military intervention not only expanded

American international activism but also generated dozens of newspaper articles in the United States about the mal-treatment of Americans at the hands of foreigners. Many reports included personal stories of expatriate suffering. Chicago readers in 1895, for example, learned of the life and death of a Hawaiian-born American, Charles Carter, who fell victim to violence during a rebellion of natives and Asian immigrants encouraged—so the reporter claimed—by pro-vocateurs and agents of the British government.[13]

Underpinning unequal treaties and extraterritoriality, Americans' reluctance to respect foreign laws, and the will-ingness of the U.S. government to intervene on American citizens' behalf, even on foreign soil, were many of the same assumptions about racial inferiority that fueled European empire-building and immigration restriction. And of course in 1858, Americans, too, had begun to read Charles Darwin's writings on evolution and to discuss the idea that the ter-ritorial expansion of the supposedly more civilized Nordic or Anglo-Saxon races was an example of Darwin's process of natural selection or survival of the fittest. "Civilized" Americans simply could not—so the new, scientific racists claimed—allow themselves to be governed by racially infe-rior peoples or by their primitive systems of law, even when Americans lived on foreign lands, tolerated by foreign rulers, as did the Caden and Evans families in Mexico.

Rosalie Evans had made her own racial prejudices clear enough when she wrote about life in Puebla before the start of the Mexican revolution. For Evans, growing up in rough-and-tumble Galveston, Europe had seemed the home of literature, the arts, romance, and refinement; her desire to be culturally more European inspired her to learn German,

French, and Spanish and to travel to Europe as a teenager in order to consolidate her linguistic and cultural attainments. Unlike the American patriots of the eighteenth century, she had no desire to be isolated from the corruptions of Europe; rather, she instead identified with Europe as the source of America's strength and ability to expand into less-developed parts of the world. Once in Mexico, Evans never dreamed of assimilating or trying to adapt to the local culture—recall that she already knew Spanish as a European language from her travels—and she regularly described Mexico's natives in the casually harsh terms of scientific racism. Elite Mexicans she dismissed as "vicious and shallow," while peasants were "monkey-brained," "under-sized," "dark and degraded"— "the dregs of a nation." (Because she was herself Catholic, Caden did not so often attribute the natives' inferiority to their religious faith as did many other Protestant Americans and British in Mexico and elsewhere.) Like her female contemporaries who became missionaries in Asia or Africa, Evans nevertheless also hoped that she could become what she called "an active source of good" among the peasants of Puebla.[14] She even believed that local Indians preferred to work for her—a modern and ostensibly more egalitarian American woman—rather than for her "despotic and arrogant," although very wealthy, Mexican neighbors.

In her own way, Rosalie Evans saw herself as shouldering what Rudyard Kipling in 1900 called the "white man's burden" of empire-building. Unlike those white Americans whose assumptions about race were shaped through contacts with enslaved or recently emancipated African-Americans on the plantations of the American South, or in the final, fierce battles with indigenous Americans over western North

America, emigrated American empire-builders inflected domestic understandings of racial difference with their own racialized fears, developed outside U.S. borders and through their interactions with foreigners. Through such experiences, widely communicated in the U.S. press, xenophobia at home became a concomitant of American geopolitics and growing international activism; it also shaped how Americans viewed the newest of immigrants, their lives in the United States, and their completely predictable, but now suddenly visible and threatening, networks of foreign relations.

FOREIGN COLONIES AND THEIR FOREIGN RELATIONS IN A GLOBALIZING WORLD

The increasingly global economy of the nineteenth century drew into its labor market the peoples of far-flung lands who made the proletarian mass migrations of this era a far more diverse movement than the pre-1850 immigrations. Still, the newest arrivals, even after 1850, remained disproportionately European. Many other parts of the world were still more intricately linked to European than to American empires, a fact that discouraged both trade and migration between, for example, Africa and the United States. The American empire was perhaps also still too new to "strike back" powerfully through migrations of colonized peoples, although the rising proportions of immigrants with origins in the Americas and Asia (see table 1) hint at changes that would become far more dramatic in the twentieth century. Moreover, as Americans began their reassessment of the dangers of the world and of the foreign threats posed by immigrants, they focused almost exclusively on immigrants from Asia and the peripheries of

Europe. Fears of the corrupt politics and systems of government of northern and western Europe gave way to fears of the racially inferior and often colonized European residents of the German, Austrian, Hungarian, and Ottoman empires.

That the origins of American immigrants were changing was readily apparent by the late nineteenth century. In 1850 the five largest immigrant groups in the United States were the Irish (961,719), Germans (573,774), British (379,093), Canadians (147,711) and French (54,069). With the Irish and French largely Catholic, and the Canadians and Germans a mixture of Catholics, Protestants, and Jews, the overwhelming majority of these largely northern and western European immigrants were already non-Protestants. By 1920 the religions and origins of American immigrants had shifted significantly. Immigrants of German origin or Italian-Catholic birth—at roughly 1.6 million each—jostled for first position on a much longer and more varied list of peoples, with immigrants born in Russia (many of them Jews) in third place at 1,400,495. Catholics and Jews born in Poland (1,139,979), French Catholic and English-speaking Protestants from Canada (1,138,174), Protestants from Great Britain (1,135,489) and Catholics from Ireland (1,037,234) still far outnumbered immigrants from Asia (237,950) or Mexico (486,418).

Influenced by scientific racism and the reports of Americans in foreign lands, residents of the United States began to fear that these new immigrants, too, would not abandon their foreignness. The changing position of the United States in a changing world chipped away at the American myth of isolation and removed the blinders that had in the past enabled so many Americans to ignore immigrant foreign relations. And what did Americans see, once the myth of isolation no longer clouded their vision? Did they see immigrants as mobile people who, much like themselves, loved their kin and wanted to help and support them even when they traveled far from their original homes? Certainly Rosalie Evans never lost touch with her sisters after she married and moved to Mexico. In fact one of her sisters continued Evans's campaign to regain her lands long after Evans died. Did Americans see in immigrants' attachment to their birthplaces a universal human impulse that they themselves shared, as demonstrated by Rosalie Evans's frequent visits to the United States and her continued pride in American culture, language, and accomplishments?

No, these were not to be the aspects of immigrants' attachment to foreign places that figured most prominently in discussions of immigration. Instead, a new strain of American xenophobia arose that joined knowledge of Americans' own experiences and behavior as foreigners living abroad with the ideas of racism. Americans came to see immigrants as clustering—as Americans also did—in foreign colonies, where they (like Americans abroad) refused to learn new languages or to adopt the customs of natives. Americans began to perceive immigrants as disrespectful of U.S. laws and customs and even as potentially violent invaders. The same anxieties that once encouraged Americans to reject foreign entanglements now fueled hostility toward immigrants.

As merchants and investors from the United States created little outposts of American culture in Puebla, Shanghai, Canada, and Hawaii, Americans began to worry about the foreign colonies that immigrants were founding in New York, Chicago, and San Francisco. After all, Americans did not travel to Mexico or to China to become Mexicans or

Chinese. They were not trading with or investing in the countries of the Americas with the expectation that they would learn Spanish, convert to Catholicism, or embrace the customs and habits of Havana. Given Americans' own resistance to adapting culturally as they traveled or engaged in cross-cultural relations, it is scarcely surprising that many now found it harder than in the past to believe that the immigrants arriving on their shores had passed through a salt-water curtain or entered the United States eager to abandon their own ancient ways. Increasingly Americans viewed immigrants as bringing "foreignness" into the United States and as holding onto that foreignness once they had arrived— just as Americans did when they traveled abroad. Viewed through the lens of xenophobia, evidence of immigrants' resistance to Americanization could be found everywhere.

It could be found, for example, in immigrants' residential choices. Already in 1850, immigrants had clustered disproportionately in a few locations within the United States. They formed a visible presence in all the cities of the industrializing Northeast and an equally visible presence in the rural and agricultural states of the Midwest. Whole towns and districts in the American Midwest spoke, and public schools even conducted instruction in, the languages of the immigrants. In the West, most notably in California, immigrants clustered in both rural and urban settings, while in the South (apart from a few cities such as New Orleans, Birmingham, Ybor City, and Tampa), the foreign accents of immigrants were less often heard. In 1860 nearly half of New York and San Francisco's residents were foreign-born. By 1880 that number had risen to 60 percent. Yet few in the United States in 1850 had entertained the notion that the

Stilles and Krummes were building a new Germany in and around Cincinnati, even though Germans often named their new hometowns after their birthplaces in Europe and continued to speak German in them.

By 1900, the urban clustering of immigrants had diminished somewhat. Immigrants constituted only 25 percent of San Francisco's population and 40 percent of New York's. But natives' awareness of foreigners and their children—and the relative visibility of the immigrants—had nevertheless grown. That visibility was as much a product of their foreignness as their skin color, for the vast majority of immigrants in 1900 were still white Europeans, albeit not the Anglo-Saxon or Nordic Europeans whom scientific racists preferred.

Urban guidebooks provided evidence of urban clustering among immigrants but portrayed it somewhat positively by recommending that American tourists "travel to foreign lands" by visiting immigrant colonies in nearby cities. "Seeing the sights" in American cities increasingly included "views" of visible foreigners and their foreign ways. James W. and Daniel B. Shepp's *New York City Illustrated* promised an introduction—to "how two million people live and die, work and play, eat and sleep, govern themselves and break the laws, win fortunes and lose them"—that was little different from equally voyeuristic reports on U.S. colonies in the Philippines or Puerto Rico. Noting that New York housed the largest Jewish city in the world, the Shepps began their tour on the Lower East Side, with a written portrait of the "Wandering Jews" of the Hebrew Quarter along Baxter and Bayard Streets. They then literally walked readers across the Bowery to the "squalid Italians" of the Mulberry Bend colony, pointing along the way to Turkish and Syrian shops with their embroidered textiles. "New China" along Mott Street was the next stop, then the "African Quarters" to the west and "Germany," to the east and north, with a brief nod along the way toward the "ubiquitous and loquacious" Irish.[15] Twenty years later on the West Coast, Clarence Edwords described *Bohemian San Francisco* in similar terms. "One feels that he is in a foreign land," he wrote, adding that, in this "good gray city . . . one might well imagine himself possessed of the magic carpet told of in Arabian Nights Tales, as he is transported in the twinkling of an eye from country to country. It is but a step across a street from America into Japan, then another step into China. Cross another street and you are in Mexico, close neighbor to France. Around the corner lies Italy, and from Italy you pass to Lombardy, and on to Greece. So it goes until one feels that he has been around the world in an afternoon."[16]

While tourist guides promised easy and inexpensive tourism, shopping, and even pleasure in foreign colonies, newspaper headlines told a different and more dangerous story of foreigners disrespecting American laws and customs. Dangers lurked around every corner of the foreign colonies, journalists claimed. Foreigners there lived so completely among their own kind that they had no incentive to learn English. News reports claimed to document immigrants' destruction of formerly clean and desirable American neighborhoods with their ancient habits of passion, filth, intrigue, and crime. Screaming headlines in even relatively staid newspapers—"Drunken and Quarrelsome Swede Murdered by a Rowdy"; "Woman Is Victim of a Murder—Mrs. Katherine Gurka Found by Son Stabbed to Death, Police Seek for Victor Kowoski, a Boarder; Son Brings Mother from Poland, Find

Breadknife Used as Weapon"—fueled fear of dangerous foreigners who refused to respect U.S. law.[17] Immigrants may not have enjoyed the privileges of extraterritoriality but many journalists portrayed them as claiming it for themselves and ignoring American laws.

Repeatedly, too, Americans in the late nineteenth century asked why it was that so many foreigners from rural backgrounds insisted on crowding together in cities when a huge continent beckoned settlers. Xenophobic racists seemed unable to credit the fact that most factories, and thus most industrial jobs, not only in the United States but around the world, had developed in urban areas, encouraging urbanization on a global scale. Instead, they described immigrants as swarming insects or dumb animals who "herded together" unthinkingly. Unflattering comparisons of immigrant and native "stock"—as if the two were separate populations of breeding animals—abounded. For example, in 1889, social reformers attending a Buffalo meeting of the Association of Charities and Corrections heard Congregationalist minister Myron W. Reed of Denver disparage first the Chinese and then "Huns and Poles" as light-shunning insects and reptiles that huddled together under rotten logs.[18]

Foreign colonies, once labeled as such, came to symbolize immigrants' incapacity for independence, individual achievement, and language learning. Beginning in 1906, the United States insisted, for the first time, that all immigrants seeking naturalization prove that they understood the English language. The evidence that immigrants were not learning English? In cities such as Chicago, New York, and San Francisco, newspapers published in immigrants' languages appeared on every newsstand. In Chicago alone, immigrants read newspapers in more than twenty different languages. News-papers certainly did provide immigrants with a steady stream of news from their countries of origins. But scholars now agree that foreign-language newspapers functioned mainly as mechanisms of Americanization, introducing immigrants to the news and politics of their new country and shifting over time toward bilingual publication, as immigrants' children matured.

Needless to say, immigrants viewed the so-called foreign colonies and the use of their mother tongues in far humbler, more emotional terms. Living outside an immigrant enclave seemed to immigrants a lonely necessity at times, but it was rarely a desirable choice. Thus, the daughter of a woman who had followed her parents from California to Mississippi reported that for her mother "Chinatown was home, [so] that when we visited San Francisco, it was not just the feeling that you were in Chinatown with all these other Chinese people, but that you were home with your family and the people that always made you happy."[19] Chain migrations guaranteed that immigrant colonies (and their foreign-language newspapers) persisted, often over decades, even though individual immigrants often moved quickly out of the foreign colonies, learning English as they did so.

The strongest expressions of xenophobia came from those conspiracy theorists who saw foreign governments as the organizers and instigators of immigration and accused them of "planting" foreign colonies as part of a warlike, aggressive strategy. In this view immigrants were soldiers and invaders who had been encouraged to migrate by their religious or governmental leaders. Notions of immigrants as invaders mobilized from abroad originated not only in fears of paupers, as expressed by the Philadelphia writer of the 1830s, but also in long-standing anti-Catholic prejudice among American Protestants of British origin, as figure 3 suggests. In the aftermath of the U.S. War with Mexico (which had raised only very slightly the population of Catholics living on U.S. territory), Protestants in the United States dredged up deeply rooted British prejudices that positioned the Irish as inherently rebellious and priest-ridden followers of an unabashedly international Catholic Church. Catholics, they alleged, would follow the leadership of the Pope—ruler of a foreign country, the Papal States in central Italy—rather than giving loyalty to the United States. The Pope would sway immigrants as they became American voters, creating a large population of potential traitors. Many Protestants also perceived a threat to American independence in the expanding Catholic religious orders, with their international memberships and transnational geographies. Easily identifiable and highly visible on account of their communal living, celibacy, and distinctive clothing, Catholic nuns and priests worshiped in the Latin language and followed rules or orders established by "mother houses" in Canada, Ireland, France, and Italy. Fears regarding Irish Catholic voters in particular and the loyalties of all immigrant Catholics in general persisted among Americans for over a century, fueling the organization of both the "Know-Nothing," nativist American Party of the 1850s and the American Protective Association, founded in 1887. The notion that this "foreign faith" dictated by a foreign government posed a serious threat long remained a central feature of American xenophobia, as expressed for example in the rapid growth of the Ku Klux Klan in the north in the 1920s. As late as the 1960 presidential election, a

THE AMERICAN RIVER GANGES,

Figure 3. "The American River Ganges," Thomas Nast cartoon. Provided courtesy of HarpWeek.

New York Times editorialist concluded that "millions of votes are certain to be cast for and against the Democratic candidate [John F. Kennedy, a Catholic] because of his church."[20]

Nor did fears of foreign invasion affix themselves only to Catholics. In the years preceding World War I, significant numbers of serious scholars and social scientists had come to agree that foreign colonies were being planted, however spontaneously, by immigrant invaders following no ruler, only the urgings of their primitive, racial heritage. "Truly a wonderful invasion! A stupendous army!" wrote one particularly dramatic and influential specialist, describing the arrival of all recent immigrants, and not just the Catholic Irish.[21] This trope of immigrant invasion drew on popular images of the civilization of Ancient Rome falling to barbarian invaders; it proved wildly popular, and was repeated many times in publications of the immediate prewar years. In 1913, Henry Pratt

Fairchild even insisted that the label "immigrant" needed to be reserved carefully for those persons who moved on their own personal initiative (rather than under the influence of church, steamship agent, or racial heritage) from one economically developed country to another; all other foreigners were either invaders (if coming from less developed societies) or conquerors (if coming from more developed societies).[22] In discussing immigration, Americans reversed the power dynamics of imperialism, so that it was they, the powerful natives of an emerging world power, who were under attack.

Reinforcing generalized fears of immigrant invaders was the growing awareness that it was now European—not American—merchant shippers who earned vast profits in the Atlantic passenger trade. Americans claimed that foreign shippers (and their sub-agents, like D'Anna's fellow villager in Sambuca) promoted emigration through "solicitation or inducement" rather than by selling tickets to "passengers who have determined to come of their own accord."[23] The specter of European governments "shoveling out paupers" into the United States remained a powerful image.[24] Exaggerated reports of what we today call "trafficking" on a very large scale—of Italian *padroni* and their immigrant "slaves," of Jewish women tricked into prostitution as "white slaves," and of Chinese contract laborers sold as "coolie slaves"— enjoyed wide readership.

Describing immigrants as slaves of foreign exploiters called attention to the very real human suffering that could accompany international migration. Migrants were often exploited, both by Americans and by those of their own background— sometimes even by their own kin. Still, Americans' frequent recourse to images of slavery when discussing immigrants' foreign connections documented mainly their unwillingness to imagine immigrants as capable, rational, and loving persons who in their motivations and attachments to home differed little from most Americans. The magic and tragedy of scientific racism was its power to transform migrants simultaneously into invading armies and hapless victims, while linking victims and invaders alike to the recently abolished but still contentious legacy of an institution—slavery—that had in fact split the United States into warring segments just a few decades earlier.

In Americans' worries over invasion, foreign colonies, and foreign accents, we can recognize the dawning recognition that immigrants did not sever their ties to their foreign homelands as they traveled. Yet most recent scholarly studies of transnational immigrant life suggest that immigrants' ongoing relations with their places of origin may have played a greater transformative role abroad than in the United States. The transfer of money from the United States to relatives in their countries of origin, for example, became a large-scale business with very real consequences for both Europe and China. In Italy, remittances sent by immigrants eliminated Italy's annual trade deficit. Italy's migrants in the United States sent home so much cash—peaking at 981 million lire in 1906—that Italians too began to speak of migrants as the country's most valuable "export."[25] Economic historians now even claim that remittances eventually transformed Italy's place in the world economy, turning an impoverished exporter of labor into a wealthy nation that itself attracts immigrants today.

In Sambuca, the local impact of remittances was substantial. Remittances purchased and improved houses (usually

called *case americane* or American houses) and allowed families to eat more meat, fish, pasta, and cheese, to purchase
modern clothing, to invest in small plots of land, to provide
dowries for daughters, or to open modest workshops. Sambucari abroad sent money to transform a former Ursuline
convent into an orphanage and, later, into a home for the
aged. Elsewhere in Italy, remittances funded patron saints'
festivals, beautification projects, such as a promenade or park,
or infrastructure, such as electric lighting or piped water systems. The returned "Americans" wore American clothes and
had often learned at least some English. In Sambuca, *back-
ousa*—meaning "backhouse" or "outhouse"—became the
preferred term for a new, and much-desired, domestic inno-
vation—a private toilet, which became a standard feature
of the American houses built by returners to this Sicilian
town. (And where did the sanitary porcelain items originate?
Often, they were produced in and then imported from the
United States.)

In southern China, too, natives quickly saw the impact of
remittances and returners. One observer insisted that Chinese Americans sent home 10 million Chinese dollars yearly.
Although they constituted only 2 percent of the Chinese
population living outside China, mainly in Southeast Asia,
the Chinese in America reportedly sent almost half of all
remittances.[26] In American Chinatowns, "Gold Mountain"
businesses called *jinshanzhuang*—many of them starting
as grocery stores—developed mechanisms for transferring
money to China, where most villages had neither banks nor
post offices. Yitang Chang's relatives in China honored the
financial support he had sent over the years by building an
ancestral hall to honor him, even before his death; ostensibly

built for Chang's kin, the hall also functioned as a school for village children.[27] Remittances built and improved houses and even new villages in China; they financed schools, they educated children, and they purchased land for peasants. Scholars estimate that the families of Chinese emigrants received three-quarters of their cash income from abroad. Some migrants and returners invested in businesses as small as an artisan's shop; others financed more extensive (and expensive) ventures such as a theater or the publication of hometown, clan, or lineage magazines that sold in China and abroad. One of the best-known investments by a returner to China was the Xinming Railroad, initiated by Chen Yixi (1844–1928) who had migrated to the United States in 1862 and prospered as a merchant in Seattle. After touring North America and Southeast Asia seeking investors, Chen Yixi built the first line of the railroad system he planned in 1909. He also constructed six adjoining houses (for his six wives) in Taishan, his hometown in Guangdong province. Chen Yixi's wives lived in houses that were taller and grander than most local homes, distinguishing the family as that of a man returned from "Gold Mountain."[28] Taishan also claimed the first middle school in the region, financed by remittances from Canada; not to be outdone, the Chinese in the United States built a magnificent high school. The raw materials for ancestor halls and schools drew on architectural and construction expertise and fine quality building materials from four continents.

Few Americans in the United States knew or cared much about the Americanization of southern Italy, southern China, or even western Canada. Fewer still knew of or cared about the arguably cosmopolitan imaginations that developed among immigrants during this industrial era of globalization.

By 1910, an illiterate man from Italy—whether or not he was himself an emigrant—might comfortably claim that "*tutto il mondo è paese*"—a proverb meaning, roughly, that "all the world is a single village"—and a Chinese man might assert instead that "*si hai zi nei jie xioing di*"—meaning, roughly, that all people around the world are siblings.[29] Nevertheless, as Americans focused negatively on immigrants as invaders and on immigrant neighborhoods as colonies, they came to a new awareness of how migration could, in fact, empower migrants. Soon, they also began to see how the power that emerged from immigrants' moves, earnings, and ongoing ties to foreign lands could also become politicized. Emigration abroad had built the foundation for American international power and leadership; when threatened, Americans living abroad could and did call their government to their rescue and assistance, whereupon marines often appeared on the scene to protect their lives and property. Would immigrants, with their own networks of foreign relations and their own ties to countries of birth, prove to be any different?

DISCOVERING THE POLITICAL MOBILIZATION OF IMMIGRANTS' FOREIGN RELATIONS

Immigrants had of course long known of the empowering consequences of migration. In Ohio, knowledge of Atlantic travel and of American life had made Wilhelm Stille seem smarter even to his sister Wilhelmina, who in the 1830s boasted to relatives in Germany of her brother going "all around" to talk with "all the clever people about all kinds of business and so on."[30] Although often poorly educated, immigrant letter writers seemed to enjoy their new status as privately influential "literary illiterates," who freely and knowledgeably dispensed advice about travel and foreign life and customs to relatives still in Europe or China.[31] Letter writers also consistently celebrated their release from the taxes and debts of their homelands, from demanding landowners, and from military service to distant and unappreciative rulers; the European migrants pointed also to their liberty to acquire property, enjoy religious toleration, and read a free press. Some saw newfound liberty in migration itself. For example, a Scottish immigrant described himself as "a bird liberated from its cage . . . so much do I prefer liberty to confinement."[32] Over time, a steady 20 percent of the letters, diaries, and oral histories collected in one large digital archive of immigrant writings referred to the liberty and freedom available to those moving to the United States.[33] European migrants probably did as much to spread an Atlantic-wide image of the United States as a land of political liberty and economic opportunity as did all the political treatises written by American patriots. Conversely, however, as the Chinese Imperial Vice Commissioner of St. Louis, Wong Kai Kah, asserted in 1904, "every Chinese ill-treated in America or sent back from it spreads the story of [American] wrongs amongst his friends and their acquaintances."[34]

Most of the empowerment immigrants accrued through migration served very ordinary ends. In Sicily, Sambucari gossiped over newly obstreperous returned migrants who refused to kiss the hands of their wealthier neighbors or who rejected their fathers' or mothers' control over their marital choices. A few also noted, with curiosity, that half of the first socialists of Sambuca had once sojourned in New York City.[35] Still, newfound and personal empowerment rarely translated into the ability to request or get assistance from the governments of their home countries. The Italian immigrants who demanded a formal protest from Italian consuls after eleven Sicilians were murdered in a New Orleans jail (while awaiting trial in the killing of a local police official) had much the same experience as Rosalie Caden Evans. Often enough, foreign governments could do little to protect their emigrants in any practical way once they were in the United States, and they rarely even tried—or so Italy's radicals claimed. China's rulers regularly objected to the ill treatment of the Chinese in the United States, but their protest had little impact outside Washington.

Explicitly political mobilizations nevertheless became a predictable and durable feature of the lives of most groups of immigrants in the United States, and the goal of these movements was almost always change in the countries they had left. The Irish revolutionaries of the early national era were, as we shall see, by no means unique. What was new by the second half of the nineteenth century was Americans' increasing awareness of such mobilizations and their increasing tendency to view politically active immigrants as threatening their own well-being. Although natives' xenophobia can strike today's readers as extreme and quite irrational, it is important to understand the basis for their anxiety, for it was the fear of radical immigrants that most tightly linked the demise of American isolation, the rise of American empire, and Americans' demands for immigration restriction. To understand natives' fears, it is helpful to review how the United States responded to several particularly controversial and violent transnational mobilizations among immigrants that occurred between 1850 and 1914.

The long history of Irish opposition to British colonial rule that had roiled domestic American politics already in the 1790s continued before and after 1850. Significantly, the Young Ireland nationalist movement collapsed in Ireland just as the protracted consequences of blighted potato harvests in the late 1840s drove millions of the residents of Ireland to seek sustenance elsewhere. In response, Americans and Irish alike again began to paint portraits of the politically charged figure of the "Irish Exile."[36] Like political exiles before and after them, considerable numbers of Irish immigrants in the United States in the 1850s remained committed to their homeland cause—a free Ireland—and willing to take action in pursuit of this goal. The Irish arguably became both the best-known and the longest-term diaspora nationalists among the many immigrants living in the United States.

During the 1850s, Irish republicans regrouped, in the United States and elsewhere, as *na fiannam*—"Fenians" English-speakers called them. By 1865, as many as 125,000 young Irish immigrant Fenians had fought in the American Civil War and many had begun to imagine using their new military skills on behalf of the anti-imperial Irish cause. At their 1865 annual meeting in New York, immigrant Fenian leaders such as John O'Mahony and Thomas Francis Bourke advocated an organized return to Ireland to fight. (Once there, Bourke would be convicted of treason and spend most of the rest of his life in prison).[37] However, the largest group of Fenians assembled in New York argued for a different strategy; mobilizing as a government in exile, they gathered around a new Fenian "Secretary of War," Tom Sweeny, who was a veteran of both the Mexican-American and Civil Wars. These Fenians committed themselves to distracting British troops from a renewed republican mobilization in Ireland by forcing Great Britain to defend itself in nearby Canada.

The new Fenian chief executive approved the plan; he had met the new American president Andrew Johnson and he believed (perhaps with cause) that he had Johnson's sympathies. (Johnson, like many supporters of the Union in the Civil War, felt that Britain's wartime neutrality had strengthened the hand of their Confederate enemies, the main suppliers for Britain's cotton textile factories.) Fenians knew that they also enjoyed considerable support from New York's Tammany Democrats: if military action could "place Canada in the hands of Fenians," wrote one expansive New York Democrat, then Canada too might become part of "our representative federal system."[38]

The largest and most successful of three planned Fenian raids into Canada left from Buffalo in June 1866. After capturing Canada's Fort Erie, and marching on toward the commercially important Welland Canal, armed American Fenians encountered hastily organized Canadian troops, who soon received reinforcements and were able to capture some of the invaders and drive the others back toward the United States. As late as 1871, the residents of Canadian Manitoba believed they had repelled yet another Fenian attack from the United States, this one formed by an alliance of Catholic Fenian Irish-Americans and Catholic Metís ("French-speaking half-breeds," according to the leader of the Canadian defense expedition.)[39]

How did the U.S. government respond to these gun-toting immigrants with their own secretary of war, armaments, and foreign policy agenda? After receiving an appeal from the British, the United States in 1866 sealed its northeast border to prevent additional Fenian exits. But it then remained completely silent, at least in public, as the battle in Canada raged. The United States also chose not to prosecute Fenians returning from Canada: the attack, after all, had not been against the United States but against Canada and against Great Britain. Perhaps the Fenians had been correct in assessing the sympathies of President Johnson. In any case, the reactions of the federal government did little to warn off other immigrants considering political, even quite violent, transnational mobilizations.

Neither did the United States respond vigorously to an even more dramatic attack—this time by anti-capitalist Italians calling themselves the "men without a country"—that captured American headlines thirty years later. On August 29, 1900, Gaetano Bresci, an anarchist who had returned to Italy from Paterson, New Jersey, assassinated Umberto, the King of Italy, with a gun purchased in the United States. Like the far better known Italian anarchists Sacco and Vanzetti (who would be executed in the United States in 1927, accused of the murder of an American), Bresci hated the tyranny of all national governments, even as he hated capitalism for its oppression of workingmen and hated organized religion for tricking workers into quiet submission. Bresci (like Sacco and Vanzetti after him) also impressed his American friends, it must be admitted, as a peaceful, thoughtful, and good man who had become sufficiently Americanized to marry an English-speaking woman of Irish origin.

Gaetano Bresci was no stranger to transnational radical politics. He had been imprisoned in Italy before fleeing to the United States, where he worked in the silk mills of Paterson and joined Paterson's "Right to Existence" anarchist club. Unlike Sacco and Vanzetti (who may have explicitly advocated assassination as a political action), Paterson's anarchists generally preferred strategies like the revolutionary education of workers, labor or workplace organization, and industrial or general strikes.[40] The assassination of Umberto by Bresci may have surprised Paterson's anarchist community, but anarchists in the town nevertheless immediately expressed solidarity with their comrade and sprang to his defense with a flood of newspaper articles, pamphlets, and poems. Exploitation by capitalists, priests, and tyrannical government officials, these publications and public demonstrations by anarchists suggested, often drove decent men to desperate acts.

European and American responses to the regicide in Italy could scarcely have differed more. Bresci had visited France and Switzerland before the attack on Umberto, and arrests of anarchists with connections to the Paterson anarchists followed in Switzerland, Sweden, and even Egypt. European governments also rather quickly changed their extradition laws in response to the crime, and they continued discussions (and the exchange of national police records and information) that would culminate later in the formation of a multinational Interpol police force to combat anarchist and communist revolutionary activities. The European response, in other words, was swift and it was multilateral.

In the United States, by contrast, Americans seemed both appalled and fascinated by Bresci's deed. Within five days, a figure of the assassin appeared in the "room of horrors" of a New York wax museum. Newspaper reports described anarchist connections linking most of the cities of Europe, the United States, and Argentina. One American reporter insisted (without any evidence) that Bresci had carried in his pocket a list of international leaders slated to be killed. Another described a complex terrorist strategy, with anarchists in one country planning a murder to be committed in a second country by an assassin recruited in a third country. Ultimately, however, the New York Italian consul's demand for a full investigation of Paterson and its anarchists and a forceful response from the United States went unsatisfied. Local police in Paterson insisted they already maintained sufficient surveillance over the local anarchists. The U.S. Treasury Department was almost alone in taking action against the newly uncovered immigrant threat—and all it did was to repress temporarily the publication of Paterson's anarchist newspaper, *La Questione Sociale*, after accusing its editors of failing to pay import duties on the many foreign newspapers they received.[41]

By contrast, two years later, after the murder of U.S. president William McKinley by an American-born assassin with immigrant parents, whose name was Leo Czolgosz, the American government responded more swiftly and conclusively. Congress in 1902 forbade any anarchist from henceforth entering the United States, a law that proved almost impossible to enforce in the absence of American involvement in the exchange of international police information. The American decision to exclude anarchists nevertheless represented a first important step toward eliminating Bill of Rights protections of the freedom of those wishing to enter the country. By passing anti-anarchist legislation, the United States Congress—unlike European nations—again responded unilaterally to a foreign threat. It engaged in no international discussions or alliances to counter the global threat of anarchist terrorism but instead passed a law that could not be effectively enforced. (Both Sacco and Vanzetti, for example, migrated to the United States after the implementation of the anarchist exclusion.)

The impact of a subsequent mobilization of Chinese merchants in 1905, by contrast, registered very prominently with the U.S. State Department, although the department's response was almost certainly not what white Californians or most congressmen wished it to be. For years, missionaries and American businessmen in China had warned of the possibility of a violent backlash as Chinese merchants repeatedly suffered harassment both at the border and in their everyday lives in the United States. Sympathetic U.S. observers had already seen evidence in the 1900 Boxer Rebellion and murder of Western missionaries of a growing backlash against Americans, their racism, and their xenophobia. Like Italy's radicals, the Chinese merchants too brought repeated complaints about discrimination in the United States to their consuls and to the Zongli Yamen, China's Foreign Ministry, without receiving satisfying results. As Yitang Chang's son observed, a "weak nation has no diplomacy to speak of," and cannot adequately defend its citizens abroad.[42]

In 1905, emigrated merchants from China scattered around the Pacific acted powerfully—but also peacefully—when they proclaimed a Pacific-wide boycott of all American trade goods. The idea of the boycott had been circulating through Chinese-language newspapers around the Pacific for the previous two years. The result was a short-lived but impressive demonstration of immigrants' ability to mobilize transnationally and across vast distances. The movement linked merchants in China's cities to the foreign colonies of Chinese merchants and laborers in the United States, Hawaii, and Southeast Asia. It was a political movement broad enough not only to threaten the ability of American exporters to sell increasing volumes of their products to the huge Chinese market, but also to endanger the U.S. State Department's Open Door policy on behalf of free trade in China. The boycott revealed how widely China's intellectuals and students, statesmen and social reformers understood and resented the treatment of the overseas Chinese and how much they hated both the unequal treaties and the extra-territoriality that had transformed parts of their cities into colonies where foreigners lived as if at home, exempt from the laws and isolated from the cultures and languages of the natives, toward whom they, in any case, felt contempt.

In the United States, the Chinese merchants' boycott quickly brought tempers to a boil. According to a *Los Angeles Times* reporter, one evening in early March, Chinese migrants were "vigorously discussing the present uprising in their native land," whereupon some Japanese onlookers recognized a unique business opportunity. The Japanese businessmen acquired "dozens of small American flags" and installed them in their shooting galleries. Angry Chinese immigrants eagerly paid their admission fees and began firing away at the stars and stripes. Such "insults to the American flag," the reporter for the *L.A. Times* editorialized solemnly, would not "be condoned in Los Angeles. This was impressed on the Chinese and Japanese element yesterday by prompt revocation of shooting gallery licenses."[43] Tellingly, the Los Angeles reporter had transformed what was in reality a peaceful, international boycott organized by overseas Chinese into a "rebellion" and an attack on America fomented in China. Other alarmist voices were also heard: one American observer of the boycott predicted a race war that would pit "yellow" nations against "white" ones.[44] Rather quickly the Chinese merchants' Pacific boycott fell victim to its own conflicting goals, exacerbated by opposition from China's imperial ruler and the devastation caused by the San Francisco fire and earthquake of 1906. It nevertheless had proved surprisingly successful. Part of that success was economic. Gleeful Canadian and British competitors of American merchants in China pronounced it "the greatest commercial disaster that the United States has suffered for a long time."[45] Exports to China from the United States had quadrupled between 1897 and 1905 to $57 million. In 1907 they fell to $26 million. (It is impossible to know, however, whether the boycott or a financial crisis that also occurred that year was more responsible for the reduction.)

Unlike the Fenian invasion or Bresci's regicide, the Chinese boycott was aimed directly at the United States, and it sparked an immediate and—from the perspective of the merchants—surprising response in Washington. Learning of the boycott, President Theodore Roosevelt intervened quickly with his secretary of commerce and labor (the office that had recently assumed oversight of immigration, replacing the Treasury Department), asking him to assure that its immigration agents carefully followed instructions and avoided harsh and unfair treatment of Chinese merchants, travelers, and students. A department circular was issued that reminded immigration agents that "the purpose of the Chinese exclusion laws is to prevent the immigration of Chinese laborers and not to restrict the freedom of movement of the Chinese. . . ."[46] Roosevelt saw the justice of the merchants' complaints and understood the boycott for what it was—a political protest by merchants against the relentless racial harassment they, and all Chinese-origin peoples, experienced while living peacefully and lawfully in the western states. Interested in expanding American influence and trade in Asia and responsible for protecting the lives and well-being of American merchants who lived in China, Roosevelt understandably wanted to honor diplomatic reciprocity. His response made him no friends among anti-Chinese white voters in California who cared little for diplomatic niceties and less for the feelings of the Chinese.

As these examples of transnational immigrant political mobilization suggest, millions of Irish, Chinese, and Italian immigrants gained a firmer sense of their power and, in some cases, also of their national identities while living abroad as foreigners in the United States. Far from threatening the United States, diaspora nationalists like these usually focused on effecting change in their countries of origin. Dozens of newspapers and hundreds of small immigrant associations in Chinatowns, Little Italys, and Irish neighborhoods sought political change, and even revolution, in their countries of birth. Italian or Irish republicans in New York and New Orleans and Chinese republicans in San Francisco and Honolulu wanted to unseat the Italian king, the British imperial rulers, or the Chinese empress. Far smaller were the numbers of those who wanted revolution in the United States. More often immigrants admired the United States for its representative form of government, and some even saw it as a model for political change in the countries they had left behind. Chinese republicans, along with anarchists, socialists, and, later, immigrant communists often expressed sharp criticisms of the United States—a country which symbolized for them the evils of both racism and capitalism—but in most cases, even these activists mainly celebrated traveling agitators from the home country and focused on providing intellectual and financial support for opposition movements there. After Mussolini seized power in Italy, for example, many exiles and Italian Americans seemed to fear mainly that fascism might "come to America" (and one promised to "push it back into the ocean" if that happened).[47]

As we have seen in the case of remittances, transnational immigrant politics had its largest impact on the countries from which the immigrants had departed. Many leaders of nationalist movements had worked abroad as immigrants, including Italy's Benito Mussolini (who had traveled to Switzerland as a worker) and Sun Yat-sen, the revolutionary and founder of the Chinese Nationalist Party, who was the main leader of China's 1911 revolution. Sen had traveled to Hawaii with his older brother, a merchant, and had gone to school there between 1879 and 1883. He even learned to speak English before returning to China. He maintained close ties to Hawaii, and he traveled there at least five more times (as well as to the United States, Europe, Japan, and Southeast Asia) as he pursued his revolutionary republican cause. When the Chinese emperor listed Sen as "wanted" for his illicit revolutionary activities, his mother, wife, and children again relocated to Hawaii, fearing that he might need to take refuge with them.[48] After the successful (and peaceful) revolution of 1911, republican China continued to care deeply about the political loyalties and financial support of China's migrants, including men such as Yitang and Sam Chang.

In only a few cases did diaspora nationalism directly threaten the United States. Like Sun Yat-sen, the Cuban exile José Martí (who visited in Florida's Ybor City and who escaped an assassin's attack there) and revolutionaries plotting against Porfirio Díaz (such as Francisco Madero and the brothers Enrique and Ricardo Flores Magón) often sought funds and supporters or issued plans and calls for change at home from the nearby United States. Given the power and influence of Americans in Cuba and Mexico, their mobilizations did sometimes threaten the privileges of Americans living abroad. After the United States acquired its own colonies in Puerto Rico and the Philippines, migrations from these islands to the United States always included a vocal minority of diaspora nationalists who wanted the Puerto Ricans and Filipinos living and working in the United States to help their fellow countrymen end American domination of the home country.

Dramatic events involving arms and armed violence (or even just immigrants in shooting galleries) understandably garnered a great deal of negative attention from Americans already nervous about the changing place of the United States in the global economy and its assertive entry into the world of international relations alongside imperial European nations. Even when immigrants supported organized, armed violence, however, that violence more often erupted in the immigrants' countries of origin and rarely threatened Americans. Still, it is difficult to read Americans' discussions of immigrant foreign relations in this era without wondering what a psychoanalytically inclined historian or poststructuralist philosopher fascinated with textual silences might make of such discussions. No writer in the United States ever acknowledged the obvious parallels between the behavior of Americans abroad and Americans' perceptions of immigrants in the United States. Was this a telling "silence," or did too few Americans actually know enough about both groups to venture such a comparison? It is striking that Americans insisted upon the racial inferiority of immigrants from outside of Anglo-Saxon or Nordic northern Europe yet at the same time perceived them as invaders capable of permanently transforming the government, culture, and people of the United States. Is it possible that Americans projected onto immigrants their own growing international power and their own powerful reluctance to learn the languages or to respect the laws and customs of the many countries where they emigrated to live, invest, and work as empire-builders?

Perhaps it is more sensible simply to note the growing numbers of Americans in the late nineteenth century who raised questions about how well, fervently, or effectively their own government protected them from foreign threats. In the three highly dramatic cases described above, official responses by elected officials reflected the foreign policies and the place of immigrants' homelands in American geopolitics, not the desires of American voters rightly or wrongly frightened by immigrants' ability to mobilize transnationally or to carry guns across borders. In 1900, as in 1849, much of the formulation and conduct of American foreign affairs, and of immigration policy, too, still lay beyond the reach of electoral politics and of the American voter.

When migratory American empire-builders living abroad demanded protection, they often enough received it, and promptly. Even if we reject the blatant racism and xenophobia of Californians hostile to what they called the "yellow peril," we can acknowledge that President Theodore Roosevelt did seem more interested in strengthening his empire of trade in China than in responding to voters' racialized fears of Chinese immigrants. As more and more Americans came to believe they needed protection from the threat of immigrant invaders, more also became convinced that they needed a new way of governing immigration. Where once the goal had been to isolate the United States from threats such as entangling alliances or foreign imports, increasing numbers of Americans now sought to isolate themselves from immigrants. And once again, they turned to their elected representatives to protect them by preventing immigrants from entering the United States.

3

IMMIGRATION AND RESTRICTION

Protection in a Dangerous World, 1850–1965

Reminiscing thirty years later about the politics of the 1890s, former congressman Richard Bartholdt recalled that "the most discussed subjects at that time were immigration, the financial question, and the tariff."[1] Prominently missing from his list were empire-building and the growing opposition to American global activism that ultimately culminated in isolationist backlash and draconic restrictions on immigration. More than his contemporaries in Congress, Bartholdt probably understood that for American voters the tariff and immigration had been anything but domestic matters in the 1890s: congressmen debated these two issues with fervor precisely because they saw them as closely linked strategies for protecting American citizens from the dangers they perceived in their country's growing global activism.

Richard Bartholdt understood the passions stirred by the changing place of the United States in the world in part because he was himself an immigrant deeply interested in international affairs. After Bartholdt abandoned his *Gymnasium* (high school) studies in Germany, he had been drawn, like many other young European men of the nineteenth century, into a family migration chain. In 1872, he had followed his father's brother to Brooklyn where he worked as a printer for the German-language newspaper operated by his cousin.

When he subsequently moved west to Missouri, the young immigrant became a reporter, an editor, and an American citizen. After his election to Congress as a Republican in 1892, Bartholdt returned for the first time to Germany in order to celebrate the achievement with his aging father. It was the first of more than fifty transatlantic steamship trips for the naturalized American congressman.

Bartholdt became an internationalist activist who believed that the United States had a special role to play in world affairs. While growing numbers of American voters came to see legislated restrictions on immigration as a necessary protection against foreign dangers, Bartholdt, along with a small group of foreign-born congressmen even younger than himself, instead sought ways to protect immigrants and their foreign relations. The opposition they faced was massive, global—and sometimes personal. It became personal for Richard Bartholdt when American xenophobia ended his political career: during World War I his German birth made Richard Bartholdt unacceptable as a candidate for higher political office.

The international migrations of the nineteenth century provoked reactions in many, many countries, not just in the United States, especially as war and economic crisis came to dominate international relations. The so-called "American Century" would not be a peaceful one; on the contrary, one historian has labeled the wars and revolutions of the twentieth century a "descent into barbarism."[2] Death tolls related to political violence around the world became truly terrifying: no fewer than 100 million civilians and soldiers had died during wars, revolutions, and civil conflicts by the century's end. To the short list of official wars fought by

American soldiers (the 1898 Spanish-American War; World War I, 1917–18; World War II, 1941–45) can be added the longer list of U.S. military interventions (Haiti, 1915; Mexico, 1914 and 1916; Korea, 1950–53; Guatemala, 1954; Cuba, 1961; the Dominican Republic, 1965; Vietnam, 1957–1975) and of violent revolutions affecting Americans who lived or did business abroad (Mexico, 1910; Russia, 1917; China, 1949; Cuba, 1959; Chile, 1973). A forty-year-long Cold War with the Soviet Union, 1945–1989, further exacerbated Americans' concerns about domestic security. After 1935, as free trade and the lowering of tariffs worldwide became the official U.S. formula for global peace and international cooperation, and as international migration plummeted globally, domestic polls in the United States documented persistent and sometimes sizable popular support for reducing still further the numbers of immigrants.

During the long, symbolic reign of the myth of American isolation, immigration had arguably been as important in connecting the United States to the world as either foreign trade or the country's official international relations. Over the course of the twentieth century, immigration's importance in creating a global America diminished dramatically. Unlike histories that examine immigration restriction as a product of domestic racism, a history of American immigration from a global perspective situates the racism and xenophobia that drove immigration restriction within a century-long political struggle over American foreign policy and its governance. That battle originated with the rise of the United States as a global power and its abandonment of the myth of isolation. Battles between internationalists and isolationists repeatedly pitted the executive branch, and especially the American president, against Congress. An examination of three funda-mental political conflicts—over federal governance of foreign relations, over the balance of power between the executive and legislative branches in regulating immigration and trade, and over the appropriate mechanisms for selecting among immigrants once their numbers were restricted—suggest how the United States was transformed from an isolationist country of high tariffs and relatively free immigration into a global power that advocated free trade while seeking to control and limit entry across its borders.

Decades-long battles produced new mechanisms for the governance of American foreign relations, with trade policy increasingly emerging from grand, multilateral, executive-branch geopolitical strategies, and immigration policy increasingly falling under unilateral, domestic, and legisla-tive control. As these two formerly entwined dimensions of foreign policy diverged, immigrants' mobilizations on behalf of their foreign friends and kin and their homelands also shifted in focus. At first, immigrant voters had mobilized through domestic electoral politics and congressional lob-bying. Soon, however, politically savvy citizens of recent immigrant origin recognized that the concern of Ameri-can presidents with foreign policy could at times make the executive branch into a useful ally in countering the impact of restrictive laws. By 1965, the alliance of presidential and immigrant-origin immigration reformers could even claim some successes. Still, as immigrants increasingly sought advantage for their individual kin, they became less likely to pursue structural change through the kinds of transnational political mobilizations that had been common in the nine-teenth century.

CHANGING AMERICAN FOREIGN RELATIONS:
STATE OR FEDERAL GOVERNANCE?

Although the American Constitution explicitly restricted the conduct of international relations to the federal government, federal governance of both trade and immigration faced repeated challenges by the states. South Carolina had threatened secession over a federal tariff in 1832, and when the Supreme Court in 1849 invalidated state and municipal immigration laws, it did so in the midst of an escalating, passionate, and ultimately violent regional conflict over states' rights. It would take much more than a single, evenly divided, Supreme Court judgment to convince states to abandon their efforts to protect their citizens by restricting immigration.

As southerners in the 1850s continued to advocate for the rights of states to preserve slavery, lower tariffs, and define citizens' rights—in other words, to behave as sovereign— state and local efforts to regulate immigration and naturalization also persisted. New Yorkers again tried to raise revenues to support the state-operated immigrant processing center, Castle Garden, through head taxes and other fees imposed on shippers or passengers. In the aftermath of the 1848 U.S. war with Mexico (and the consequent acquisition by the United States of a new population of dark-skinned Catholic residents), xenophobic voters in many parts of the country began to elect officials from the secretive American Party (usually called the "Know-Nothings"), which promised to pass laws to limit access to naturalization, citizenship, and public office by Catholics and aliens. White Californians imposed a head tax on foreign miners, required merchant shippers to post bonds for Chinese migrants, and imposed taxes on Chinese businesses. Despite court rulings, states' challenges continued until the Civil War.

After 1860, with the seceded southern states no longer represented in Washington, the federal government began to consolidate its control over immigration more vigorously, even as it raised tariffs to finance its war against the southern rebels. Abraham Lincoln created a short-lived Immigration Bureau to recruit immigrant workers from Europe, while Congress prohibited the transportation to the United States on American-owned ships of "coolies" (indentured Chinese) and proclaimed aliens who had declared their intentions to naturalize (a privilege still limited to whites) eligible to apply for western homesteads.

Postwar constitutional amendments and federal civil rights legislation that defined the status of newly emancipated slaves aimed to resolve these federal-state conflicts. A report to the president in 1873 began with the assertion that "citizenship is national," and a matter of "national, not individual state, sovereignty" and ended by proclaiming: "It is the nation and the nation only that can make and un-make citizens,"[3] an issue of interest to both newly emancipated slaves and to immigrants. Soon thereafter, the Supreme Court again invalidated a New York head tax, along with several West Coast anti-Chinese laws—some for violating the Commerce Clause, others for violating federal Civil Rights laws, the Fourteenth Amendment or, in the case of western anti-Chinese laws, the 1868 Burlingame Treaty. Summarizing what he surely hoped would be the final round in the battle over states regulating immigration, a federal judge argued that "between this [California law against Asian immigration] and the 'firing on

Fort Sumter,' . . . there is the difference of the direct and the indirect—and nothing more."[4]

State-level efforts to regulate immigration had reached the same dead end as southerners' challenges to federal tariffs in the 1830s. As states'-rights challenges ended, federal administrative oversight of immigration transferred from the Department of State to the Treasury and then to the Commerce and Labor Department, removing the examination of immigrants from the hands of customs collectors. A new Bureau of Immigration created in 1891 oversaw the building of immigration processing centers on Ellis Island in New York's harbor (it opened in 1893) and on San Francisco's Angel Island (opened in 1910). In 1906, Congress created uniform naturalization procedures, limited naturalization proceedings to federal courts, and joined the Bureaus of Immigration and of Naturalization to administer both entry and the making of new citizens.

In the cases of both tariff and trade policies and immigration policy, however, consolidation at the federal level merely shifted the venue for longstanding conflicts. For most of the century after 1860, battles continued to rage over whether and how tariffs and immigration restriction protected Americans from foreign threats. Meanwhile, the system of federal governance that linked trade and immigration policies began to unravel in Washington.

CHANGING FOREIGN RELATIONS: EXECUTIVE OR LEGISLATIVE GOVERNANCE OF TARIFFS?

It can be very difficult, from the vantage point of the twenty-first century, to understand the "sheer volume" of rhetoric that "spewed forth" from late-nineteenth-century politicians, editors, and voters on the subject of the tariff.[5] It can be even more difficult to understand the relevance of these debates for immigration restriction. Nevertheless, tariffs were the most important nineteenth-century expression of Americans' desire for protection from negative, foreign influences. And foreign trade and immigration had also been inextricably linked in the governance of U.S. foreign policy. The passionate, but also repetitive, tariff debates are not only crucial to our understanding of the history of immigration restriction, they also hold clues to how immigration came to be regarded, and regulated, as a domestic matter. In fact, it is in the tariff debates of the late nineteenth and early twentieth centuries that the governance of foreign trade and of immigration began to come uncoupled.

Throughout the nineteenth century, advocates of economic protection through high tariffs had battled supporters of low or no tariffs, who increasingly called themselves advocates of free trade. Even after violently contested elections, however, changes in tariffs legislated by Congress were typically incremental, often raising or lowering import duties on particular goods from particular countries by only a few percentage points. Even relatively small changes were hotly debated and candidates' positions on tariff issues figured prominently in election-year debates. As congressional seats changed hands between parties, and the balance of party power shifted back and forth, voters could often see no long-term trends toward either raising or lowering tariffs. Although tariffs had at times climbed considerably higher, the 1913 Underwood Simmons Act fixed tariffs at an average of 27 percent—just above their level in 1855. As the constant raising and lowering of tariffs absorbed congressional energies and generated vituperative election-year debates, many identified an emerging political stalemate for which there seemed no obvious solution. No wonder that a weary supporter warned Congressman Richard Bartholdt, who was preparing to write his memoirs, "Whatever you do, don't write about the tariff; it is too dull and threadbare a subject!"[6] And that is indeed how many readers today think of the nineteenth-century tariff battles.

In the resolution of this political stalemate over tariffs, however, it is possible to perceive how immigration policy became domesticated and separated from the regulation of foreign trade. Whereas in the 1850s, Whig observers had insisted that "the higher the tariff, the higher the figure of immigration" (since tariffs raised U.S. wages, which in turn attracted workers from abroad),[7] an editorial writer of 1909 instead resented the fact that "the smart men who control our business methods" had been "shrewd enough to teach the rank and file of voters that a tariff on the products of labor is a protection to the laborer himself." The writer then demanded instead a "Duty on Immigrants; as a Means of Directly Protecting American Labor."[8] In short, critics began to argue that tariffs did not protect American workers, since the real threat to their jobs came not from imported goods but rather from immigrants. By 1913, the American Federation of Labor agreed with Frank Julian Warne when he concluded that "the enlightened American workingman objects to unlimited or free trade in immigration," which he characterized as an invasion. Workers, Warne emphasized, wanted protection from immigrants, not protection from imports.[9] By the time he wrote, in other words, congressional debates over protective tariffs were already giving way to debates over immigration restriction as the preferred mechanism for protecting Americans from foreign threats.

The extrication of immigration regulation from the governance of foreign trade hinged on this new understanding of protectionism that made immigrants, not imports, the invaders Americans most feared. As Congress increasingly focused on protecting Americans from immigrants, they were also able to rethink the governance of foreign trade, especially after the passage of a federal income tax in 1913 promised to replace revenues that had been generated earlier by tariffs.

Congressmen, presidents, and State Department officials who supported American commercial expansion and international leadership (but who needed regular revenue streams to accomplish these ends) worked to transform the tariff, in the felicitous words of one economic historian, from "a tool of national survival to one of international integration."[10] They increasingly sought to remove the determination and fine-tuning of tariffs from the hands of Congress, where the conflicting interests of democratic politics too easily resulted in political stalemates. Their goal was to gain congressional consent for an increased State Department role in the negotiation of reciprocal or bilateral treaties, different from the commercial treaties of the past and aimed specifically at lowering tariffs. Vehemently pro-tariff, Republican congressman Nelson Aldrich hated such "modern diplomatic inventions."[11] Despite considerable opposition in the House of Representatives, the 1890 McKinley tariff nevertheless empowered the executive branch to increase U.S. tariffs when European nations raised rates on U.S. exports. The 1897 Dingley Tariff also expanded the bargaining powers of the

executive branch, and Democratic president Grover Cleveland appointed a "reciprocity commission" to advise him on
the kinds of reciprocal tariff reductions his diplomats might
have the opportunity to negotiate. With Congress's responsibility for raising revenues fulfilled through a federal income
tax, another foundation for political wrangling over tariffs
fell aside.

Thus, even when the House raised tariff rates again, as it
did in 1922 and in 1930, it allowed the executive branch to
modify rates as diplomatic opportunities arose. Democratic
president Franklin Roosevelt gained still more authority over
tariffs after arguing that the 1930 Smoot Hawley Tariff had
precipitated a disastrous trade war, exacerbating the domestic effects of the global Great Depression.[12] In 1934, Congress
created a Reciprocal Trade Agreements Program (RTAP)
that further shifted governance of tariffs toward the executive branch. President Harry S. Truman continued to argue
that high tariffs had made the Second World War inevitable.
The United States "must lead in cutting tariffs," he argued
in early 1947, in order to avert renewed "economic 'war.'"[13]
Republican president Dwight Eisenhower agreed: multilateral free trade agreements were the best foundation for
global peace. From the United Nations in 1945 and the North
Atlantic Treaty Organization (NATO) in 1949 to the General Agreement on Tariffs and Trade (GATT—superseded
in 1995 by the World Trade Organization, WTO), postwar
international organizations followed American leadership in
advocating for free trade. By 1965, U.S. tariff rates had fallen
by more than half. However, over the past century, as its
power to set tariffs diminished, Congress sought to fulfill its
protectionist role by instead restricting immigration.

CHANGING FOREIGN RELATIONS: EXECUTIVE OR LEGISLATIVE GOVERNANCE OF IMMIGRATION?

As the governance of tariffs moved increasingly into the executive branch, governance of immigration moved away from its moorings in commercial diplomacy and into Congress. The shift was not easy or swift. A pitched and prolonged battle between Congress and the executive branch poured the foundations for immigration restriction by legislation and also made Congress the main site of power for those seeking immigration reform.

The two branches first collided over Chinese immigration under the provisions of the 1868 Burlingame Treaty. The Senate had ratified the treaty during Reconstruction, when egalitarian radical Republicans were briefly in the ascendant and former Confederates, largely Democrats, excluded from Congress. Famously, the Burlingame Treaty extended to the Chinese the same liberty to travel, trade, and reside freely that had figured in earlier trade treaties with Europe. China's rulers had long sought such reciprocity with Western nations but had rarely gained it. The outcry against the Burlingame Treaty from voters in the western states was enormous and immediate. In 1875 Congress placated California voters with a law requiring consular inspection of immigrants from Asia and excluding prostitutes, indentured laborers ("coolies"), and convicted criminals (without however specifically naming China as the source of these problems). Desiring to expand trade with China, the executive branch then warned Congress against insulting China's emperor by restricting only immigration from China.

In 1880, soon after California's latest Constitutional Convention asked Congress for further relief from the purportedly baneful effect of Chinese immigration, a particularly blunt *New York Times* editorialist offered his own cynical solution to the festering conflict between legislated restrictions and commercial diplomacy. In the past, he observed, the United States "made numerous treaties with our Indian tribes and violated them whenever the Northwestern voter . . . desired to seize [their] land." Thus, he continued, "one of the fundamental principles of our Government [is] that we are under no obligation to keep treaties" with the "weak and powerless" nations of the world. On the contrary, he continued, "We keep treaties made with nations like England and France, who are able to resent bad faith and dishonesty on our part, but the Indians can be cheated with impunity. We can apply the same reasoning to the treaty [with China]." China could not "possibly invade our coasts with a powerful fleet and batter down our towns." In his view, China's weakness made respect for the Burlingame Treaty mere "sentimental nonsense."[14]

The State Department remained committed to the "sentimental nonsense" of diplomacy, however, and it was a new treaty, negotiated with China in 1880, that opened the way for Congress to exclude laborers from China for ten years, beginning in 1882; the same treaty continued to protect merchants' liberties to travel and reside. Congress renewed the ban on laborers again in 1892. In 1902, over China's renewed diplomatic protests, Congress's exclusion of Chinese laborers became permanent. Emboldened, Congress also imposed head taxes on all immigrants; it excluded paupers, lunatics, the deaf, the blind, and convicts, along with any infirm persons or others (for example women or young children traveling alone) deemed unlikely to work and thus liable to become a public charge, as well as contract (or indentured) laborers.

The Supreme Court not only supported Congress's expanding role in governing immigration, but also declared congressional power over immigration exempt from almost every constitutional review or limit. The precedent for its far-reaching conclusion was an 1889 case brought by a detained Chinese laborer, Chae Chan Ping.[15] Associate Justice Stephen Johnson Field (whom Lincoln had appointed to the court because he was a westerner) wrote the majority opinion in the case, which confirmed the power of the United States to exclude from its territories any person or group of people that Congress deemed a threat. Field argued that treaties held no greater power over immigration than did Congress. He argued further that once the courts of the United States had acknowledged Congress's power to regulate immigration (as they now had), they should limit their interventions to applying law to specific cases and should not further challenge Congress's powers to restrict or exclude. (Significantly, it was the refusal of the Supreme Court to review the cases of aggrieved Chinese merchants that sparked the 1905 boycott.)

Field reiterated many of the same points raised in the 1849 Passenger Cases. He noted that international law required governments to protect their subjects or citizens. But Field described protection more broadly as including the power to exclude anyone deemed threatening, for any reason, from the nation's territories. Indeed, Field continued, the power to exclude was the foundation for every nation's jurisdiction over its own national territory; the power to exclude was, he insisted, "part of its independence" and survival, and thus a key to national sovereignty. In Field's formulation, the obligation of the government to protect existed prior to and outside the provisions of the Constitution. It could not be legislated away; it could not be negotiated away by diplomats; it could not be limited by courts. Field strongly implied that every foreigner was an invader, for he devoted many words in his argument to a comparison of Congress's right to expel foreigners with its constitutional power to declare war. On this basis, Congress soon found it unproblematic to exclude anarchists—its first ideological exclusion of immigrants—in 1902. More restrictions would follow.

Although Ping v. U.S. seemed applicable only to immigrant foreigners, its assertion of Congress's unlimited (so-called plenary or full) power to protect the nation, its territory, and citizens from foreign threats had significant implications for the governance by the United States of foreigners living in its foreign, colonized territories as well. The so-called Insular Cases called attention to how plenary power linked the governance of immigration and empire. As Senator Joseph B. Foraker, an advocate of American expansion, explained, under the Insular Cases of 1902, "the Constitution does not follow the flag."[16] The Constitution and the rights it guarantees apply only in U.S. territories in North America, Alaska, and Hawaii; any alien could be denied entry to these territories, and, conversely, foreigners admitted as immigrants could enjoy constitutional protection only in these territories. In other, U.S.–governed foreign territories, there would be no constitutional rights for colonized "foreigners" native to those "foreign" places. Similarly, foreigners seeking admission to North America or Hawaii as immigrants to the United States remained unprotected by the Constitution. Until immigrant foreigners actually gained admission and entry into U.S. territory in North America, their constitutional status was little different from foreigners residing in and native to American colonies established abroad.

Once the court had endorsed this breathtaking expansion of congressional governance of immigration, almost every subsequent president and secretary of state of the United States found cause to challenge it, along with many of the immigration restrictions that Congress subsequently passed. Restrictions on immigration often insulted countries whose goodwill (and usually also trading opportunities) the executive branch and its consuls wished to have. Fearing negative consequences for Americans living in China, the State Department argued repeatedly against extending restriction to Chinese merchants, students, and ministers. As the United States recognized Japan as a rising and rapidly modernizing power in the Pacific, formal complaints from the Japanese government about the segregation of Japanese children in San Francisco also landed on the desk of President Theodore Roosevelt in 1906. Quiet negotiations produced an informal gentlemen's agreement whereby Japan prohibited further emigration of laborers, but Roosevelt then felt it necessary to warn California legislators that "The Constitution Comes First" in protecting the rights of those foreigners, including Japanese, who had been allowed to enter and reside in the United States.[17]

Roosevelt's secretary of state, Elihu Root, assessed the new governance of immigration by legislators far more bluntly. "The practice of diplomacy has ceased to be a mystery confined to a few learned men," he openly lamented, "and has become a representative [legislative] function answering to the opinions and will of the multitude of citizens."[18] In short, the governance of immigration was becoming more democratic as it became more unilateral and legislative; democratic governance would rarely respect the desires of immigrants or of the executive branch to maintain or extend relations to other parts of the world. In the halls of Congress, the popular scientific racism and isolationism of many American voters soon prevailed.

East Coast scientific racists mobilized as the Immigration Restriction League (founded in 1894 by prominent New Englanders at Harvard) and began to argue for the restriction of "elements undesirable for citizenship or injurious to our national character." They suggested that a literacy test would mainly exclude those groups—Asians, Mexicans, and southern and eastern Europeans—with the least racial capacity for democratic governance.[19] Insisting that they wanted to protect democracy, restrictionists in Congress repeatedly sought to impose a literacy requirement on all prospective immigrants, only to see both Democratic presidents Grover Cleveland (in 1897) and Woodrow Wilson (in 1914 and 1917) and Republican president William Howard Taft (in 1913) veto their legislation. On the eve of the U.S. entry into World War I in 1917, Woodrow Wilson used his veto to address the troubling implications of restricting migrants from European countries that were about to become U.S. allies. It was also presidents, and the occasional foreign-born congressman, who spoke of restriction as an insult to American citizens of immigrant origin.

Americans' still-powerful desires for isolation mixed potently with the rebalancing of executive and legislative governance of foreign affairs as the United States went to war in Europe. It is no accident that immigration restriction triumphed during and just after World War I. Nothing symbolized better the U.S. abandonment of isolation and the myth of isolation, its continued entanglement with Europe, and the exposure of its citizens to foreign dangers than a foreign war, fought in Europe, as part of a European alliance (with France and Great Britain) to defeat Germany. Scholars have long recognized the unsettling effects of Democratic president Woodrow Wilson's "internationalist" agenda of lowered tariffs, a military campaign "to make the world safe for democracy,"[20] and a proposal for a postwar League of Nations. By war's end, observers of congressional politics wrote openly of a new "isolationism": indeed, it was at this time that the term was invented. So-called isolationists opposed every element of Wilsonian geopolitical strategy. The internationalism of Woodrow Wilson and the new isolationism of his congressional opponents figured prominently not only in debates over the League of Nations but also in the triumph of immigration restriction.

The impact of isolationism on immigration restriction is on clear view in the frequent political interventions on both issues of Henry Cabot Lodge, the senator from Massachusetts who was not only an early supporter of the Immigration Restriction League but also the powerful chair of the Senate Foreign Relations Committee from 1919 until 1924. Lodge was no typical isolationist. He had supported U.S. expansion and even the acquisition of new territories from Spain in 1898. He had not joined the fifty-seven congressmen who voted against the U.S. declaration of war against Germany in 1917. (In April of 1917, the sixty-seven-year-old senator had knocked down a pacifist who—by Lodge's account, at any rate—called him a coward for his support of the war declaration and tried to hit him.[21]) Lodge nevertheless detested Wilsonian internationalism, which he saw as a threat to American sovereignty. In 1919 he wondered, "How much of our sovereignty we are justified in sacrificing?" and went on to emphasize how much he loathed the thought of sharing his devotion to the American flag with what he called "a mongrel banner created for a League." Lodge's use of the word "mongrel" for both immigrants and foreign flags nicely demonstrates how restriction, scientific racism, and isolation sometimes intertwined. Lodge denied feeling any hostility to the humanitarian goals of internationalism but expressed his certainty that the United States could best promote peace and civilization "by not putting ourselves in leading strings [treaties] or subjecting our policies and our sovereignty to other nations."[22]

Within months, Lodge offered his formal "reservations" to the "mongrel" League. They included his belief that the U.S. Congress alone had "the right to decide what questions are within its domestic jurisdiction." Lodge's understanding of "domestic and political questions relating wholly or in part to its internal affairs," grew to a capacious list that included "immigration, labor, coastwise traffic, the tariff, [and] commerce. . . ." Such domestic or internal questions were, in Lodge's view, "solely within the jurisdiction of the United States"; they could not be subjected to bilateral or multilateral negotiations or treaties as part of the executive branch's conduct of foreign affairs.[23] They were, in short, matters to be governed by Congress.

Lodge's expansive understanding of domestic policies and congressional power caused more traditional isolationists— who had opposed war in 1898 and in 1917—to rally around him. In 1920, the U.S. Senate refused to consent to the Versailles Treaty with its provisions for a League of Nations.

While the United States certainly did not return to complete isolation in the years that followed, the political vigor of the new isolationists was a reminder of how controversial American international activism—whether in the form of empire, foreign wars, or participation in international organizations—had been. Isolationists would soon play a key role in the passage and long-term defense of still harsher new restrictions on immigration.

In the aftermath of World War I, many isolationists (especially those from the South, which had earlier supported free migration, free trade, and low tariffs) now became—and long remained—strong supporters of immigration restriction. Lodge's continuing campaign for restriction closely mirrored his objections to the League. Immigrant "mongrels," in Lodge's eyes, lacked traditions of self-governance and thus, like the League, posed a threat to American self-rule and democracy, symbolized best by a vigorous U.S. Congress. Lodge and other congressmen had overridden Wilson's veto in 1917 and enacted not only a law that required immigrants to demonstrate that they could read and write in their native tongue, but also prohibited immigration from much of Asia (referred to as a "barred zone"). For South Carolina's Ellison Smith, chair of the Senate Immigration Committee in 1917, the very survival of the United States as a sovereign nation rested on the maintenance of what he called, in the language of scientific racism, a "pure, homogeneous American people,"[24] and the exclusion of racially inferior peoples. Congressional acts passed in 1921 and in 1924, the year of Lodge's death, excluded immigrants from all of Asia, reduced to 150,000 the total number of immigrants allowed to enter from the rest of the Eastern hemisphere, and apportioned visas by means of national-origins quotas that privileged immigrants from western and northern Europe over immigrants from southern and eastern Europe. No clearer statement can be found of Americans' desire to withdraw from foreign dangers.

Albert Johnson, a western Republican and the House sponsor of the 1924 law, recognized the significance of immigration restriction for isolationists when he called it "America's Second Declaration of Independence." Restriction sought to sever immigrants' connections to Europe and Asia as surely as the Senate's rejection of the League separated the United States from Wilsonian internationalism. Together, Johnson seemed to suggest, restriction and isolation would safeguard American independence, providing security from foreign turmoil. Johnson warned a meeting of the Daughters of the American Revolution that a country that would not protect its sovereignty through restriction of immigration invited attack. Johnson even viewed Japan's response to the exclusion of Japanese emigrants—it tellingly and immediately imposed a 100 percent tariff on U.S. imports—as itself constituting a threat of war. He did not regret the ensuing destruction of American businesses in Japan; such losses were the price of protecting what Johnson called "our sovereign right to regulate immigration to our shores."[25]

Despite Johnson's bravado, immigration could not easily be transformed into a purely domestic matter to be governed unilaterally by Congress. Nor did the success of the isolationists actually remove the United States from the global arena. Even many congressmen of the time acknowledged that to be impossible. In debating the 1924 law, for example, Congress carefully considered the risks of insulting their country's closest neighbors and chose (with strong support from employers in the Southwest) to impose no national-origins quotas on the countries of the Americas (the Western hemisphere). Even isolationists who hated diplomatic entanglements with Europe sometimes supported Pan-American goodwill as a better alternative than "big stick" gunboat diplomacy. The "American Good Neighbor Policy," so named rather casually by Herbert Hoover, rested at least in part on the exemption of American countries from the humiliations of immigration restriction, although it acquired still larger meaning after President Franklin Roosevelt's November 1933 announcement that the United States would no longer intervene militarily or create obstacles "to the free and untrammeled determination" by Latin American countries "of their own destinies."[26]

Nor did the executive branch completely abandon its role in immigration policy after 1924. Congress placed the day-to-day implementation of the restrictive national-origins quotas in the hands of American consuls abroad, just as it had in the case of the exclusion of Chinese workers forty years earlier. Rather than have immigration inspectors grant a limited number of visas at the border, the State Department performed the work of restriction abroad. Scholars have since labeled the consular administration of immigration restriction as an exercise in "remote control." Remote control had the advantage of defusing potential problems at the border by reducing the numbers turned away. But it also guaranteed the State Department a continued role in administering immigration.[27]

As American geopolitical strategies changed over time, so did the grounds for executive complaints about congressional restrictions. Franklin Roosevelt—another vigorous internationalist and humanitarian—believed already in the 1930s that the United States should respond to the growing militarization of Nazi Germany and to its mounting persecution of its Jewish population. But in 1924 the restrictionist and racist Albert Johnson had instead promised that restriction meant an end to "the idea that the United States is an asylum for the oppressed of the world";[28] Roosevelt's contemporary, Martin Dies—a Texas Democrat who would later lead investigations of suspected communists and other alien radicals—was even harsher. "We must," he asserted in 1934, "ignore the tears of sobbing sentimentalists and internationalists, and we must permanently close, lock, and bar the gates of our country to new immigration waves and then throw the keys away."[29] For citizen voters demoralized by high unemployment, Dies's words may have rung true. But the consequences of throwing away the keys would not be felt only by foreigners, since so many Europeans were the foreign relatives of Americans. More sympathetic to the plight of Germany's Jewish refugees than either the predominantly isolationist Congress or a skeptical State Department (where vocal anti-Semites and career diplomats enforced consuls' refusals to grant visas to Jewish refugees as "liable to become a public charge") Roosevelt sponsored the 1938 Evian conference in France, hoping for an international response. Unfortunately, as a scholar of international refugee policies concluded, the United States "made no new pledges to modify its own immigration law even to the extent of permitting the entry of Jewish Refugee children."[30] The influence of openly racist and xenophobic congressmen remained formidable: during the height of the European refugee crisis of 1939, as desperate German Jews paid large sums of money to board boats in search of refuge almost anywhere, American geneticist Harry H. Laughlin issued a new report from his position at the Carnegie Institution that again portrayed immigrants and refugees as invaders from inferior cultures.[31] American borders remained closed to Europe's refugees, and existing quotas for Germany went unfilled, even as Hitler's Nazi forces occupied Europe and began their "final solution" of genocide against Europe's Jews.

Humanitarianism was not the only force driving continued executive-branch interventions in the governance of migration. In 1940, President Roosevelt relocated the Immigration and Naturalization Service (INS) administration from the Labor Department to the Justice Department in order to facilitate the deportation of suspicious, and often communist, aliens and law-breakers. Moreover, once the United States entered the war, the Justice Department sought to head off the formation of any disloyal "fifth columns" (organized groups loyal to enemy governments) by requiring all aliens, regardless of origin or political sentiments, to register with the police.[32] The most egregious case of wartime's exacerbation of racial and xenophobic prejudices was President Roosevelt's 1942 Executive Order, which responded to Japan's attack on Pearl Harbor by sending all Japanese immigrants and their citizen descendants to inland internment camps. Even the 1798 Alien and Sedition Act, which had acknowledged the threat of enemies living in the United States during wartime and provided for strict policing, was limited in its application to enemy aliens, leaving citizens exempt from persecution. Yet even an internationalist and humanitarian like Roosevelt was not immune to fears that Japanese American citizens had inherited, biologically, the racial heritage and foreign loyalties of their parents.

Challenges to restriction nevertheless continued to emerge from the executive branch during the hot and cold wars of the 1940s and 1950s. Desperate to take action in the face of a European humanitarian crisis toward the end of World War II, Franklin Roosevelt boldly invented a new executive-branch power to "parole" into the United States a token shipment of largely Jewish refugees from camps in Italy.[33] President Harry Truman warned congressional isolationists in 1945 against passing new laws that would again "prohibit or severely reduce further immigration" as contrary to the international interests of the country.[34] As commander-in-chief of the military, both Truman (a Democrat) and Republican Dwight Eisenhower responded to demands from American soldiers wanting to marry women they met while serving abroad; they managed to convince Congress to provide the required legislation, although the reluctance of southern and western Democrats to the admission of Japanese "war brides" threatened at first to scuttle the initiatives.[35] Convincing Congress to admit refugees proved even harder. Truman saw their admission as a foundation for constructing anti-communist European alliances and for establishing U.S. leadership of the United Nations Relief and Rehabilitation Administration. Only in 1948, and then begrudgingly, did Congress authorize 200,000 non-quota visas for Europe's Displaced Persons. There would be no visas at all for Asia's millions of refugees until 1960.

Both Truman and Eisenhower saw immigration restriction as a hindrance to their Cold War campaigns for global democracy and for American leadership of the new nations emerging in what was later called the "Third World" of formerly colonized lands in Africa, Asia, Latin America, and the Caribbean. Isolationists, scientific racists, and anti-communists in Congress remained unmoved. The 1952 McCarran-Walter Act did raise the numerical cap on immigrants from the "old world" to 270,000 yearly, and it ended race-based exclusions of Asians only by providing extremely small quotas for them. Contrary to Truman's hopes, it continued the use of highly restrictive national-origins quotas for Europe. (Migrants from the Americas also remained exempt from numerical limits.) The act continued to exempt some relatives from numerical restrictions, but now also privileged entry by highly skilled immigrants and banned communist sympathizers from entry. It created a small number of visas for refugees and authorized the executive parole of refugees, but it granted the power to the president's Attorney General, not to the president, and then only on an emergency basis. Furious about the continuation of the national-origins quotas, which insulted potential allies in containing communism internationally, President Truman vetoed the McCarran-Walter Act, but to no avail. Although Congress overturned Truman's veto, even Republican presidential candidate Dwight Eisenhower argued that the nation needed "a better immigration law" than the McCarran Act with its internationally offensive racial and national exclusions.[36] Eisenhower, too, would fail to achieve this goal, although he did manage to convince a Republican-dominated Congress to admit additional refugees by special legislation. Given widespread international awareness of discriminatory American immigration quotas and the persistence of domestic Jim Crow laws, American

presidents and State Departments faced constant embarrass-
ment when arguing abroad for the superiority of capitalism,
democracy, and the American way of life against their communist Cold War opponents in the USSR.

Once established, parole by the executive branch remained
an important mechanism for admitting Cuban, eastern
European, and Southeast Asian refugees. In 1956, President
Eisenhower ordered the parole of 30,000 Hungarians fleeing a failed revolution against Soviet troops. Parole status
was temporary and could be subsequently revoked, but the
majority of refugees, once in the United States, succeeded in
obtaining residency and access to naturalization and citizenship. People fleeing communist revolutions and communist-
dominated countries were almost alone in finding refuge in
the United States, however. Until 1980 the United States
ignored the 1951 U.N. Convention that defined refugees
more broadly.[37] Sometimes even anti-communists in Congress opposed increases in the numbers of anti-communist
refugees admitted: in 1956, Francis Walter, sponsor of the
1952 McCarran-Walter act, had proclaimed his certainty that
some of the Hungarians admitted as freedom fighters into
the United States "once were Reds."[38]

Thus, even after Congress had domesticated immigration policy, increasing the power of American voters to enact
immigration restriction, the executive branch retained a
lively interest in continuing and even increasing immigration. So did the millions of recently naturalized immigrants,
many of whom had become citizen voters and raised citizen
children within networks that connected their parents and
the United States to foreign lands. Both immigrants and the
officials charged with the conduct of official foreign relations

knew that no Supreme Court decision, fearful American voter, or congressional plenary power could transform immigration into a strictly domestic matter. Slowly, and often ambivalently, immigrants and the executive branch began to identify each other as potential allies in a campaign against the restrictions Congress had created. They formed a new coalition advocating immigration reform. As the Americans who felt most directly the consequences of restriction, immigrants had begun to explore their own options for protecting their foreign relations under Congress's governance of immigration policy.

THE NEW RULES OF GOVERNANCE:
THREE LIFE STORIES

Restriction terrified many immigrants; it especially terrified immigrants already accustomed to autocratic rule and hostile governments in their former homes. Apart from Native Americans and African-Americans, few Americans understood as intimately as recently arrived immigrants how fundamentally governmental agents could disrupt their lives. On the West Coast, detained immigrants from Asia left plaintive and angry poetry on the walls of Angel Island.[39] In the East, immigrants from Europe heard so many tales of families separated and persons excluded or detained that they began to call Ellis Island the "Island of Tears."[40] After 1917, immigrants faced escalating demands for papers and passports and visas that certified they were harmless or that they matched exactly the ever-more carefully delimited categories deemed worthy of admission. Under restriction, former ports of entry increasingly became sites of detention and of deportation for Europeans, too, as they had long been for the Chinese.

On December 22, 1919, Dora Lipkin, a Russian-born immigrant incarcerated on Ellis Island, personally discovered the power of American law to restrict and to exclude. She was deported by force along with two hundred other supposedly dangerous radicals. The month before, on the second anniversary of the Russian Revolution, Lipkin had been arrested together with her male companion at a Manhattan party sponsored by the Union of Russian Workers. It is unlikely that Dora Lipkin had ever heard of the 1918 Alien Act, which permitted the deportation of foreign-born persons advocating the overthrow of government, but Lipkin nonetheless became one of only three women among the two hundred so-called reds loaded onto the U.S.S. Buford and shipped to the Soviet Union. Sharing her room was Emma Goldman, the well-known and outspoken anarchist activist who would denounce communist authoritarianism soon after her arrival in Russia.

Unlike Lipkin, Goldman was a U.S. citizen; her naturalization had been revoked in order to facilitate her deportation. The deportation proceedings of the two women were closely monitored by Methodist minister Constantine Panunzio, himself an immigrant (from Italy), who immediately questioned the practice of deporting a person "merely for the possession of ideas."[41] But had anyone questioned Dora Lipkin about her ideas? Apparently not: her presence at a party sponsored by a Russian organization and celebrating the Russian Revolution and her association with an anarchist boyfriend constituted in her case "advocacy of the overthrow of government." Lipkin was deported to the country

she had left as an infant. In the aftermath of World War
I—and during later periods of international warfare, too—
Americans nervous about the dangers of the world began to
accept without question that immigrants and alien radicals
living in the United States—whether they were leaders like
Goldman or followers like Lipkin—could be denied rights
Americans claimed for themselves.

Three years before Lipkin's arrest, an explosion in a New
York–area harbor had been attributed to German spies; a
few months earlier, the New York Stock Exchange had been
bombed, presumably by immigrant Italian anarchists. Lipkin had nothing to do with these events, of course. But she
became guilty by association. A cartoon of the time portrayed
what many Americans accepted as a completely appropriate and defensive response: it showed a powerful American
eagle protecting its American nest by tossing out "reds." In
this disturbing image, both foreigners and their ideas literally became garbage—a classic device in racist and nationalist propaganda. That the deportation of people holding
objectionable ideas ("garbage") might eventually undermine
Americans' own rights to speak freely did not go completely
unnoticed at the time—the American Civil Liberties Union
was formed in 1920, the year after Lipkin's arrest—but by
then Lipkin's American life was over. After taking leave of
Goldman in Moscow, Dora Lipkin disappeared forever from
the historical record.[42]

Lipkin's encounter with immigration restriction was an
extreme one, but it was no worse than the harsh encounters of thousands of Chinese merchants and laborers with
custom inspectors or with rioting working-class vigilantes
determined to terminate the presence of the "yellow peril" in

the western states. The denial of foreigners' liberty of thought and opinion became routine as Americans rejected their liberty to move about freely and instead increasingly perceived immigrants as potentially dangerous invaders to be treated like enemy alien soldiers even in peacetime when the United States remained friendly toward their home countries.

It is scarcely surprising that immigrants reacted powerfully to restriction, or that they sought to protect themselves as best they could from the worst of its impacts. The political histories of two foreign-born American congressmen reveal how immigrants sought to do so. The two men were typical in objecting not to immigration restriction itself, and not to all restrictions, but mainly to the restrictions they perceived as most threatening to themselves, their relatives, and the constituents who had elected them. Immigrants' concerns for their relatives more often made them humanitarians and internationalists than xenophobes or isolationists, but their humanitarianism had its limits.

Consider Richard Bartholdt, the congressman who had unintentionally observed the connection between immigration and tariff debates in the 1890s and whose friend had cautioned him against writing too much about boring tariffs. In spite of the warning, Bartholdt participated personally in many congressional battles over protective tariffs and immigration restriction between 1892 and World War I. During most of his ten terms in Congress, he found himself speaking, usually rather mildly, in favor of tariffs to protect American industries and workers' jobs. He acknowledged that the world was "slowly drifting" toward free trade but in later life proclaimed himself proud that he "always voted for protection" because he believed it to be the best policy "for the time being. . . ."[43] When Congress addressed immigration restriction, by contrast, Bartholdt's voice grew louder, he intervened more actively and more often, and his colleagues also recognized his authority as a spokesman for the growing population of naturalized immigrant citizens of the United States.

Soon after Bartholdt's election to a third term in 1896, Congress considered a literacy bill introduced by supporters of the Immigration Restriction League. Although relatively new to the Congress, Richard Bartholdt chaired the House of Representatives' hearings on the bill. That same year, he also became one of a small group of foreign-born congressmen who proclaimed for the first time in Congress that the United States was a "nation of immigrants."[44] Fearing (rightly) that he could not convince a House majority to reject the literacy bill, Bartholdt instead took what pleasure he could in making a fool of the anti-Chinese Californian, Congressman (and later Customs Collector in San Diego, where he would examine Yitang Chang) William Wallace Bowers. Years later, Bartholdt recounted how Bowers had moaned during the hearings about "the alleged physical deterioration of the American people on account of the wholesale admission of foreigners." At that point Bartholdt called into the hearing room a very tall Swede, whom he had invited to remain outside the hearing room, awaiting the right moment to introduce him as "one of those consumptive specimens of immigrant, so well described by the last speaker."[45] Bartholdt's practical joke revealed Bowers as a racist and xenophobe, and Bowers did not forget the humiliation; he subsequently introduced an unsuccessful bill to prohibit foreign-born citizens such as Bartholdt from holding public office.[46] Like other elected officials of foreign birth, Bartholdt also personally

experienced the impact of rising xenophobia in the late nineteenth century, although, as a northern European, he was
largely exempt from the most violent expressions of American
racism. Nevertheless, the American Protective Association
(the main anti-Catholic organization of that era) declared
that Bartholdt, a Protestant, had fallen "under Catholic influence" when he accepted hospitality from a priest during his
travels around his district in 1899.[47]

Bartholdt was not so much a critic of restriction as a
critic of literacy as the appropriate mechanism for imposing restrictions. Rather consistently, in fact, he distinguished
between more and less desirable immigrants, and he supported the exclusion of Chinese laborers, whom he portrayed
on occasion as heathens and barbarians. In his memoir, the
usually pragmatic Bartholdt warned that Americans would
either "have to change our attitude towards those who are
willing to come through our Eastern gates or open our
Western gates to the influx of Orientals."[48] And if he ever
spoke out against the exclusion of immigrant anarchists or
of the deportation of immigrants like Dora Lipkin, we find
no record of his objections.

Despite his involvement in domestic politics, Richard
Bartholdt was decidedly internationalist in his thinking,
and he maintained throughout his life a special interest in
the continent of his birth. Bartholdt voyaged frequently to
Europe to attend meetings of the Interparliamentary Union.
A nongovernmental organization (NGO) formed by a mixed
(Lodge might have said "mongrel") group of European and
North American elected officials, the group was committed
to fostering the peaceful resolution of international disputes

through arbitration (a goal the League of Nations would also try to realize). Bartholdt even hoped for a time that American schools might embrace the teaching of Esperanto, a language invented in 1887 to facilitate international communication and world peace. Given his advocacy of peace, and his adamant rejection of German nationalism, Bartholdt understandably felt unfairly pushed from public life by the sudden rise of anti-German xenophobia among voters in Missouri during and just after World War I. He had hoped to run for the Senate after retiring from the House in 1912, but he soon discovered that he would never again be able to secure a nomination for public office.

New foreign-born opponents of restriction replaced Bartholdt in Congress, but their numbers seemed to dwindle after the 1920s. Among this group was Chicago Democrat Adolph Joachim Sabath, a Jewish lawyer born in Zabori, an Austrian town that later became part of Czechoslovakia. (Today it is in the Czech Republic.) In 1881, at age fifteen, Sabath immigrated to join a cousin in Chicago. While attending public high school, he worked odd jobs to pay for steamship tickets so his parents, brothers, and sisters could reunite their family in Chicago. Then, after studying law and dealing in real estate, Sabath became a political protégé of Illinois governor Peter Altgeld, who appointed him a justice of the peace and a police magistrate. Sabath attracted negative attention from xenophobes in Chicago already during these early years, for, when necessary, he conducted court business in the many languages spoken by the petty claimants who appeared before him.[49] The fact that Sabath, like many Central European immigrants, was multilingual surely helped him also in attracting naturalized immigrant voters when he ran successfully for Congress in 1907.

Sabath, like Bartholdt, consistently opposed a literacy requirement as a means for selecting among immigrants in order to restrict their total numbers. He opposed the Alien Act that resulted in Lipkin's deportation, and he remained skeptical of ideological exclusions of any kind. Sabath was less hostile to non-white immigrants than Bartholdt; although he rarely spoke out against the exclusion of Asians, he voted against every bill that excluded them. In 1924, Sabath was confronted about his opposition to restriction by the openly racist Texas congressman John Box, who objected to exempting Mexicans from the national-origins quotas then under discussion. Box accused his opponent of failing to acknowledge the threat posed by Mexican migration, of failing to see the importance of "guarding that border,"[50] and of refusing to contemplate "what will prevent them [Mexican migrants] from going where they please and staying where they please?"[51] Sabath declared himself willing to accept numerical restrictions on immigration, but only if they could be applied equitably to all countries.

Sabath's main focus was on the unfairness of small national-origins quotas for stigmatized, working-class immigrants hailing from southern and eastern Europe.[52] These were his relatives and his constituents in Chicago; they were the voters who sent him for so many terms to Washington. Throughout his life, Sabath gave heavily accented speeches against the national-origins quotas and in support of U.S. aid to Czechoslovakia and to Israel, the two countries (other than the United States) that he cared about most deeply. His humanitarianism, too, was broad, but not without limits. He objected when first President Hoover and then President Roosevelt instructed depression-era consuls to refuse visas to working-age adults who as immigrants might add to the ranks of the unemployed and could thus be labeled as "likely to become a public charge." In the 1930s and 1940s, Sabath worked with Jewish organizations to pressure Roosevelt into taking executive action on behalf of Europe's Jews, and he collaborated with fellow Jewish congressmen in introducing several unsuccessful bills to admit groups of refugees from Germany. He showed less interest in the problems of other immigrants and refugees, however. There is, for example, no evidence that Sabath knew or cared about the yearly campaign by western social workers, employers, and government officials in both the United States and Mexico to encourage the "repatriation" or deportation of seasonally unemployed Mexican agricultural workers, along with their citizen children.[53] (Relief agencies in California and Texas subsidized at least 30,000 such deportations or repatriations.) The rules of representative democracy also encouraged such parochialism, for it was citizens of Chicago, and not California or Texas, who voted on Sabath's candidacy every two years.

After World War II, as Congress begrudgingly considered authorizing 200,000 non-quota visas for Europe's Displaced Persons, Sabath argued for the admission of still greater numbers. Because so many isolationists and conservatives in the immediate postwar years viewed almost all Jews as sympathetic to left-wing causes, and thus as potential security threats, Sabath became the target of constant criticism and accusations. When he objected to investigations by the House Un-American Activities Committee (headed by

Martin Dies) as undermining the Constitution or criticized southern colleagues for their racism and xenophobia, Sabath found himself accused of "friendliness to the Reds."[54] He died in 1952, aged eighty-two, and was the longest-serving member in the House of Representatives. Later that same year Congress passed the immigration bill named after its security-minded, anti-communist co-sponsors, Pat McCarran and Francis Walter, over Truman's veto.[55]

Over the course of their lives, both Bartholdt and Sabath became astute observers of the limits of American democracy. Sabath was particularly aware of racial prejudice. Restriction encouraged both men to participate in debates over immigration without terminating their interest in their places of origin, in their foreign friends and relatives, or in international issues generally. Both became outspoken opponents of restriction and saw themselves as representing constituencies that included large numbers of foreign-born and foreign-origin voters who, like them, were mainly from Europe. Sabath proved far the more sympathetic of the two to the common ground that Europeans and Asians shared under restriction and exclusion, but his legislative activism remained firmly rooted in local Chicago-based politics. He did not attempt to speak for the Asian immigrants of the West Coast or for the Mexican immigrants of the Southwest. Finally, although both Sabath and Bartholdt devoted their political lives to Congress, Sabath in his final three decades more often found himself in agreement with the executive branch on both the importance of a more humanitarian refugee admissions policy and on the necessity of eliminating national-origins quotas.

EXECUTIVE AND LEGISLATIVE STRATEGIES FOR PROTECTING IMMIGRANT FOREIGN RELATIONS

Immigrants like Richard Bartholdt and Adolph Sabath, along with their immigrant-origin supporters, saw electoral politics and congressional legislation as their first and best strategy for protecting immigrants from the worst effects of restriction. The Constitution blocked either man from presidential ambitions and, in any case, legislative office had been the most important portal into political activism for new citizen voters since 1789. Over time, however, immigrants such as Sabath came to realize that their best allies more often occupied the Oval Office of the White House than the halls of Congress.

Bartholdt and Sabath were by no means the first or even the best known of the many naturalized immigrants who sought elected office and political influence. They probably did not know that the proportion of foreign-born men serving in Congress had peaked long before they arrived in the United States, but they were certainly aware of the difficulties involved in forming legislative alliances to protect the rights of foreigners after the 1890s. In the nineteenth century, Bartholdt numbered among a small group of foreign-born congressional representatives, mainly from the rural Midwest—Missouri, Minnesota, Wisconsin, Illinois—and from New York. By 1933 Sabath was among an exceedingly small and very select group of naturalized citizens in the U.S. Congress, most of them from cities in the urban Northeast and urban Midwest. Only three percent of his fellow congressmen were foreign-born—two senators (from Canada and from Germany) and thirteen representatives (two each from England, Italy, and Sweden and one each from Canada, Czechoslovakia, Germany, Ireland, Norway, Scotland, and the Ukraine).[56] Vastly outnumbered, this small group of foreign-born legislators included many of Congress's firmest opponents of race-, class- or ideologically based categories of exclusion.

Strange as it might seem, restriction gave immigrants living in the United States in the twentieth century far higher incentives than their predecessors to become politically active, yet immigrant candidates with strong international interests also experienced far greater difficulties in gaining election after World War I, as the story of Richard Bartholdt demonstrates. In part, this was because recent immigrants naturalized at a slower rate than they had in the age of Crèvecoeur and Wilhelm Stille. Their inability to mount a successful assault on restrictive legislation reflects yet another stark reality—that the goals of immigrants and the children of immigrants diversified over time. Bartholdt, for example, was no fan of Chinese immigration but opposed the literacy requirement, while Pat McCarran—Sabath's nemesis and the coauthor of the 1952 McCarran-Walter Act—was the son of an Irish immigrant as well as a strict restrictionist. More important, the intertwining of xenophobia and racism with isolationism and anti-communism created huge hurdles for foreign-born candidates for public office. Their children, especially those raised in the foreign colonies of big cities like New York or San Francisco—men such as Emanuel Celler, the grandchild of Jewish and Christian grandparents who was raised among the Jews and Italians of his native Brooklyn—seemed better able to gain nomination and election. But even candidates with immigrant parents regularly faced xenophobic and racist opposition. An historian of the 1928 presidential campaign of the Catholic Democratic candidate Al Smith (yet another son of an Irish immigrant) tells of a message written to the wife of Smith's Republican opponent Herbert Hoover by a friend, claiming that the Pope had secretly arrived in the United States in anticipation of Smith's election and that Smith had opened the Holland Tunnel connecting New York to New Jersey because "the Pope wanted a navy and an army and an outlet to the sea."[57]

Even when wildly irrational in its expression—as in this case—xenophobia remained an influence on American voters confronted with second-generation candidates. Many rural American natives could not bring themselves to vote for a candidate with urban American roots or ties to what later came to be called the "ethnic voting blocs" of Jews and Catholics. Not until 1960 would Americans elect to the presidency a man—John F. Kennedy—who was not a Protestant. And they have done so only once. (Pundits would later joke that the Episcopalian George W. Bush became the country's second Catholic president because he surrounded himself with advisers of that faith.[58])

Despite daunting odds against them, immigrant-origin citizens looked to Congress for a remedy to restriction, because Congress by the twentieth century was the maker of most of the rules governing immigration. Rather than contest restriction itself, they focused on challenging a handful of the many restrictions that Congress imposed. None proposed laws that might reinstate the liberty to travel, reside, and trade that the nineteenth-century trade treaties and commercial diplomacy had created. Their goals were more modest, but even exceedingly modest goals proved difficult to attain. Lobbying to influence Congress often seemed a more promising strategy than striving for nomination and election to office.

Already in the 1890s, immigrant citizens had joined forces with European shipping companies and with Joseph H. Senner, an Austrian former editor of the *New York Staatszeitung* and Commissioner of Immigration at New York, in forming an "Immigration Protective League" to oppose restriction through a literacy requirement.[59] Similar defense and protective groups registered their objections during every subsequent congressional hearing on the literacy bills; these were the first "ethnic lobbies." Leading opposition to the Literacy Act and to the 1921 and 1924 restriction laws were men such as Louis Marshall, president of the American Jewish Committee, which had been founded in 1906 to promote the understanding of Jews and to defend them from anti-Semitic myths. Marshall could not prevent passage of the Literacy Act in 1917, but he lobbied successfully among enough congressmen to guarantee that illiterate religious refugees would be exempt from its requirements. In 1921 and 1924 the American Jewish Committee found new allies—the American Jewish Congress, the Polish American Alliance, the Italian League, the Czechoslovak National Council, the Lithuanian National Alliance, and the National Croatian Society, to name but a few—but this multiethnic alliance found only a few congressmen—most of them representing large urban and northern Catholic and Jewish immigrant constituencies—willing to oppose national-origins quotas.

With the battle over restriction lost in 1924, congressmen still found themselves responding to demands from immigrant-origin voters among their constituents. So many foreign-born friends and relatives of naturalized citizens had no record of their admission to the United States prior to 1921, and so many demanded relief from their representatives, that Congress in 1929 chose to allow aliens to purchase an entry record for twenty dollars. When the deportation of immigrants without proper papers—a group whose numbers grew after restriction made visas increasingly difficult to obtain— threatened long-term separations for recent immigrant families, the citizen voters in those families also turned to their elected representatives. Even congressmen sympathetic to restriction hesitated to reject requests from potential voters. Many arranged through contacts in the Immigration and Naturalization Service for the paperless relatives to depart to Canada and then to reenter the country legally. On the West Coast, by contrast, no sympathetic congressman took on the case of Yitang Chang's paper sons; in fact, no congressman with immigrant roots in Asia was elected to the Congress until 1957. And, in the 1950s, when the INS allowed Chinese paper sons to confess to their crimes and to normalize their status as residents, many paper sons feared their confession would trigger deportation. Only 30,000 participated in the program.

The most frequent focus of immigrant lobbying on behalf of foreign relatives was the political quest for either the exemption of immigrants' kinfolk from numerical restrictions or, failing that, privileged access to numerically limited visas through preferences for family unification. Family unification was central to the long-time immigrant strategy of chain migration, which had figured so prominently in the lives of Yitang Chang, Hector St. Jean de Crèvecoeur,

Wilhelm Stille, Baldassare D'Anna, and Adolph Sabath. In a by-now familiar story, the first exemptions of kin from restrictions had emerged not from acts of Congress but from bilateral commercial treaties. The Supreme Court in 1900 confirmed the treaty right of a Chinese merchant to sponsor the emigration of his minor child or his wife. In 1907 the informal "gentlemen's agreement" between Japan and the United States also allowed Japanese laborers already in the States to sponsor wives, including "picture brides" married through proxy. (Another informal agreement—sometimes called the "ladies' agreement"—ended that provision in 1922.[60]) Congressmen opposed to the Literacy Act could not prevent passage of the bill in 1917, but they were able to gain exemptions for illiterate wives of American citizens. The 1921 and 1924 restrictions, too, defined wives and children of Europeans, much like all immigrants from the American hemisphere, as "non-quota immigrants" to be admitted without numerical limits; it also allowed up to half of all quota visas to go to the husbands or parents of U.S. citizens. Even the McCarran-Walter Act exempted the husbands of U.S. citizens from numerical limits, while creating a preference system to allocate limited numbers of national-origins visas to the spouses and minor children of permanent resident aliens and to the parents of U.S. citizens. In every debate over restriction, opponents of restriction sought to widen the circle of exempt or preferred kin, while restrictionists struggled to limit the numbers of eligible foreigners.

The postwar story of Baldassare D'Anna's family illustrates the successes and failures of immigrant citizens' legislative mobilizations on behalf of their foreign relations. As Italians, the Sicilian-born D'Anna siblings faced persistently small national-origins quotas; their main resource in navigating restriction was their American-born sister in Rockford, Illinois. When World War II ended, the children of Baldassare D'Anna again began receiving packages of clothing and cash gifts from her and from other relatives in Rockford and Chicago. Meanwhile, over the course of the next decade, more than half of the remaining U.S.–born *americani* of Sambuca, including several more D'Annas, departed for the United States. Baldassare D'Anna's oldest son, also an American citizen, joined his sister in Rockford in 1950 and then renewed the family's chain migration by signing an official affidavit promising to provide financial support for his wife, minor children, and mother-in-law, allowing them, too, to enter the country.

Ultimately, however, none of the three adult, Italian-born siblings of the Rockford D'Annas could join their siblings in the United States. There were no visas for adult siblings of citizens or of immigrant "legal permanent residents" (LPRs). Ironically, the best educated and most highly skilled of D'Anna's children could not migrate either. Trained as a shoemaker, this son had joined Sambuca's clandestine communist party in the 1920s and had been briefly imprisoned under the fascist regime of dictator Benito Mussolini. Political ideology closed the door to the United States to him; he saw his American siblings only when they began visiting Sicily in the 1960s.

Exemptions from restriction for wives and minor children of immigrants have continued—down to the present—not only because immigrant citizen voters and lobbyists desired them, but also because American notions of appropriate gender and family relations made them palatable. Even restrictionists generally believed a man should enjoy the company of his wife and children, and even staunch anti-communists were comfortable allowing a man to sponsor dependent members of his immediate family. (Immigrant women—because they were imagined still as dependents—could not sponsor their husbands until the 1950s; minor children who are citizens may not sponsor their foreign-born parents at all, even today.)

In 1924, a newly elected naturalized immigrant congressman, Samuel Dickstein of New York, harangued restrictionists who rejected exemptions for immigrants' parents, trying to make such exemptions seem politically expedient. Would the exclusion of parents "meet with the general favor of the American people amongst your own constituents?" he challenged opponents. "Now, some of you might sneer and some of you might laugh," he continued, "but I tell you, my friends, that some day, you will be called upon to account for your action to-day, when you go to an American citizen who has been in this country for many years and tell that American citizen that, although he has not seen his mother for 15 years, she does not come within the nonquota class. . . ."[61] As he pleaded for the exemption of parents from restriction, Dickstein demonstrated a sophisticated knowledge of American gender stereotypes.

He then continued on to more dramatic levels of hyperbole, anticipating the form that immigrants' concern for their foreign relations would take during the refugee crises that resulted from twentieth-century warfare. Dickstein worried over the mother who "might be alone in the world; that poor woman might be friendless over in Europe. . . ." and he reminded his opponents that "the only child she might have is her boy, a loyal citizen of the United States."[62] There were in fact many such mothers in Europe and in Asia during the 1930s and 1940s. And immigrant citizens, especially American Jews, became horrified when they realized how little they could do to rescue their relatives and coreligionists from Nazi Europe. Reminding congressmen of their right to "sponsor" their very closest kin within the numerically limited national-origins quotas, Jewish American lobbyists pleaded for unused quota visas for persecuted brothers, sisters, aunts, uncles, nephews, and nieces, and even for Jewish strangers. In 1938, almost one hundred sections of the Jewish War Veterans of New York State pledged to sponsor German Jewish veterans if only Congress would permit them to do so.[63] In 1938 and 1939, Congressmen Sabath, Dickstein, and Celler worked closely with Jewish organizations, with labor organizations representing large immigrant memberships (especially the Congress of Industrial Organizations, or CIO), and with immigrant Catholic and Protestant religious leaders. They introduced several proposals to admit larger numbers of European refugees. In each and every attempt, they failed. Without citizenship or congressional representatives, Chinese immigrants could not even make such proposals after Japan invaded first Manchuria and, then, China. Not surprisingly, earlier immigrants and religious organizations working closely with immigrant and ethnic communities later organized many of the voluntary agencies (or "Volags") that assisted in the relocation of Displaced Persons and refugees after World War II. Almost all refugees—like exempted relatives—were sponsored by individuals and religious groups that guaranteed to support newcomers through their initial period of adjustment. Sponsorship apparently overcame restrictionists' reservations about refugees becoming a drain on public coffers.

Immigrants' mobilization on behalf of their kin was strenuous but also, it would seem, often invisible. How else could one explain the thinking of philosopher Hannah Arendt who reached grim postwar conclusions about the inevitability of the Holocaust that destroyed Europe's Jews? When national governments ignored the rights of their minority populations, Arendt suggested, "no authority was left to protect them and no institution was willing to guarantee them."[64] Like many internationalists, Arendt looked to the United Nations, with its 1948 Declaration on Human Rights and its 1951 Convention on Refugees, to prevent future tragedies. And like most people in the United States in the nineteenth century, she either could not see or she chose to ignore immigrants' efforts on behalf of their foreign relations. In the foreign colonies of the United States, immigrant advocates for Europe's Jews had been plentiful throughout the interwar and immediate postwar years. But while numerous, they were rarely politically powerful. Too many restrictionist, isolationist, and anti-communist congressmen, with no significant immigrant-origin voters among their constituents, continued to see humanitarian policies as sentimental and dangerous to the security of the United States

Over the long twentieth-century history of immigration restriction, interest in the plight of their countries of origin increasingly encouraged immigrants to consider internationalist presidents as their best allies. During World War I, Woodrow Wilson's support for self-determination for the minority groups ruled by the Austro-Hungarian (but not, significantly, the Ottoman) Empire had unleashed a flurry of mobilization in immigrant colonies; Czech-Americans liked to attribute Wilson's support for self-determination to the influence of Czech patriot Tomas Masaryck, who was then living in exile in the United States. In 1934, Sabath joined the Jewish organization B'nai B'rith in presenting President Roosevelt with a petition, signed by 250,000 "American citizens of various faiths and all stations of life," urging action against Germany as it stripped its Jewish citizens of property and rights.[65] Bonds between immigrant foreign colonies and the executive branch solidified during World War II. The new Office of Strategic Services (OSS, a precursor to the CIA) created a "Foreign Nationalities Branch" (headed by DeWitt Poole, a long-time State Department official and diplomat) to recruit citizens of recent immigrant origin as operatives and intelligence-gatherers. Immigrant citizens knew the languages and local politics of Europe, China, and Japan. At the same time, however, the FBI often put anti-fascist and anti-communist refugees under surveillance once they arrived in the United States, suspecting them of communist sympathies; the U.S. Department of Justice required even those immigrants raising money for the American war effort to register as potentially dangerous "foreign agents."[66] Working on behalf of one's country of origin carried risks; while considerable numbers of immigrant citizens accepted that risk, their efforts rarely launched successful political careers.

After the war's end, the OSS's Poole also created and led a "Committee for a Free Europe," that again worked closely with the many anti-communist refugees and immigrants entering the United States from Europe, and eventually also from China. The postwar years also saw Jewish Americans mobilize again on behalf of European refugees who had fled (illegally, in 1945 and 1946) to Palestine and in support of the new, embattled nation of Israel, while anti-communist refugees, once arrived in the United States, organized groups such as the Assembly of Captive European Nations (ACEN), which sought to restore "freedom and independence" to Albania, Bulgaria, Czechoslovakia, Estonia, Hungary, Latvia, Lithuania, Poland, and Romania.[67] The State Department and Oval Office both drew privately on advice proffered by the many professionals and intellectuals in refugee and immigrant communities. To anti-communist refugees, the executive branch offered public statements of support, applauding the refugees' goals and hinting at support for any future military action the émigrés might organize. If the refugees had expected President Dwight Eisenhower to send troops to Hungary in 1956, however, they were sorely disappointed. Having the president's ear was no guarantee that the United States would risk war on behalf of immigrants' foreign relations, even when official and immigrant foreign relations converged almost perfectly, as they did in this case. Worse, executive branch collusion with Cuban anti-communist refugees' schemes of return and conquest, through the invasion of Cuba's Bay of Pigs, ended in disaster.

Despite the engagement of millions of immigrant citizens, political activism usually wrung only small concessions from Congress. In 1943, a committee of China experts, including Pearl S. Buck (an American born in China), convinced Congress to repeal the Chinese Exclusion Act, but restrictionists in Congress then again insulted this important U.S. wartime ally by imposing a minuscule quota of only 105 visas annually. A year later, when Brooklyn congressman Emmanuel Celler appealed for still greater "breaking down of immigration and naturalization barriers" for India and the Philippines, he reminded his listeners how "Jap propaganda" had highlighted U.S. prejudice toward Asians.[68] Congress remained stalemated in support of the status quo, however, and the McCarran-Walter Act, despite its small concessions to both the executive branch and immigrant voters in the shape of a minuscule quota for Asians and quota exemptions for family unification, thoroughly, if only temporarily, demoralized not only the presidential candidates of both parties but also the immigrant-origin citizens who had sought an end to national-origins quotas since the 1920s.

Ultimately, the opponents of restriction—whether in the White House or in groups such as the Ukrainian Relief Association—had to confront the racists, anti-radicals, xenophobes, and isolationists who continued to support restriction and who remained powerful in both houses of the U.S. Congress, especially among the powerful southern Dixiecrat Democrats. U.S. leadership of a global Cold War had more successfully undermined the legitimacy of isolationism and economic protectionism than it had immigration restriction. Immigrant citizens continued to chafe under the social and cultural stigma of restriction, and several of the large labor unions of which they were members now joined ethnic community lobbies in demanding change. Although President Eisenhower at times called for overall increases in immigration in response to the voracious labor market of the postwar economic boom, raising the number of immigrants was not the reformers' main focus. And, as scientists after 1940 vigorously denounced the tenets of scientific racism and African-Americans mounted a new civil rights movement against domestic Jim Crow restrictions, racial equity, transnational family relations, and humanitarian internationalism became the main areas of focus for a new reform coalition of younger and largely second- and third-generation immigrant-origin congressmen representing eastern and urban districts and states. In 1960, John F. Kennedy entered his own brief presidency as an avid advocate of immigration reform. Hopes among immigration reformers soared and then crashed again with Kennedy's assassination. A more positive development for the reformers were African-American campaigns to end scientific racist domestic policies, which chastened defenders of national-origins quotas, even when they remained fiercely committed to restriction.

A later generation of restrictionists would claim that the Hart-Celler Immigration Reform Act of 1965—which, after being passed by sizable majorities, finally eliminated the national-origins quotas—constituted a radical departure from the past and one that "opened the floodgates" to a new "immigration invasion."[69] That is not how the American president, Lyndon Baines Johnson, or the congressional immigration reformers themselves saw it in 1965, however. Following on complex negotiations between President Johnson, reformers, and hardcore restrictionists, the new rules that Congress devised to govern immigration seemed harmless enough at the time. The 1965 law created a global cap of 290,000 visas annually, slightly increasing available visas for the Eastern hemisphere to 170,000, while imposing numerical limits of 120,000 for the first time on immigrants from the American hemisphere. Spouses, unmarried minor children, and the parents of U.S. citizens remained exempt from numerical limits, while the new law also reserved three-quarters of Eastern hemisphere visas for an expanded group of relatives—unmarried adult children of citizens, the spouses and unmarried children of resident aliens, the married children of U.S. citizens, and the brothers and sisters of adult U.S. citizens. (Similar provisions for immigrants from the American hemisphere came somewhat later, in 1976.) Another 10 percent of visas went to professionals and to specially qualified scientists or artists; and a further 10 percent were available to skilled and unskilled workers—but only in occupations for which the Department of Labor had certified a shortage of native laborers. Refugees could claim the few remaining visas.

Older immigrant communities were understandably pleased with the 1965 law. They had lobbied hard for the expanded provisions for family unification, for example with Mike Feighan, the conservative and restrictionist Democrat who generally voted with the southern Dixiecrats on immigration issues. Feighan headed a key immigration subcommittee and used his power to introduce—and insist on—a numerical limit (with no preferences for relatives) on immigrants from the Americas. According to the *New York Times*, Feighan had "felt the heat" from the "Poles, Hungarians, Slovaks and Byelo Russians [*sic*]" in his Cleveland district on the issue of exemptions and preferences for kin.[70] But Feighan's constituents may also have been surprised by their sudden success. That success was facilitated mainly by a highly unusual Democratic congressional landslide that accompanied the defeat by Johnson of conservative Republican presidential candidate Barry Goldwater the previous year.

The *New York Times* found the new law to be "far-reaching" because it eliminated national origins quotas, but it also noted the significance of extending numerical limits to the countries of the American hemisphere for the first time.[71] When President Johnson signed the Hart-Celler bill into law at the Statue of Liberty on October 4, his speech predicted only limited change ahead. He hoped the new grounds for admission constituted a "fair test" for all. But while he celebrated the end of the "harsh injustice of the National Origins Quota System," Johnson also confirmed that "the days of unlimited immigration are past."[72]

Immigration restriction was the long-term legacy of scientific racism, of the xenophobia sparked by American empire-building, and of the resurgent isolationism that followed U.S. participation in World War I and Wilson's internationalist dreams of a League of Nations. While many isolationists and restrictionists gradually gave up their opposition to U.S. global leadership, in part because of their hatred of fascist and communist totalitarianism, restrictionists retained power over the governance of immigration by Congress into the 1960s. Only repeated challenges by the executive branch, horrified by the global Cold War public relations problems caused by racially discriminatory U.S. immigration and domestic policies and further influenced by the concerted and long-term mobilizations of immigrant-origin citizens on behalf of their foreign relatives, had prevented isolationists and restrictionists from realizing their goal "to close, lock, and bar the gates" of the country and "then throw the keys away." Restriction did not end with the elimination of the national-origins quotas in 1965, however. In fact, neither the executive branch nor immigrant communities nor immigration reformers had mobilized to that end. Immigrants sought mainly relief for those closest to, and most like, themselves.

The rules governing restriction and the impact of restriction would change again after 1965 as the United States and the world again experienced the tumult and change that accompanies globalization. Immigration too would change in ways that few of the 1965 act's supporters had anticipated. But restriction itself remained firmly in place. Arguably, the 1965 Hart-Celler Act even extended the reach of restriction into the American hemisphere. In a world in which the United States had become a "super power," American voters' desire for protection, restriction, and fewer not more immigrants had not changed. Restriction, much like high tariffs in an earlier era, still struck Americans, and indeed most other people of the world, as a necessity for national survival; almost no one imagined the elimination of immigration restrictions as an opportunity for international integration as free trade was now understood to be, not only in the United States, but also worldwide.

4

|||||||||||||||||||||||||||||||||||||||||||||||||||||||||||||||||||||||||||||

IMMIGRATION AND GLOBALIZATION, 1965 TO THE PRESENT

In the forty-five years that followed President Lyndon Johnson's signing of the 1965 Immigration Act, few could ignore changes occurring both within the United States and beyond America's borders. By the millennium's turn in 2000, these changes had acquired a brand new label—"globalization." Invoked 200 times in the *New York Times* during the 1980s, the word appeared in 910 articles in the 1990s and then almost daily between 2000 and 2007. Globalization furnished a shorthand explanation for just about any change— positive, negative, economic, social, or cultural—underway anywhere in the world.

Dictionaries defined "globalization" as "the development of an increasingly integrated global economy marked especially by free trade, free flow of capital, and the tapping of cheaper foreign labor. . . ."[1] Globalization also revived Marshall McLuhan's vision of the world as a tightly integrated "global village."[2] With such familiar associations, globalization could also easily be understood as the cause of the increases in immigration that had followed the passage of the 1965 immigration reforms. Rather than reflecting Americans' new comfort level with their country's active leadership role internationally, rising levels of immigration instead continued to confound and disturb many voters. Already in 1981 a member of a congressional select committee on immigration and refugee policy had summed up the long-term trend rather sadly: "As a general rule, the American public . . . has been negative toward the admission of immigrants and refugees."[3] Yet, once again, voters seemed unable to obtain what they wanted—which was fewer immigrants. Was Congress at fault? Was the federal government? Internationalists? Immigrants themselves?

While some saw globalization as driven by activist nation states, including the United States, or by international cabals committed to a "new world order," other popular explanations traced globalization to the agendas of multinational corporations or, more benignly, to the digital reproduction and circulation of images and words made possible by new communication technologies. Theorists of globalization encouraged alarm by predicting far-reaching consequences that included the demise of nation states unable to control flows of people, money, images, ideas, and goods across their borders; the homogenization of national cultures; and the proliferation of fragmented and fluid human identities detached from any emotional loyalty to particular places. Nationalists worried that globalization would undermine national sovereignty, while radical internationalists claimed it generated vast wealth for the few while impoverishing the many, driving ever greater numbers to migrate, often unwillingly. While world historians dared to suggest that globalization was nothing new, theirs were lonely voices lost in a cacophony of millenarian claims.

To many Americans, those millenarian claims seemed on the verge of coming true. The United States was no less involved in the world in 2010 than it had been in 1945, but neither its continued military might and involvement in foreign wars (in the Persian Gulf, Afghanistan, and Iraq) nor the global impact of its vast financial and consumer markets could hide the economic dynamism of the industrializing "Asian Tigers"—South Korea, Singapore, Hong Kong, Taiwan and, most recently, China—the oil-rich countries in the Middle East, or the newly united countries of the European Union (EU). Just a decade after its long-term nemesis the Soviet Union collapsed in 1989, the United States experienced terrorist attacks on its largest city; before the decade was over it faced financial crisis and an increasingly multipolar world of shifting international relations.

These were not changes likely to diminish the xenophobic fears that had long fueled Americans' desires for immigration restriction. Just as empire-building and the exercise of international power had transformed Americans' views of immigrants in the late nineteenth century, so too perceptions of American decline in a changing world fostered a revival of xenophobia. In renewed political debates about immigration, some Americans now insisted—as did an expert witness before Congress in 1983—that the borders of the United States were "out of control."⁴ As anti-immigrant hostility escalated after the 2001 attacks on the World Trade Center, it was also obvious that discussions of immigration had settled into the kind of passionate yet also repetitive, "dull and threadbare" rhetoric that Congressman Bartholdt's friend found so tiresome in the nineteenth-century tariff debates. Discussions of American foreign policies—the nation's wars in the Middle East and its advocacy of free trade (which had produced trade deficits that increased even more rapidly than did immigration—failed to spark the same kind of sustained debate. In part, at least, this reflected the governance of immigration as a domestic issue, by Congress. Americans could not control globalization; they still could not directly or easily influence their country's foreign policies. What they could do was vote. They could choose their representatives and they could insist that their representatives protect them from the threat of immigration.

IMMIGRANT LIVES IN A NEW ERA OF GLOBALIZATION

While Americans' new awareness of both globalization and the possibility of American decline helped make immigration appear newly threatening and unlike the migrations of the past, the lives of post-1965 immigrants reveal, however, surprisingly familiar patterns, most notably in their own foreign relations. To a considerable degree, immigration to the United States after 1965 mirrored the geography and history of American empire-building in Latin America, the Caribbean, and Asia, and that, in itself, seemed a dramatic change. As one waggish group of British scholars put it, empires do tend to "strike back" through the migration of "post-colonials" to their former colonizers' home countries.[5] Worldwide, the result has been a profound shift from the east-west transatlantic and transpacific moves of the nineteenth century toward the south-north moves of our own times. Diversifying these post-colonial migrations of migrant laborers and refugees were the corporate managers and administrators, international students, engineers, technical specialists, scientists, professionals, intellectuals, and bureaucrats who more often symbolized the global economy of the late twentieth century. The 1965 immigration law had created particularly sharp distinctions between immigrants seeking family unification visas, refugees seeking asylum, and highly skilled immigrants on the one hand, and working-class labor migrants with few opportunities to obtain visas on the other. As a result, American immigration after 1965 would not, despite the familiarity of the newer immigrants' foreign relations, exactly replicate the proletarian mass migrations of the nineteenth century.

The life of one woman immigrant from Southeast Asia demonstrates how U.S. foreign wars drove demands for visas for both family unification—in her case, for wives or children of American soldiers and military workers abroad—and for refugees. Born in central Vietnam during the year of China's 1949 communist revolution, Le Ly Thi Phung grew up amidst campaigns against the French colonizers of Vietnam and a civil war that divided the southern and northern branches of her family.[6] Earlier subject to occupation by China, the people of Vietnam had no particular love for either Chinese or French rulers; many saw the arrival of the United States military in the 1950s as just the latest in a long sequence of heavily armed foreign empire-builders who threatened their well-being.

Phung's peasant family demanded hard work from all its members, cultivating sweet potatoes, peanuts, taro, and rice. Life became more difficult with the division of Vietnam in 1954. Like many families in central Vietnam, the Phungs had kin fighting on both sides in the ensuing civil war. Phung's father and brother supported the Viet Cong, who had fought the French and who now identified with communist North Vietnam. Phung initially became a Viet Cong supporter, too, while her mother maintained relations with a brother who was a prominent republican in nearby Danang, where

American military advisers had replaced the French as advisers to the republican South Vietnamese fighting against the communist Viet Cong.

Arrested in 1964 as a Viet Cong supporter, Phung gained release through her uncle's connections. Sensing ideological betrayal, two former Viet Cong allies then violently raped the young woman; shamed and horrified, her father drank acid, while Phung and her mother fled to Danang, where they secured permission to travel to Saigon, the capital of South Vietnam. There, Phung found work as a domestic servant; like many poor servants before her, she was impregnated by her wealthy employer and then fired. Phung soon found work in the illicit marketplaces of Danang, selling contraband goods to American and Vietnamese customers in order to support herself and her child. She also began a series of intimate relationships with American military men, and she dreamed of escape from ceaseless warfare. Phung eventually married a kind, elderly American military contractor, Ed Munro, and in 1970 she traveled to the United States as Munro's wife, accompanied by her older son and an infant fathered by Munro. As dependents of a U.S. citizen, they were exempt from numerical caps on immigration. When the family arrived in San Diego, only eighteen thousand other Vietnamese lived in the United States. That would change quickly after Saigon fell in 1975, ending the American military's campaign against communism. Ed Munro had died by then, and Le Ly Munro, now the mother of three, had married a violent American veteran named Dennis Hayslip.[7] As more than a million Vietnamese refugees sought relocation to the United States, Le Ly Hayslip divorced her violent husband and again began to support herself and her children.

By the time Ly Le Hayslip had recovered a measure of personal stability in California, two men born in Puebla just before Rosalie Evans lost her life there had built very different lives for themselves in far-flung locations in the United States. In New York, Don Pedro lived and worked without papers; in El Paso, Arnulfo Caballero, a small businessman and citizen, had succeeded in launching his family into the American middle class. Access to lands expropriated from foreigners like Rosalie Evans had at first allowed the parents of both these men to remain at home while millions of Mexicans from other regions fled to the United States to escape poverty and the chaos of the Mexican Revolution. Young men from Puebla began departing for the United States only in the 1940s. Thereafter, they tuned their lives to accord with dramatic changes in U.S. policies toward Mexico, a country long affected by American empire-building.

At some point in the 1990s, Don Pedro suggested to a New York ethnographer that he was the first Poblano to have ventured to New York City—a suggestion that others disputed.[8] He had fled his hometown of Ticuani in 1942 to escape the same kind of violence over land that had resulted in Evans's death; he traveled with a cousin to Mexico City, where the two young men hoped to bribe a Mexican government official and obtain papers and tickets to travel to the United States as temporary contract laborers (*braceros*). Faced with a labor shortage during World War II, the United States had created the Bracero Program by negotiating a bilateral treaty with the Mexican government. Under that treaty, Mexico recruited and paid for the transport of its young male citizens to the northern border, where U.S employers selected them to fill jobs abandoned by American soldiers or by workers who had taken better-paying jobs in war industries. The program would continue until 1964, albeit largely under unilateral U.S. control.

The luck of Don Pedro and his cousin improved when they met an American tourist, named Montesinos, who offered to drive them to New York City. Presumably the two Poblanos possessed no visas—that would have required more bribery—but with the help of their friend the duo crossed the border without difficulty on July 6, 1943. Montesinos offered further advice in New York and the two quickly found work "because of the war," Don Pedro later reported, referring to war-induced labor shortages. Although he lacked papers, Don Pedro continued to find work easily after the war ended. In the 1950s, he helped fellow villagers who could not obtain visas to join him. Americans disparaged them as "illegal immigrants" or "wetbacks."

Among those who succeeded in enrolling in the Bracero Program during World War II was Arnulfo Caballero, a Poblano who must have had better luck, wider connections, or a fatter pocketbook than Don Pedro. Holding a paper contract, Caballero and fifty-four other men from Puebla journeyed with government-subsidized tickets to the U.S border in 1944. From there, U.S. employers arranged their travel to jobs with the New York Central Railroad. Caballero later claimed to have written *A. Caballero aquí*—"A. Caballero was here"— inside the crown of the Statue of Liberty during his sojourn in the North.[9] After working on New York railroads for a year, Caballero—unlike Don Pedro—returned to Puebla and settled into marriage and the operation of a small business.

But Caballero's immigration story did not end with his return to Puebla. Frustrated by limited business opportunities in his hometown, Caballero moved again ten years later to Ciudad Juárez, just across the Mexico-U.S. border from El Paso, Texas. His wife and children accompanied him. Many Poblanos lived in Juárez, providing a ready clientele for the restaurant and dry cleaning establishment the family opened. Once in Juárez, Caballero saved money, learned English, and applied for a visa to enter the United States. He began sending his son Cesar across the border daily to attend school in the United States. (In the 1950s a streetcar line still connected the Mexican and U.S. halves of the twin cities of Juárez and El Paso, and thousands crossed the border casually each day to go to school, shop, and work.) Once he had obtained a green card, making him a LPR (Legal Permanent Resident), Caballero took a job in an El Paso restaurant; he crossed the border daily to be with his family, who continued to operate their businesses in Juárez. After five years of international commuting, Caballero naturalized and became a U.S. citizen. He immediately applied to sponsor his wife and children as immigrants. Their wait was not a long one. After the Caballero family relocated to El Paso, on the U.S. side of the border, Caballero's wife chose to remain a citizen of Mexico, but Caballero himself became such a fervent American patriot that he was shocked when he learned that his son Cesar—inspired as a university student by the civil rights and black power movements of African-Americans—had joined protest groups demanding equality for Chicanos and protesting the Vietnam War.

While the businessman Caballero successfully navigated U.S. immigration laws, most post-1965 Poblano migrants were like Don Pedro in having no access to visas. The United States eliminated the Bracero Program in 1964 shortly before the new immigration law of 1965 imposed a numerical cap on migrations from Mexico. A later law, passed in 1976, required all Mexicans to compete for only 30,000 visas annually: the close kin of previous migrants and green-card holders claimed almost all of them. With only a handful of visas available for blue-collar workers, poorly educated or unskilled Mexicans again regarded bribery, which many could not afford, as part of the cost of authorized migration to the United States. Most instead followed the route of Don Pedro, migrating without papers and accepting the risk of living in illegality, often with the assistance of family and friends. They easily found low-wage work, for Americans had few qualms about hiring them, even without papers. Only in 1986, under the Immigration Reform and Control Act (IRCA), did Don Pedro gain a green card and status as a LPR. By then, he had been in the United States for more than forty years.

In apparent sharp contrast to the working-class, paperless Poblanos were highly educated persons from around the world who sought to study in the United States or to work in technical, managerial, or professional positions in business, science, and industry. Even they could experience difficulties in gaining LPR status, however. Typical of these elite labor migrants was Indra Nooyi, who in 2007 became chairman and chief executive officer of PepsiCo.[10] Nooyi was born in 1955 in Chennai, Tamil Nadu, India; she described herself to reporters as having been a wild and somewhat rebellious daughter who played soccer and performed in an all-girl rock band, despite having been raised in a conservative, comfortably middle-class Brahmin family. After graduating from a Christian college and completing a postgraduate degree in one of the only two management programs that existed in 1970s India, Nooyi accepted a managerial position in a British textile company. She then moved to a position with the American corporation Johnson & Johnson. Nooyi's supervisors were happy to have a woman as a manager; they assigned her the task of marketing Stayfree sanitary pads, an item unknown at the time among female consumers in India. Working in international, corporate settings, Nooyi soon learned of opportunities beyond her native country, which sparked in her a new surge of restlessness. Knowing her family valued education, she began to plan a migration that would allow her to study abroad.

In 1978, Nooyi gained her family's reluctant approval to travel to the United States to enroll in Yale University's brand-new School of Management. Her family worried—unnecessarily as it turned out—that the decision would make her unmarriageable. Undaunted, Nooyi soon learned that the Yale program had attracted many "brain drain" students like her. And, like many of these international students, Nooyi succeeded in remaining in the United States after she had completed her M.A. in public and private management, but only with considerable assistance. Her first U.S–based employers, and their lawyers, helped her to fulfill the complex bureaucratic requirements for exchanging a student visa first for a temporary work visa and then for a green card.

Nooyi's path to leadership was a swift one that took her through varied corners of the corporate world, including a Swiss-based multinational firm. As she rose in the corporate world, she married an India-born engineer with whom she had two children. Once at PepsiCo, she vowed to move the company away from junk food and toward less sugary beverages and packaged foods.[11] In 2007, she insisted that PepsiCo could make sizable profits while doing good, and expressed the hope that by 2010 half of PepsiCo's profits in the United States would come from healthy foods.

With a large income and outstanding credentials, Nooyi and her family easily found acceptance in upper- and upper-middle-class communities such as the one in Greenwich, Connecticut, where they currently live. To her American neighbors, Nooyi scarcely seems like an immigrant. She is not poor; she speaks English fluently; she not only works for a prominent American corporation but she exercises great authority in her workplace. Some have called immigrants like Nooyi "cosmopolitans" or "citizens of the world." She and others like her give an attractive, personable face to globalization, and many Americans have begun to argue that they are exactly the kind of immigrants the United States needs if it is to compete successfully in a changing global economy. Yet even Nooyi obtained her temporary visa and green card only through the interventions of expensive and highly expert legal professionals. Attaining the status of a legal permanent resident (LPR) was a not a sure thing, even for her.

It is, in fact, not rare for professional job-seekers to experience difficulties when migrating to the United States. For example, the human consequences of one apparently small change in American immigration law shocked the Korean computer engineer Jay Cho into desperate action.[12] After working, marrying, and having two children in Seoul, Cho moved to Seattle in 1993 with a green card, sponsored by his own mother, a naturalized U.S. citizen. There, he found work as a computer programmer. Unfortunately, Cho arrived in the United States just as Congress—seeking ways to increase the number of employment-based visas available to highly skilled immigrants like him—reduced the number of family-based visas available to close relatives of green-card holders, a decision that immediately lengthened waiting lists for family unification visas. Like many green-card holders, Cho applied immediately after arrival for visas for his wife and young children, but he learned they would have to wait for five years.

Cho regarded the long separation as "torture"; three years later, he arranged for his wife, daughter, and son to fly to Vancouver. His son, Simon Cho, aged five at the time, later recalled walking with his mother and sister across a muddy field to join his father on the U.S. side of the border. Cho's wife and children then lived without papers until they rose to the top of the waiting list and received their green cards in 2001, whereupon they traveled back again to Canada and reentered the United States legally; several years later, all became U.S. citizens. Nevertheless, when their son Simon's achievements as a speed skater in the 2010 Olympics revealed their story of illicit entry, this "model minority" family could read web-based diatribes accusing them of being criminals and calling for their deportation. As the world had changed, so had Americans' tolerance for illegality and their understanding of which foreigners deserved entry into the United States.

IMMIGRANT FOREIGN RELATIONS

While none of these most recent immigrants' lives began in Europe, their attachments to their places of birth resembled in many ways those of earlier European migrants. Chain migration figured prominently in the lives of almost all of them. Even the wealthy and accomplished Nooyi, who did not come to the United States as part of a migration chain or sponsor members of her family to follow her, remained in touch with India. Migrants from Asia, Africa, and Latin America provided financial support to relatives abroad. Lacking papers and access to citizenship, the New York Poblanos remained interested in the politics of their home villages; along with Nooyi and the wife and son of Caballero, many became active in public and private initiatives to foster improved relations between their countries of origin and the United States. As in the past, too, immigrants' transnational politics could spark intense controversy, especially when accompanied by violence.

Given immigrant-origin voters' decades-long mobilizations around family unification, and given the large proportion of visas actually allotted to relatives under the 1965 Immigration Law, it is scarcely surprising that chain migration continued among post-1965 immigrants. The 1965 law created what scholars, observing the rapidly increasing numbers of migrants from Asia and Mexico, began to call an immigration "multiplier effect"—the multiplication being the expansion of chain migration under the preferences system created as part of restrictive laws.[13] LPRs like Jay Cho could sponsor only spouses and dependent children, but once they obtained citizenship, the list of their kin eligible for unification visas expanded slightly, initiating spiraling visa applications across kin networks. Nor was there a limit on the number of closest relatives of citizens who could enter the United States.

The specific requirements for family unification visas nevertheless produced quite different outcomes for the Hayslip and Caballero families, on the one hand, and for the

Poblanos, most Vietnamese migrants, and Jay Cho, on the other. Just prior to the American evacuation of Saigon in 1975, for example, Hayslip's husband Dennis, a Vietnam War veteran, had traveled to Vietnam to rescue one of his citizen wife's sisters and her children—all of them eligible for family unification visas. Thereafter, however, Le Ly Munro Hayslip could do little for the millions of people, including hundreds of thousands of Vietnamese of Chinese origin, who fled on rickety boats from Vietnam to refugee camps in Southeast Asia. She received but she could not respond positively to heart-wrenching pleas for sponsorship and assistance from friends and family in the camps. While generous, American visas for family unification defined kinship quite strictly, even for U.S. citizens—no cousins, aunts, nephews, or grandparents, let alone in-laws or friends, were eligible. Furthermore, the 1965 law had allotted less than 10 percent of available visas to refugees. Most who fled Vietnam thus waited long years in camps for sponsorship by humanitarian strangers—usually members of American churches and synagogues—or they entered either under the provisions of viciously contested, special acts of Congress (the Indochina Migration and Refugee Assistance Act of 1974; the Refugee Act of 1980; the Amerasian Homecoming Act of 1987) or under executive-branch parole.

Although relocation agencies consciously scattered incoming refugees, hoping to defuse hostility against Asians, relatives among the refugees often reunited once they became familiar with life and work in the United States. Like many labor migrants of the past, the Vietnamese soon clustered—in coastal Texas, for example, and in California. Somali and Hmong refugees formed large enclaves in

Minnesota and in California; Cuban refugees concentrated in New Jersey and Florida. Haitians—who experienced great difficulty in making claims for asylum, also clustered in Florida and New York.

Prior to 1976 it was impossible for Poblanos and other Mexicans to obtain visas for family unification, and it remained difficult even thereafter. Since he lacked a green card, and could not become a citizen, Don Pedro, unlike Arnulfo Caballero, could not sponsor a wife or child to enter the United States with a family unification visa. Still, illegality had its own multiplier effect, generating both more illegality and the growing use of forged papers as relatives sought to reunite with earlier unauthorized migrants. After Don Pedro gained a green card under the IRCA (see the "IRCA spike" in numbers of immigrants in 1987 in figure 1, which is estimated at 2.3 million), he and others responded by returning to Mexico to visit or to marry and by applying for visas to bring wives and children to New York. Through chain migration, the approximately 25,000 Poblanos in New York in 1980 facilitated the arrival and job searches of friends and family who still could not obtain work-based visas but who nevertheless risked entering the United States as the regional economy of Puebla stagnated and the economy of New York boomed. After the 1994 North American Free Trade Agreement facilitated the export to Mexico of low-priced midwestern corn, Mexican farmers' incomes collapsed and emigration from Puebla again increased. By the early twenty-first century, more than a million Poblanos—about a quarter of the resident population of Puebla—lived in the United States. The largest groups from Puebla lived in Texas and California, not far from the border. But some 300,000

Poblanos and their children also lived in the New York City, where they constituted half the Mexico-origin population of the city.[14]

Unlike the Chos, whose middle-class, professional way of living allowed them to avoid detection despite their visible, Asian appearance, working-class Poblanos—also a visible minority—soon saw their detention and deportation rates soar. Anxiety rose throughout this large, transnational community, for Poblano families and households typically united persons of differing immigration status. In a single family, one might find a paperless father or older son, a wife or mother in possession of a lapsed tourist visa or forged green card, and one or more citizen children (who could not sponsor their own parents for green cards until they reached age twenty-one). Worldwide, large numbers of potential migrants competed for only 10,000 visas available for unskilled or semiskilled employment. Even potential migrants with a green-card-holding spouse or parent faced long waits (of up to thirty years), so many continued to risk illicit entry or to overstay temporary or tourist visas, raising further the population living in illegality.

Regardless of their immigration status, post-1965 migrants proved to be just as involved in transnational families and communities as earlier immigrants. Computers, cell phones, jet travel, e-mail, and the World Wide Web all made it easier than ever before to remain in touch with relatives and friends abroad. Canadians, Mexicans, and immigrants from the Caribbean made the most frequent visits home, but transnational family ties mattered to migrants from Asia, too. With large numbers of married women working in the United States, for example, the poorest Chinese families sometimes sent pre-school-aged citizen children to China to be raised by their grandparents until they were old enough for all-day school. Indra Nooyi claimed that she still spoke twice daily with her mother in India after twenty-five years in the United States. In 2007—just as she consolidated control at PepsiCo—she and her husband, Raj Kishan Nooyi, also bought a large apartment in Chennai's posh Poes Garden neighborhood, home to many government officials and wealthy film stars.[15]

While the amount of money that Nooyi transferred to India for a home purchase was surely higher than average for an immigrant in the United States, remittances remain an extremely common form of connection between migrants and their families and friends in their country of origin. Migrants from Mexico remitted upwards of $16 billion to families in Mexico in 2005 alone; money transfers purchased in the United States by migrants thus exceeded all direct foreign investment in Mexico and generated almost as much currency revenue as Mexico's most lucrative export—oil.[16] In the twenty-first century, unlike the nineteenth, many governments, along with the World Bank, understood that remitted flows of currency sometimes surpassed the value of foreign trade or of foreign aid offered by the United States or other wealthy countries. In 2009, the World Bank estimated that migrants worldwide sent abroad more than $414 billion in remittances for the support of family and friends. The Philippines, like Italy before it, identified a bank to assist immigrants in remitting funds, and it began to celebrate the financial achievements of its migrants and to encourage firmer ties to home. India, Pakistan, and the Philippines all actively encouraged migrants to invest in homeland enterprises. While some of the amounts remitted to Mexico may have been invested in businesses and land, remittances from New York Poblanos to their home villages more often constructed private homes. By paying the costs of education for children, remittances also helped to expand the Mexican middle class. Scholars debate whether or not such small-scale remittances, even when aggregated, will foster long-term economic development, but the World Bank remains hopeful that remittances generated during migration can help to end global economic inequality.

As in the past, emotional attachments to their countries of birth also continued to encourage public activism. Indra Nooyi resembles many corporate leaders in taking on leadership roles in charitable foundations and public service organizations—but more than a few of her activities directly benefit India. She has served, for example, as chairperson of the U.S.–India Business Council, and she was appointed by President Obama to the U.S.–India CEO Forum in 2008. In more modest ways, Arnulfo Caballero's librarian son and his Mexican-citizen wife have promoted cultural and folkloric exchanges between El Paso and Mexico. Like the Italians before them, Catholic Poblanos in New York financially support the building of village infrastructure and return to Mexico to celebrate patron saint holidays; they also celebrate the same saints in their Queens and Brooklyn neighborhoods and exchange videos of the celebrations with fellow villagers elsewhere.

By the late twentieth century, observers impressed by the rapid pace of recent globalization began to notice the many nongovernmental actors playing influential international roles as founders, funders, and volunteers operating hundreds of international NGOs, many of them with humanitarian aims. The immigrant and refugee Le Ly Hayslip numbers among these highly visible non-state actors in international relations. As she became increasingly familiar with conditions in the refugee camps of Southeast Asia and in her birth country, Vietnam, and as the numbers of Vietnamese refugees living in the United States rapidly grew, Hayslip began to imagine returning to Vietnam to assist in some way. She described meeting American veterans who were as concerned as she was about the plight of people they had come to know, like, and admire during their military service in Southeast Asia. With the waning of the Cold War, Hayslip traveled back to Vietnam for the first time. Accompanying her were several former GIs. The group emphasized how both refugees and soldiers could feel pride at having done their duty in Vietnam, while also insisting "we have important new roles to play," based on their intimate knowledge of the country.[17] Soon afterward, Hayslip founded the East Meets West Foundation, an NGO that describes itself today as "a nonprofit, humanitarian organization that partners with the people of Vietnam to improve their health, education, and economic conditions in an effort to ease poverty and encourage self-sufficiency."[18]

In a somewhat different way, the working-class and often paperless Poblanos in New York also mobilized on behalf of their country of origin. Migrants from Don Pedro's home village of Ticuani organized themselves as a committee to collect funds to build a potable water system in Mexico. With growing resources at its command, the committee soon also became embroiled in the complicated municipal politics of Ticuani, their participation facilitated in part by the Mexican government's decision to allow Mexicans living abroad to vote in Mexican elections. By 1998, candidates for office in the Puebla region campaigned among Poblanos in New York and elsewhere in the United States; and emigrated Poblanos from Ticuani successfully supported a reform candidate for leadership of their village. Without papers, most of these Poblanos had few hopes of becoming American citizens, so their political loyalties remained based in Mexico. When asked, however, many indicated a desire for dual citizenship. (Dual citizenship is created through bilateral negotiations; relatively few countries worldwide allow it, and the number of dual citizens living in the United States—while assumed to be growing—is actually unknown. Many countries, such as China, resist opening dual citizenship to their migrants.)

Of course, diaspora nationalism—political mobilization by immigrants on behalf of their home countries—is nothing new. And in the twentieth-first century, as in the past, it has the potential to generate political violence. Americans' reactions to immigrant support of political violence have been as quixotic in the twentieth and twenty-first centuries as they were one hundred years earlier. For example, Irish Americans who raised funds in the 1980s for the Irish Republican Army—a group Britain had declared to be terrorists—generally escaped notice and prosecution in the United States.[19] By contrast, the United States government in 2007 arrested former CIA ally and Hmong military leader General Vang Pao, claiming he was plotting the overthrow of the Laotian government.[20] The official foreign policies of the United States—not the potential for violence—determined how immigrant and refugee activists fared in cases like these.

U.S.–born citizens of recent immigrant origin also continued to enjoy greater rights than the foreign-born to express unpopular political beliefs.

Until recently, average Americans have demonstrated little interest in immigrants' political mobilizations, even when they threaten political violence abroad. But that indifference disappeared as concerns about Middle Eastern immigrants' political loyalties intensified after the terrorist attacks on the World Trade Center towers. In his address to the American nation on September 20, 2001, President George W. Bush insisted firmly: "The enemy of America is not our many Muslim friends. It is not our many Arab friends." Careful scrutiny of Muslim and of Arab immigrants nevertheless increased and gave rise to fears of their foreign ties and to occasional violence by Americans against foreigners perceived as originating in the Middle East.[21]

No deep knowledge of the history of immigrant foreign relations informed these developments. On the contrary, most Americans were unaware of immigrants' long history of involvement in the political struggles of their homelands, so much so that when a *New York Times* journalist in 2009 reported on a group of Somali refugee boys returning to Somalia to fight in the ongoing civil war there, she did not question the assertion of FBI Agent Ralph S. Boelte, who stated, "This case is unlike anything we have encountered."[22] Every story of transnational politics is unique in its details, but the transnational politics of Somali refugees living in the Cedar-Riverside neighborhood of Minneapolis, Minnesota, tell a tale that is consonant in many ways with earlier immigrant armed struggles, and for historians studying this issue, the records of the Bureau of Investigation and the FBI (its successor) have been important sources. The refugees accused of becoming involved in Somalia with a terrorist organization were all young men, as were the Fenians and the Italian anarchists of an earlier time. Most of the Somali fighters had arrived in the United States at an early age; their American acquaintances considered them (like the Fenians) to be both likeable and thoroughly Americanized: they were lovers of basketball and dedicated students planning American professional careers while studying at the University of Minnesota. Like the Catholic Fenians, the Muslim Somali fighters desperately wanted to assist their troubled homeland, and their fervor drew on the uncomfortable experience of belonging to a mistrusted religious minority. Even FBI evidence suggesting the young men had attempted to recruit friends to do violence in the United States mirrored Italian anarchists' earlier transnational strategies.

Regardless of how one assessed the actual domestic threat posed by these Somali refugees and their political affiliations and actions in Somalia, there were precedents for their behavior. But elements of the myth of earlier immigrants who lived completely isolated from their countries of birth continued to work its magic, suggesting that globalization and militant Islam were generating totally new—and therefore even more terrifying—threats to American security. By rendering invisible the extremely common, and sometimes violent, political passions of earlier immigrants, domestic histories of immigration actually heighten fear of newer immigrants. Predictably, such fears of foreigners and of the changing world from which they have come found expression also in battles over U.S. immigration policy in the years after 1965. As in the past, many Americans wanted protection from the threats that they believed immigrant foreigners posed—to their jobs, their culture, and even their lives.

A DOMESTIC IMPASSE: THE POLITICS OF IMMIGRATION AFTER 1965

Every poll of American public opinion since 1938 has reported the largest group of Americans as preferring less immigration, even when immigration volumes were at their nadir. Yet significant numbers of Americans have also continued to value their country's long history of immigration and to celebrate the United States as a nation of immigrants. According to Susan Martin, Americans tend to value past immigration but not the immigrants of the present day.[23] By the end of the twentieth century this conflicted view had given rise to an apparently irresolvable conflict over American immigration policy. The new restrictionists, who claimed that immigration was "out of control," drove the debates. They attributed three disturbing changes to the 1965 Immigration Act: rising volumes of immigration, large numbers of immigrants living in illegality, and declining immigrant "quality."

Restrictionists were correct in noting that—contrary to predictions—immigration had increased after 1965. These increases were uneven and small during the stagflation of the 1970s, but accelerated during bursts of economic growth—to seven million during the 1980s and nine million during the 1990s (see figure 1). After 2000, and until the financial crash of 2008, an average of one million immigrants entered the United States annually. Almost every year, too, immigration surpassed the annual numerical limits set by Congress—of

290,000, 1965–1980; 270,000, 1980–1986; 540,000, 1986–1991; 700,000, 1992–1994; and 675,000 after 1994. But these figures were scarcely evidence of out-of-control migration, for the surplus immigrants were almost all either relatives legally exempted from numerical caps or refugees admitted by Congress or the executive branch.

The estimated ten to eleven million immigrants who live and work in the United States without visas permitting them to do so contribute greatly to the perception that migration is "out of control," and they have in recent years been the focus of most negative attention to immigration. Concerns with illegality have understandably fueled a new restrictionist movement. Some believe that illegality signals the diminishing power of nations to maintain secure borders. But illegality, too, is neither new nor the result of the 1965 act's abandonment of restriction. On the contrary, every restrictive law Congress passed since 1882 has generated illegality; Americans actually invented the term "illegal immigrant" to describe Chinese laborers and paper sons as early as the nineteenth century. Already in 1927—long before Congress imposed numerical limits on Mexican immigration—a Catholic Church study found a million Mexicans living illegally in the United States; most were border dwellers, like the Caballero family, who crossed borders casually, even daily, as they often had for many years prior to 1965, without bothering to obtain permits and papers.[24] At the height of the Bracero Program, federal agents deported a million "wetbacks" from borderland Texas. Soon after the elimination of the program, 1965 reforms placed numerical caps on Mexican migration. Nevertheless, by 1971, estimates of a million paperless immigrants still about equaled the estimate of 1927.

Thereafter, however, estimates rose, to three million during the 1980s. After 1990 they had quadrupled. Moreover, contrary to critics' charges, budgets for border patrol, detention, and deportation increased along with illegality, beginning in 1996 under Democratic president Clinton and continuing under the presidencies of both Republican George W. Bush and Democrat Barack Obama.

Eliminating illegality through stricter policing became restrictionists' key demand. One angry writer, "Galactus988," responded to an online forum about speed skater Simon Cho by proclaiming, "They are still criminals and should be deported. I think anyone who comes here illegally should never be allowed to become a U.S. citizen. Period."[25] Galactus988 would be displeased to learn that unauthorized entry into the United States is actually a relatively minor misdemeanor under American law. It is punishable only by deportation. Immigrants living in illegality can escape it—if they can afford to—by employing the same strategies and following the same course as Indra Nooyi took in turning to her employers for assistance and sponsorship.

To Galactus988, even middle-class wives and children reunifying their families counted as criminals. And widespread perception of immigrants as outlaws further inflated a common perception among Americans that the "quality" of immigrants had declined after 1965. But how could such an argument be made when one-third of adult immigrants after 1965 were highly educated professionals and another third were white-collar workers? In 1984 journalist Robert Pear pointed to the preponderance of women and children among immigrants and, ignoring the fact that most immigrant women also worked, suggested that female migration would not "generate as much economic growth" as past immigration.[26] Others charged that highly educated migrants like Indra Nooyi could not obtain visas because so many were reserved for family members who are presumed always to be either less ambitious and educated or less capable than those seeking work-based visas. There is no evidence that this is the case. Claims that immigrants drove up health, education, and welfare costs also carried the implication that recent immigrants were less independent or work-oriented than earlier ones, thus imposing a burden on American taxpayers. In the words of a child of earlier Finnish immigrants trying to explain American immigration history to an international student: "The old immigrants were givers; today's immigrants are takers."[27] Observations like these are difficult to reconcile however with persistent concerns that immigrants take Americans' jobs.

Soon after alerting readers to the feminization of immigration, Robert Pear also introduced them to the "browning of America." In 1970, the origins of the ten largest groups of immigrant residents in the United States were in Europe (Italy, Germany, Canada, the U.K., Poland, the U.S.S.R., Ireland, and Austria), with Mexico (in fourth place) and Cuba (in eighth) the only exceptions. By 1990, persons born in Mexico were 21 percent of all foreign-born residents, followed by immigrants from China, the Philippines, Canada, Cuba, Germany, the U.K., Italy, Korea, and Vietnam. Citing scholar Lawrence Fuchs, Pear pointed ominously towards a future non-white majority.[28] For Americans still inclined to see racial change in negative terms—Fuchs firmly declared that he did not—the "browning of America" clinched assertions about diminishing quality. Meanwhile, others responded with horror to the blatant racism of such charges. In Texas, Arnulfo Caballero's son again became politically active in the 1980s when he perceived local INS agents harassing Mexican-American citizens "just because of our brown skin."[29] In his work as a librarian and educator, Caballero instead celebrated the cultural diversity of newer immigrants, asserting the existence of a multicultural America.

Nevertheless, Nathan Glazer's weary 1997 conclusion that "we are all multiculturalists now"[30] was demonstrably inaccurate, for angry debates about immigration policy and demands for renewed restriction continued. Just as readers today are puzzled by the sheer volume of rhetoric that tariff policies generated a century ago (see chapter 3), future Americans may well be puzzled by the passionate and repetitive immigration debates of the late twentieth century. Indeed, the 1965 Immigration Law had scarcely been fully implemented (in 1968) when Congress began to hear demands for change. Illegality and immigrant labor were both of special concern during the economically sluggish 1970s. Both housewives and western farmers traveled to Washington to complain when the Labor Department refused to certify shortages of native domestic servants and agricultural workers, denying employment-based visas for low-skill immigrants. But when Representative Peter Rodino suggested that "an increase in the number of visas for immigrant workers" might be required, protests from American workers fearing immigrant competition squashed congressional action.[31] Congress continued to hear complaints about employers hiring workers without papers and about employers' difficulties in obtaining either qualified job applicants or certifications of labor shortages. In the West and Southwest, angry voters again demanded action from their state legislators and, in 1976, the Supreme Court ruled that states could prohibit employers from hiring unauthorized workers under certain conditions.[32] Labor organizations such as the United Farm Workers and even the American Federation of Labor and the CIO (which had earlier advocated immigration restriction) instead now demanded penalties on employers and argued that abuse of undocumented workers harmed all workers.

Ever alert to popular resistance to increased immigration, Congress continued its Cold War battles with the executive branch, even as the Cold War waned. When Congress resisted a request for refugee assistance in 1975, Republican president Gerald Ford fumed that congressmen wanted to "turn their backs" on the Vietnamese. "We didn't do it to the Hungarians," he declared, "we didn't do it to the Cubans, and, damn it, we're not going to do it now."[33] Ford prevailed. Congress also heard from members of American Jewish communities and advocates for human rights who sought visas for the Jews of the Soviet Union. Senator Alan Simpson complained that such petitioners needed to learn to distinguish "between the right to leave the Soviet Union" (which he supported), and the right to enter the United States (which he did not).[34] As in the past, advocates found a more sympathetic audience in the Oval Office, especially under anti-communist president Ronald Reagan. By 1993, 250,000 Soviet Jews lived in the United States.

When President Jimmy Carter, a self-declared humanitarian, used executive branch parole powers to admit still more refugees from Southeast Asia, Congress again resisted. The Refugee Act of 1980 was the result. It constituted a compromise between the two branches over the governance of refugee admissions, broadening the U.S. definition of a refugee to match that advocated by the U.N., but also requiring that presidents who wished to admit more than 50,000 refugees had to negotiate with Congress. Frustrated when Congress failed to respond quickly and affirmatively to his requests, Ronald Reagan simply ignored Congress and again used his parole powers to admit anti-communist refugees from Cuba, Southeast Asia, and the Soviet Union. (Meanwhile, the Immigration and Naturalization Service continued to refuse refugee status to Haitians and Central Americans fleeing right-wing authoritarian allies of the United States, despite the fact that they qualified under the U.N. definition of "refugee.") Complaints from citizens about refugees also continued to flow toward Capitol Hill. From Florida, Robert Graham charged the federal government with failing to reimburse his state for the costs of a 1980 Cuban "boatlift."[35] Refugees especially were seen as taking rather than giving, as earlier immigrants supposedly had.

If congressmen by 1986 hoped that the IRCA would eliminate illegality and quiet restrictionists' main complaints, they were disappointed. The IRCA was, in the words of a critic, "Christmas-Tree-Legislation" that offered "something for everyone" (excepting, notably, those few who wanted more employment-based visas for low-skill workers).[36] Honoring restrictionists' and labor's demands, the act imposed sanctions on employers who knowingly employed undocumented workers, and it increased border enforcement. Honoring humanitarians' goals, it created a regularization program that allowed Don Pedro to claim a green card. Concerned that restrictionists' angry objections to what they called an amnesty for Mexican criminals would insult Mexico just as the United States was pursuing delicate free trade negotiations with Mexico and Canada, President Reagan insisted "the problem of illegal immigration should not . . . be seen as a problem between the United States and its neighbors."[37] As Reagan's successor, George Bush, pursued the creation of a North American "common market," it became apparent that NAFTA, once implemented in 1994, would allow for free movement of commodities but not the liberty of people to move about freely as they chose.

Rapid increases in immigration after the signing of NAFTA especially spooked restrictionists who feared for Americans' jobs. In 1992, economic protectionist and presidential candidate Ross Perot had predicted a "giant sucking sound" created by American investment and jobs rushing into Mexico. But his protectionist campaign failed to upset Democratic presidential candidate Bill Clinton, who instead promised the creation of 200,000 new "NAFTA jobs" in the United States. Offering Mexico (like other countries in the past) "trade, not aid"[38] may have pleased disgruntled taxpayers who hated foreign aid, but it did nothing to protect jobs in aging U.S. industries. As industrial production relocated abroad and U.S. trade deficits soared, construction sites, hotels and restaurants, meatpacking plants, and private individuals throughout the United States became employers of millions of newly arrived, low-skill workers, many of them without papers. At the same time, however, unemployment levels among Americans also dropped. Illogically, this did little to assuage fears of foreign job-seekers; as unemployment levels fell, even mainstream economists continued to warn of American workers facing "a sea of low-paid, low-skilled competitors."[39] On the border, INS agent Michael

Teague observed thoughtfully that "The great majority of them are decent people coming here to work. . . . You have to sympathize with them to a point . . . we know that they're going to keep coming as long as our grass is greener. And we also know that we can't catch them all."[40] Teague dismissed restrictionists' newest demand—for border walls or fences—as expensive and unworkable. But he also warned, "If you open the border wide up, you're going to invite political and social upheaval. . . ."[41] In Washington, the sponsor of yet another restrictive bill, Lamar Smith, agreed: "We just can't admit everybody who wants to come."[42]

Demands for further restrictions intensified as the population of paperless immigrants surged in the 1990s. By 1996, former anti-NAFTA crusader and economic protectionist, Patrick Buchanan (a descendant of Catholic immigrants from Ireland) promised voters in Waterloo, Iowa, that if his presidential campaign succeeded, "I'll build that security fence, and we'll close it . . . and we'll say 'listen José, you're not coming in.'"[43] Western employers instead demanded a new guest worker program; labor unions promptly joined the U.S. Chamber of Commerce in opposing it. Once elected, Bill Clinton seemed concerned mainly with the difficulties faced by "high-tech" corporations seeking visas for their engineers or programmers; perhaps they had tired of the high legal costs involved in transforming students such as Indra Nooyi into legal permanent residents.

In 1996, Congress sought another compromise. The Illegal Immigration Reform and Immigrant Responsibility Act (IIRIRA)—which drove immigrant engineer Jay Cho into despair—reduced the availability of some family unification visas, increased the numbers of immigrants to be admitted, doubled the size of the U.S. Border Patrol, and mandated construction of fences along parts of the border with Mexico. It created a diversity lottery, broadened the list of crimes triggering deportation and the grounds for detention, and imposed an income test on immigrants sponsoring their kin. It also created a pilot database to assist employers in checking the immigration status of job applicants. Significantly, the act denied access to all welfare programs (except emergency medical care) to all immigrants, whether green-card holders or "illegals."

The 1996 law's linkage of heightened restrictions to enhanced numbers of visas for highly skilled workers failed again to break restrictionists' momentum. President George Bush's campaign promise to engage Mexican president Vicente Fox in bilateral discussions of a new guest worker program went unrealized as Bush instead declared a war on terror and as wars begun by the United States in Afghanistan and Iraq predictably heightened xenophobia—just as wars had so often in the past. Immigration and Customs Enforcement (ICE) agents, working within a new Department of Homeland Security, raided workplaces and detained and deported thousands of immigrant workers, and municipal and state governments began passing laws to penalize "illegal immigrants" in other ways: by denying them rental housing or drivers' licenses, for example. Self-described patriots in the Southwest threatened to begin patrolling the borders themselves. A 2007 immigration bill that would have created a guest worker program, increased temporary visas for high-tech workers, and crafted an arduous and punitive regularization program for workers without papers failed despite co-sponsorship by the liberal, pro-labor Democratic senator

Ted Kennedy from Massachusetts and the conservative, pro-business, Republican war hero from Arizona, Senator John McCain. The subsequent presidential campaigns of McCain and Barack Obama avoided all discussion of immigration. As financial crisis engulfed the United States, ideas for change floated in Congress promoted policies that had already failed or had been recently rejected. Still, restrictionists escalated their demands; in October 2010, seven Republican senators demanded an estimate of the cost of deporting every alien identified by law enforcement agents as residing illegally in the United States.[44] Globalization may have been on the lips of millions of Americans in the early twentieth-first century, but by turning only to their elected representatives to solve immigration problems, voters continued to assume that immigration was a domestic problem, requiring a domestic solution. And on that point they were wrong.

GLOBAL PERSPECTIVES ON A DOMESTIC DEBATE

In a world where vast circulations of capital remain completely invisible, and where consumers must look hard to see tiny labels identifying the origins of imported goods, nothing makes the challenges of globalization more visible—or more terrifying, apparently—than mobile people. While Americans focused on immigrants entering their own national territories, two social scientists instead wrote of a new global and worldwide "age of migration."[45] They described contemporary mobility as unique in involving, for the first time, people from every corner of the world. In 2005, U.N. statisticians counted 191 million people living outside the countries of their birth; higher estimates of between 214 and 219 million have since appeared. Recent refugees account for 16 to 19 million of that total. Rates of short-term travel, whether for tourism or business, ranged much, much higher, with estimates extending from 800 million to a billion or more annually. While temporary and short-term international travel for business and pleasure clearly is a new and unprecedented development, facilitated by new technologies, many historians view the current number of international migrants as impressive but—at 3 percent of the world's populations— still below nineteenth-century levels. Why would levels be lower today than in the past? The answer in all likelihood has to do with nation states' restrictions.

Worldwide there is no agreement about what constitutes normal or desirable levels of international migration. Business and tourist travel is usually understood to be desirable; it is the much smaller movements of workers and refugees that raise suspicion. In the 1920s, as the United States began to restrict immigration, labor economists asserted that the "ideal rate" of annual immigration for a sparsely populated country (like the United States) was close to 2 percent of the resident population.[46] The 700,000 plus immigrants admitted annually into the States after 1990 instead constituted .3 percent of U.S. residents (see figure 1). About a fifth of all recent international migrants currently live in the United States, or about the same proportion as in the nineteenth century. The United States has admitted more immigrants since 1965 than any other single nation in the world, but it is by no means the home of most immigrants in today's world. Migrations from the relatively poor nations of the global south toward the nations of the relatively wealthier global north have transformed populations not only in the

United States, but also in parts of eastern, southern, south-eastern and western Asia, in the nations of Canada and Australia, in almost all of the countries of western Europe, and in the Southern Cone of South America, as well. Ongoing migrations of rural Chinese toward the industrializing cities of coastal and southern China equal or even surpass these international migrations in scale and provoke just as much controversy and negative comment within China as international movements do elsewhere.

The overall demographic impact of post-1965 immigration on the United States also falls far short of the numbers recorded in other countries, as table 3 demonstrates. The latest census figures show 36.7 million foreign-born persons living in the United States, or 11.8 percent of a population of over 310 million. This is well below peak historical levels of almost 15 percent. One third of those foreign-born persons, moreover, are not aliens but naturalized citizens, who in the statistics of other countries would not even figure in counts of foreign population. The sizable population of immigrants without papers in the United States, if fully counted, might raise the proportion of the foreign-born in the States to its historic peak. But even then the United States would not merit inclusion in table 3.

Like the United States, all the countries listed in table 3 restrict immigration and privilege particular types of immigrants. The oil-rich countries of the Middle East admit foreigners only as temporary contract or "guest" laborers; Israel accepts mainly Jewish immigrants. Canada, which falls just below New Zealand in its proportion of foreigners, uses a point system to encourage immigration by well-educated, professional, and high-skilled workers who can provide evidence

Table 3. Top Ten Countries with the Highest Share of International
Migrants in the Total Population, 2010

Qatar	86.5%
United Arab Emirates	70.0%
Kuwait	68.8%
Jordan	45.9%
Singapore	40.7%
Israel	40.4%
Oman	28.4%
Saudi Arabia	27.8%
Switzerland	23.2%
New Zealand	22.4%

Note: Countries with 1 million or more residents.

Source: MPI Data Hub: Migration Facts, Stats, and Maps, http://www
.migrationinformation.org/datahub/charts/6.2shtml. Accessed May 10,
2011.

of speaking French or English and of their own "adaptability"
(as measured largely by their level of educational attainment).

Almost all the countries listed in table 3 also regard immigration as undesirable and as a problem. The democracies
near the low end of table 3 have all experienced vigorous
recent debates over immigration. Switzerland, New Zealand,
and especially Australia have seen the rise of powerful anti-
immigrant political movements that express intense hostility
to the presence of large numbers of foreigners, to their illegality (for it is not only in the United States that restriction
encourages clandestine movements), and to their quality—
usually measured by the degree of their racial, religious, or
cultural difference from long-time residents, even in multilingual nations. (However, complaints about immigrants
as drains on state-funded welfare services are somewhat less

common, for example, in Europe or Canada, than they are in the United States—a strange pattern, since both Europe and Canada offer a wider array of public entitlements than does the United States.)

While the more authoritarian government of the United Arab Emirates has at times sought to expel as many as 300,000 (mainly South Asian and African) workers who have overstayed their visas, it—like most other wealthy countries in a global economy characterized by sharp inequalities—has found no way to develop its industries or to maintain public and private services without foreign workers. With some of the wealthiest European nations in very real demographic decline—to put matters simply, their populations no longer reproduce themselves—and with many poorer nations still growing demographically, immigrants do necessary reproductive work, too. They care for children and the elderly; and their children outnumber natives in public school systems. In this context, thoughtful scholars have suggested that the almost universal restrictions imposed on international migration worldwide by nation states are efforts to institutionalize global inequality—or what one scholar referred to as a regime of "global apartheid."[47] Despite such judgments, the World Bank continues to dream of migrants' remittances righting the imbalance.

Beyond U.S. borders, one also finds considerable evidence of bilateral, multilateral, and international efforts to identify and address migration as an international, rather than a domestic problem. In the years before, during, and after World II—and in countries such as the U.A.E. even today—nation states have negotiated bilaterally to create contract labor programs in the pursuit of national interests. All of

Germany's postwar guest worker programs emerged from bilateral negotiations with Italy, Yugoslavia, Spain, Portugal, and Turkey: Germany needed labor, while the other countries typically had high unemployment rates. Italy had earlier also offered Belgium the opportunity to recruit its unemployed laborers for work in Belgian mines, gaining in return a Belgian promise of cheaper prices for the coal Italy imported. (In North America, by contrast, similar efforts have faltered: Mexico withdrew its support from the Bracero Program treaty, claiming that the United States had refused to protect Mexican workers from job-based and racial abuses. The United States then continued to operate the program unilaterally until it was abolished completely in 1964.)

Perhaps because it is itself a product of international treaties, the E.U. has handled international migration very differently from NAFTA. The complex, multilateral, and long-term negotiations that produced the E.U. focused not only on the removal of barriers to trade and employment (in addition to the creation of a shared currency) but also on the removal of barriers to the free movements of people. Today, as new states—many of them former Warsaw Pact allies of the collapsed Soviet Union—join the E.U., their citizens acquire—sometimes incrementally—the right to travel, live, and work anywhere in Europe.

As the E.U. instituted free trade and free movement within Europe, it also however began to construct what has been called "Fortress Europe" by tightening control of its peripheral borders in order to prevent immigration by non-Europeans, a tightening that had devastating consequences as political rebellions spread across the Muslim countries of North Africa and the Middle East in 2011. Most European countries admit non-Europeans only as refugees, asylum seekers, or family members, not as workers. As a result, clandestine migrants—those who have entered the E.U. from bordering states or after traveling by boat to Italy, Greece, and Spain from Africa or Asia in order to seek work—spark just as much hostility among Europeans as illegality does among Americans. Still, recent German and Dutch debates about the perceived failure of their own multicultural experiments with immigrant integration focus less on the behavior of recent arrivals (who are few in number) than on the long-term consequences and multiplier effects of the postwar labor migrations that terminated already in the early 1970s. Somewhat more than a third of recent immigrants entering the Netherlands do so to form or unify families—a sharp contrast to the United States, where such migrants are the majority. Another third are asylum-seekers from outside Europe. Only 20 percent are job-seekers, and almost all of them are from other E.U. countries or from North America.

While regional approaches to the management of south-north migrations in response to global inequalities have developed over the past half-century, especially in Europe, international organizations too have studied and addressed the phenomenon of international migrations by both job seekers and refugees. Since its refusal to join the League of Nations, the U.S. government has a long history of rejecting the international regulation of labor migrations, and it has been only modestly more sympathetic to international oversight of refugee aid and resettlement. American international relations have never, it would seem, completely escaped from the isolationist suspicions of the 1920s. Here, too, is a sign of American insistence on the domestic nature of the immigration problem. Although still the preeminent nation of immigrants in the 1920s, the United States played no role in the International Labour Organization, an agency of the League of Nations that collected data on international labor migrations as a first step toward finding multilateral solutions to the problems and conflicts caused by cross-national job-seeking. After joining the ILO in 1934, the United States withdrew again in 1977, protesting the behavior of trade unions from Soviet-bloc countries. (It is again currently a member, but remains reluctant to adopt ILO protocols on the fair treatment and rights of workers.)

Since the United States played a large role in creating the United Nations, it is not surprising that the 1948 U.N. Declaration of Human Rights closely mirrored American national strategies for regulating human mobility. Article 13 of the Declaration established that "everyone has a right to freedom of movement and residence within the borders of each state" and a "right to leave any country, including his own,"[48] but it offered no corresponding article or right for an exiting person to actually then enter any other country. Such a right would challenge national sovereignty, as the United States and many other countries still understand it. The U.N. Declaration of Human Rights thus seems to accept, tacitly, the reality of illegality, clandestinity, and asylum-seeking. While people are free to leave any country, no country has to admit them, and without the right to enter, needless to say, there is no real right to exit, except the "right" to exit into illegality.

Resisting international standards, the United States also failed to adopt the broad definition of "refugee" offered in 1951 by the newly created Office of the United Nations' High Commissioner on Refugees (UNHCR). According to UNHCR, a refugee is anyone with a "well-founded fear of being persecuted for reasons of race, religion, nationality, membership of a particular social group or political opinion" who is living "outside the country of his nationality" and who "owing to such fear, is unwilling to avail himself of the protection of that country."[49] Until 1980, as noted above, the United States reserved its own offers of asylum to refugees fleeing communism.

Since 1950, the UNHCR has coordinated international actions to protect refugees and to resolve refugee problems. It operates refugee camps, typically in countries adjacent to those the refugees have fled. (Most refugees originate in western Asia and Africa, and that is where most also find refuge—and not, as is commonly believed in both the United States and in Europe, in the wealthier nations of the global north.) Many American voluntary agencies cooperate closely with the UNHCR in relocating refugees, and the United States continues to accept more refugees than any other single nation. Nevertheless, smaller nations—such as Canada and Sweden—have created far stronger reputations for their humanitarianism within the UNHCR. To this day, the United States requires refugees to repay the costs of their transportation to the United States, for example. Yet, when asked, refugees who prefer not to return to their homelands often state a preference for being relocated to the United States rather than to the E.U. with its stronger welfare services or to Canada with its stronger reputation for humanitarianism. The history of the United States as a nation of immigrants may be viewed ambivalently by American citizens, but it continues to work a positive influence on potential migrants around the world.

Unlike the majority of Americans engaging in the intense, repetitive immigration debates of the late twentieth century, immigrants and their children have always known that immigration is an international and not an exclusively domestic matter. Like their counterparts in the past, post-1965 immigrants have also sought to create, to extend, and to preserve and protect their networks of family and friends living abroad. Often enough, down to the present, immigrants mobilize politically on behalf of their countries of origin or to protect the few privileges—notably their access to visas for family reunification—that U.S. immigration law allows them. During the most recent American elections, commentators speculated endlessly about the eventual political impact of rapidly growing populations of naturalized citizens of recent immigrant origin, and especially about the political influence of growing numbers of Mexican- and Latin-American-origin immigrants, who are believed to have the most extensive and intimate involvements with relatives and friends living in illegality. As visas for family unification have increasingly come under criticism both from restrictionists and from those advocating more employment-based visas for the highly skilled, and as rates of detention, harassment, and deportation of those living in illegality have soared, it seems logical to expect that concern for their families and friends will, as they did in the past, motivate these more recent immigrants to naturalize, and that the same concerns will affect their political choices as voters and citizens. But what choices they will make about immigration is not clear; historically immigrants have sometimes divided, even on issues of restriction.

Angry Americans like Galactus988 insist that evasions of immigration law reflect immigrants' shocking disrespect for American law and thus their incapacity for responsible American citizenship. But foreigners prohibited from entering the United States are able to evade detection in large part because American citizens, too, disrespect, oppose, and ignore laws they perceive as restricting their liberties. The American who carried Don Pedro across the border in 1943 seemed unperturbed about violating American law. Eleven million foreigners without papers can live in the United States in part because Americans themselves have resisted systems of population registration and national identity cards that are routine in other countries. Citizens willingly hire migrants without papers, rent houses to them, and buy the products and services they produce. Large corporations are not the employers of the largest numbers of workers without papers: millions of small businessmen and individual households in need of domestic servants, gardeners, and child minders are.

Such indifference to law by natives and immigrants alike is not without precedent in American history. Consider the brief, troubled decade when the United States prohibited the sale of alcohol by constitutional amendment—an act and a period that we now call "Prohibition." Early in the twentieth century, so many natives wanted protection from the "evils of drink"—symbolized at the time by German-owned saloons and foreign wine- and beer-drinkers— that Congress passed and thirty-six states quickly ratified a constitutional amendment prohibiting the sale of alcoholic beverages. But despite apparently overwhelming voter and legislative support for Prohibition, surprisingly few natives or citizens proved themselves willing to stop drinking or to cease purchasing liquor in order to drink. During Prohibition, too, it was most often the smugglers, producers, and purveyors of alcohol (many of them foreigners) who landed in prison, and not the consumers of their outlawed goods. Faced with massive evasion fueled by demand for an illicit product, the Treasury Department at first demanded ever more enforcement agents, better funding, and more and stricter enforcement. Eventually, however, even those who supported Prohibition concluded that the law was ineffective and unenforceable; with the economic collapse of the 1930s, Congress—and a second constitutional amendment—ended the Prohibition experiment and decriminalized the purchase and sale of alcohol. The United States faces a somewhat similar constellation of behaviors today, only it is the labor of unskilled foreigners that has become illicit.

No one in 2008 or 2009, in the face of the financial collapse of those years, suggested that it might be time to end restrictions on employment-based visas for low-wage workers. Instead, by pointing to global challenges to U.S. economic power, recent and heated discussions of globalization, with their emphasis on impending revolutionary changes, have fed American xenophobia without encouraging Americans to acknowledge their own role in nurturing illegality. Xenophobia has been a constant companion of periods of international warfare in U.S. history, and in 2009 the United States still had considerable numbers of soldiers stationed abroad, with many of them devoted to a vague "war on terror" or fighting to create democracies in Iraq and Afghanistan.

With both isolation and economic protection firmly rejected as strategies for limiting the domestic impact of global change, immigration restriction remains the most important legislated and symbolic defense against the dangers many Americans perceive as coming from the world beyond their borders. Almost all the immigration issues that Americans seek to address through their domestic debates and through domestic legislation are also being addressed in other countries. As the domestic impasse over immigration continues, the United States pursues its official foreign relations in a changing world, and its relationship to that world continues to change as well. Yet foreign affairs and policies rarely figure in debates about immigration, and most Americans still see immigration as a unique, domestic challenge. Fearful of globalization, aware of looming budget deficits and huge international trade deficits, and concerned that their nation's power is slipping away, Americans see rising immigrant numbers, illegality, and declining immigrant quality as uniquely American problems and as products of their own government's failure to enforce American laws rather than as global problems that require international solutions.

CONCLUSION

"The Inalienable Right of Man to Change His Home and Allegiance"

My examination of immigrant foreign relations challenges readers to think in new ways about immigrants' lives, about the relationship of immigration and globalization, about the governance of immigration and foreign policy, and about the relationship of the United States to the rest of the world. While domestic histories of American nation-building rightly emphasize the diversity of immigrants' origins, cultures, and religions as they have changed over time, the story of immigrants' foreign relations reveals more similarities among groups and more continuities over time. The most important continuity emerges from the almost universal human tendency to love and remain attached to family and birthplace. While the newly arrived face quite varied options for building transnational social networks and using them to achieve their individual or collective ends, almost all immigrants do try to remain in touch with friends and family in other countries; all have initiated kin-based chain migrations; many have assisted loved ones abroad, and by doing so some have become involved in transnational or diaspora politics, domestic American politics, and American foreign affairs.

In the nineteenth century, the social networks created by southern and eastern European immigrants overlapped little with the geopolitical strategies of the United States; during the twentieth-century era of restriction, by contrast, immigrants more often found allies in the president's office or the State Department than in the halls of Congress. Whether immigrants succeeded or failed in assisting their friends and family abroad was more a consequence of American geopolitics than of immigrants' influence or marginality. American Jewish communities mobilized on behalf of their kin and coreligionists in Germany in the 1930s and failed; in the 1970s and 1980s, their campaigns to obtain visas for the Jews of the Soviet Union succeeded. American foreign policy priorities drove the differing outcomes.

Heightened international migration has characterized every era of globalization in world history, but the foreign policies of the United States have also significantly influenced migration patterns. Whether in the early Atlantic, or the late-nineteenth-century Pacific, migrants found passage on the same ships that carried trade goods and American businessmen. Participation in foreign wars repeatedly sparked migrations of war brides and refugees, while suppressing labor migrations. The building of the Panama Canal initiated a prolonged chain migration from the Caribbean to New York City; American military withdrawal from Southeast Asia initiated refugee movements stretching over three decades. Countries with U.S. military bases continue to have higher rates of emigration and higher proportions of female migrants than countries without such bases.

Legislated restrictions on immigration have also responded to geopolitics, often to prevent foreign policies from "striking back" through increased immigration. Even before Yitang Chang entered the United States, American voters and their representatives sought legislation to reduce, restrict, and prohibit immigration from the very countries with which American presidents, diplomats, and military leaders were most deeply involved. NAFTA provides only the most recent example. Conflicts between the executive and legislative branches over immigration have resulted, on the one hand, in international conflicts that endangered Americans living and working abroad, and on the other hand, in immigration laws that failed to deliver the security voters sought. After signing NAFTA, Mexico experienced violent political rebellions in its southern provinces, high unemployment, and a currency collapse; Americans who had objected to NAFTA watched as industry relocations and unauthorized migrations increased simultaneously. Both illegal entries from Mexico in the 1990s and Americans' fears of an out-of-control southern border in the aftermath of 9/11 were driven in large part by the reorganization of the economies of the United States and Mexico under NAFTA.

Americans' ambivalence about the world beyond their borders and voters' ambivalence about their nation's international role also exhibited strong continuities over time. Of course, the dangers identified as originating from abroad also underwent changes. In the nineteenth century, Americans worried mainly about entangling alliances and "cheap" foreign imports; more recently they have been made anxious by foreign wars and "cheap" foreign workers The international leadership role and military activism of the United States for the past century has kept alive complaints about immigrants as invaders and financial burdens from whom voters demand protection. Hostility to immigrants is, at least in part, an expression of popular ambivalence toward the global activism of the United States. Isolationism and the desire for isolation have never completely disappeared as factors in American politics.

Compare the worldviews and desires for protection from foreign threats expressed by three hypothetical voters living in the United States in 2011. One voter—she might be labeled both a "protectionist" and a "nationalist"—applauds wall-building on the U.S. southern border in order to exclude Mexican criminals, and she also wants the United States to withdraw from NAFTA in order to protect American jobs; at the same time, she strongly supports the war on terror and an expansion of the war in Afghanistan as safeguards of a domestic security threatened by radical Islamic terrorists. Another voter—an anti-globalization activist and self-described humanitarian—expresses contempt for the World Trade Organization, the World Bank, and the war on terror while desiring an end to the fingerprinting of foreign tourists and an increase in the numbers of visas for refugees and family members and green cards for the many immigrant workers who do not have them. A third voter, who calls herself a conservative, celebrates free trade and the expansion of multinational corporations and supports the war on terror as a necessity, but argues that employment-based visas should be made available to highly educated technical and professional workers rather than to blue-collar workers. None of these voters wants to isolate her country completely from the world; each identifies different foreign dangers from which she wants different forms of protection. While none of these voters has much direct influence over the conduct of U.S. foreign policy—constitutionally insulated as it remains from the conflicting interests of electoral politics—all three participate as voters in debates over immigration, because it is understood as domestic policy. Their legislators have, despite repeated efforts, failed to find a compromise that satisfies the conflicting desires of these voters. All can thus agree that the immigration policies of the United States are "broken."

Yet all probably also continue to assume that restriction is necessary and that only Congress is capable of finding a way to fix what is broken. Readers of this book should, by now, have gained insight into how limiting such assumptions are. The history of immigrant foreign relations reveals how immigration was transformed from an international matter, governed through commercial diplomacy and the Commerce Clause, into a domestic matter, governed by Congress and driven by the electoral politics of protectionism. Those who debate American immigration today would do well to ponder this history.

My history of immigrant foreign relations provides surprisingly little evidence for the necessity of restriction. Many Americans believe restriction alone prevents immigration from growing to dimensions that would trigger domestic chaos or even national collapse. Yet in the nineteenth century—when commercial diplomacy opened the ports of the United States and extended the liberty to travel and reside to all Europeans and Latin Americans, and to some Asians, and when extensive, inexpensive, and transnational transportation systems were already in place—immigration neither overwhelmed the United States nor caused a national crisis. Late nineteenth-century globalization certainly pushed international migrations to higher levels relative to the figures that prevailed earlier in the century, but proportionately immigration was only somewhat greater than it is today, and immigrants never exceeded 15 percent of the U.S. population. In the absence of restrictive laws, there was no global stampede to the United States, not even across its land borders, which could be easily and cheaply traversed on foot by very poor people. The vast majority of the closest neighbors of the United States in the nineteenth century—French- and English-speaking Canadians and very poor Mexicans living along the border area—remained on their side of the U.S. borders. The vast majority of Germans, Swedes, eastern European Jews, and Italians remained in their homelands, despite harsh deprivation and persecutions. The majority remained at home while impressive migrations of their friends and families created significant emotional incentives for family unification through additional migration.

Immigrants' foreign networks were impressive and emotionally powerful, but even under a system of governance that supported the liberty to travel, they were not sufficient to transplant entire populations to the United States. In 1910, the million and more Canadians living in the United States represented about 14 percent of Canada's resident population; Italy in 1920 reported 15 to 20 percent of its resident population as living abroad (less than half of them in the United States). The only truly catastrophic domestic political or social upheaval in the years predating legislated immigration restrictions—the Civil War—was largely unrelated to contemporary immigration, although it was, arguably, the tragic legacy of the mass coerced migrations of an earlier era of globalization in the colonial Atlantic.

Today, the numbers of Mexicans living in the United States, both with and without papers, constitutes a percentage of Mexico's resident population that is about the same as Canada's or Italy's a century ago. Millenarian and ahistorical claims about the revolutionary character of recent globalization raise fears of mass relocations of impoverished peoples that have no historical precedent. The United States remains an attractive country to many people around the world, but most have never wanted to move to the States, and most do not want to do so today. Indeed, only 14 to 16 percent of people surveyed worldwide indicate any interest at all in changing their country of residence.

Nor have restrictive laws always driven the occasional historic decreases in the volumes of immigration. Figure 1 showed immigration responding most immediately and negatively to depressions and wars—whether during the years prior to 1882 (for example during the Civil War and the depression of the 1870s), during the years of mass European migration (during the depression of the 1890s and again, prior to restrictions, during World War I), or during the era of the Asian exclusions and national-origins quotas (the depression of the 1930s and World War II). Since 1965, swings in immigration have become less extreme, in part because restrictive laws privilege family reunification: migration motivated by love and emotion does not follow the dynamics of the labor market as precisely as does labor recruitment. Still, immigration has varied, and sometimes even decreased, in recent times, too—for example, briefly, during the stagflation of the 1970s, in the years just after the massive surge in regularization associated with the IRCA, and most recently in the aftermath of the 2008–2009 financial crisis. Restrictions have proved least effective during periods of economic expansion (the early 1920s, the 1950s, the 1990s and early 2000s), when their main impact has been to encourage illegality. The cases of Chinese paper sons in the nineteenth century and paperless Mexicans today document that migrants from countries where the United States actively encourages military or trade relations are particularly prone to evade restrictive laws during periods of economic expansion.

Almost no one debating contemporary American immigration today acknowledges any alternative to the congressional governance of immigration. Even those who blame Congress for the currently "broken immigration system" want mainly to replace federal legislation and policing with local or state legislation and policing. Americans seem to have no memory of the alternative forms of governance that a history of immigrant foreign relations reveals—namely, the commercial treaties, the Commerce Clause of the Constitution, and bilateral negotiations such as the first Bracero Program. And while studies of American empire-building have rightly pointed toward the negative consequences of an expanding and increasingly imperial twentieth-century presidency, the history of immigration governance instead reveals problems that have accompanied the expansion of an unchecked Congress, exercising its plenary power over human movements. Legislators in the late nineteenth century were able to force the renegotiation of treaties with China, contributing to a long decline in U.S.–China relations; in the 1970s, Congress used legislation to contain even presidential power to admit (or "parole") refugees. And more recently U.S. immigration restrictions have troubled U.S. relations with Mexico.

Once Congress gained plenary power to protect Americans from foreign invaders, immigration also became a domestic issue subject to the contradictions and interest-group conflicts of electoral politics. And since that time, there have been no easy or clear agreements about how to legislate, regulate, select, and restrict immigration. Between 1924 and 1965, and again between 1975 and the present, the basic contours of immigration debates, the shape and composition of legislative coalitions around immigration issues, and the tensions between executive and legislative interests in regard to immigration policy have produced lengthy and repetitive political conflicts that persist as political stalemates, often almost unchanged in their rhetoric, over many decades.

On this point, the history of foreign trade governance and the termination of the equally repetitive nineteenth-century debates over tariffs are instructive. That history suggests that it was a new form of governance initiated from the executive branch—and not changes in domestic political coalitions or the advent of new legislative ideas—that broke the long impasse that had rendered protective tariffs such a "dull and threadbare" subject by the 1920s. Beginning in the 1880s and 1890s, American presidents and their secretaries of state saw how legislative quarrels over tariff policies hindered their own geopolitics, then dubbed "dollar diplomacy." They repeatedly sought the greater flexibility that would enable them to negotiate changes in tariff rates with Congress. Over time, Congress accepted the appointment of neutral commissions to advise presidents on annual tariff adjustments. Voters suffering through the Great Depression and World War II accepted presidential arguments that international negotiation in pursuit of free trade would build the foundation for world peace, while protectionist laws had instead exacerbated the depression and contributed to the onset of World War II. In the 1980s, voters even accepted Ronald Reagan's demand for "fast track" presidential negotiations of tariff adjustments. The abandonment of legislative protectionism for executive leadership and bilateral trade policies has not been without its own problems. Executive leadership has further insulated trade policy from the wrath of protectionist voters, for example, but it did at least end a decades-long political legislative stalemate over tariffs.

Why is it not possible to imagine a parallel change in governance that would end the current immigration impasse? Quite stable electoral coalitions (recall that opposition to guest worker programs came from both the U.S. Chamber of Congress and American labor unions) have created an impasse over immigration that has persisted almost as long as the tariff stalemate of an earlier century. Voter frustration with the immigration stalemate has increased. More often than not, restrictive legislation has increased rather than diminished illegality. Like the protective tariffs that preceded them, immigration restrictions have failed to deliver a sense of security from foreign threats. In all likelihood, immigration policy cannot deliver that security while the United States remains at war, imports expensive foreign oil, and continues to incur huge trade deficits.

Could an alliance of foreign-origin voters and lobbyists with vigorous presidential leadership undo the legislative impasse and create a neutral Immigration Council to advise the executive branch, so that it could request annual changes in immigration numbers in keeping with the dynamics of the U.S. economy or the dynamics of American foreign affairs? In immigration policy, the Refugee Act of 1980 creates a somewhat different kind of precedent for presidential negotiations with Congress—at least over the numbers of refugee admissions. Historically, however, immigrant-origin voters have rarely challenged restriction. And, at present, only a few voices—of anarchists on the left, a few business-oriented neo-liberals, and on the right, libertarians of diverse persuasions—have called for open borders: it is doubt-ful, moreover, that any of these groups would welcome an expanded role for the executive branch in the governance of immigration, or even a renegotiation of NAFTA. Yet a North American zone of free movement of people, goods, and capital, comparable to the one created by the E.U., would certainly be the most direct path to eliminating illegality, and at least some Mexican-origin voters and American proponents of enhanced marketplace freedoms, whether neo-liberals or libertarians—along with many humanitarians—might well embrace such a solution. At the same time, however, significant U.S. allies and trading partners—notably China and India—would scarcely welcome such a change if it resulted (as it did in a unifying Europe) in diminished opportunities for their own citizens to enter "Fortress North America."

While past presidents managed to convince Americans that free trade was the best foundation for global economic integration and peace, few people today view the liberty to move as an equally powerful contribution to humanitarian internationalism or global integration. Nevertheless, international migration, even while restricted, does promote integration. Some economists now do see immigrant remittances as promoting greater equality worldwide. A few economic historians have even suggested that the freer movements of labor migrants in the nineteenth century had greater developmental consequences for poorer nations—largely by diminishing wage differentials between rich and poor countries around the Atlantic—than did foreign trade.

But it is a focus on immigrant foreign relations, not remittances, that provides the best evidence of how immigrants foster person-to-person humanitarian integration on a global scale. Nineteenth-century letters from America spread positive news about the benefits of economic opportunities and political liberties throughout plebeian Europe, while bad news about restriction and racial discrimination encouraged anti-Americanism in Asia. Humanitarian efforts by immigrants in the United States were not sufficient to prevent the murder of Europe's Jews in the 1940s, but they helped to guarantee that postwar European refugees would find at least some welcome despite otherwise restrictive laws. World War II revealed how foreign relations from below could, in times of international crises, assist the executive branch in its military activities and, in the postwar world, encourage friendly relations with postwar Europe and Japan or assist in Cold War strategies for change within the Warsaw Pact countries. The voluntary agencies and the nongovernmental international organizations to which foreigners living in the United States disproportionately contribute time, money, and leadership continue to generate positive connections to the United States that harsh immigration restrictions, illegality, wars in the Middle East, and the building of walls undermine.

If policies that treat immigration as a domestic matter seem doomed to fail, so too are foreign policies that ignore immigrants' foreign relations and that ignore the impact of immigration restriction on immigrants' international webs of communication. By insisting that immigration is a domestic matter, Americans foreclose rich opportunities to make the liberty to move, much like free trade, into a mechanism for international integration. The needs of merchants and investors matter in globalization, but so do the emotional, familial, and cultural webs that immigrants inevitably nurture and seek to preserve as they become Americans. Just as few people in the 1930s imagined that a new mechanism for the governing of tariffs would hold the key to future global economic integration, so few today think about the future of global integration when they consider how to fix a broken domestic system for governing immigration.

APPENDIX

Suggestions for Further Reading

In a short book on a big topic, my footnotes have provided only a limited introduction to the many works I consulted and learned from while writing. Here, I try to point to works of interest to readers who wish to pursue specific topics through rich historiographies and (in some cases) interdisciplinary fields of study.

General readers and students enrolled in courses on "the United States and the world" will want to understand the origins of this approach to American history, and they should begin by consulting four pioneers in the field. David Thelen, ed. "The Nation and Beyond: Transnational Perspectives on United States History," special issue, *Journal of American History* 86, 3 (Dec. 1999) links U.S. history and transnational history. The title of Thomas Bender's *America's Place in World History* (New York: Hill and Wang, 2006) speaks for itself, as does Ian Tyrell's *Transnational Nation: United States History in Global Perspective since 1789* (New York: Palgrave Macmillan, 2007). Carl Guarneri and James Davis's *Teaching American History in a Global Context* (Armonk, NY: M. E. Sharpe, 2008) builds on Guarneri's innovative work on comparative history. Although I do not agree with much of his exceptionalist interpretation, Eric Rauchway's *Blessed among Nations* (New York: Hill and Wang, 2006) also provides a provocative and very readable short survey of the growing genre of histories of the United States from a global perspective.

For students in courses on international history, which may or may not focus on the United States, I have chosen from the rich, scholarly literature on trade, diplomacy, and migration those books (and fewer articles) that seem most likely to provoke thoughts on the relationships among the three. Readers will face no shortage of choices when they seek general introductions to international history. My own work has been especially influenced by Akira Iriye, *Cultural Internationalism and World Order* (Baltimore: Johns Hopkins University Press, 1997); Patrick Finney, *Palgrave Advances in International History* (New York: Palgrave Macmillan, 2005); Robert Kagan, *Dangerous Nation* (New York: Alfred A. Knopf, 2006); Kristin L. Hoganson, *Consumers' Imperium: The Global Production of American Domesticity, 1865–1920* (Chapel Hill: University of North Carolina Press, 2007); Michael J. Hogan, *America in the World: The Historiography of American Foreign Relations since 1941* (New York: Cambridge University Press, 1995); Thomas W. Zeiler, "The Diplomatic History Bandwagon: A State of the Field," *Journal of American History* 95, 4 (March 2009): 1053–73. Among older works I would point readers to Frank Thistlethwaite, *The Anglo-American Connection in the Early Nineteenth Century* (Studies in American Civilization, Department of American Civilization, University of Pennsylvania, 1959).

The modestly shifting paradigm of the American "nation of immigrants" and the persistent attention to immigration, ethnicity, race, and nation-building in U.S. history can be explored in the works of immigration historians, past and present, beginning with Oscar Handlin, *The Uprooted; The Epic Story of the Great Migrations That Made the American People* (Boston: Little, Brown, 1951); John Bodnar, *The*

Transplanted: A History of Immigrants in Urban America (Bloomington: Indiana University Press, 1985); Roger Daniels, *Coming to America: A History of Immigration and Ethnicity in American Life* (New York: HarperCollins, 1990); Paul Spickard, *Almost All Aliens: Immigration, Race, and Colonialism in American History and Identity* (New York: Routledge, 2007). Gary Gerstle's *American Crucible: Race and Nation in the Twentieth Century* (Princeton, NJ: Princeton University Press, 2002) is most explicit in its focus on plural nation-building. In *American Dreaming, Global Realities: Re-Thinking U.S. Immigration History* (Urbana: University of Illinois Press, 2006), editors Donna Gabaccia and Vicki Ruiz instead offer a selection of recent scholarly articles meant to widen students' understandings of both "immigration" and "American history."

These nation-centered works can be contrasted to the more comparative, diasporic, and global or world historical accounts written or edited by U.S. and world historians in the past two decades. Especially useful for those wishing to think more broadly about the study of international migration historically are David Eltis, ed., *Coerced and Free Migration: Global Perspectives* (Stanford, CA: Stanford University Press, 2002); Nancy Green and Francois Weil, eds., *Citizenship and Those Who Leave: The Politics of Emigration* (Urbana: University of Illinois Press, 2007); Dirk Hoerder, *Cultures in Contact: World Migration in the Second Millennium* (Durham, NC: Duke University Press, 2002); Dirk Hoerder and Christiane Harzig, *What is Migration History?* (Cambridge: Polity Press, 2009); Jan Lucassen and Leo Lucassen, *Migration, Migration History, History: Old Paradigms and New Perspectives* (Bern: Peter Lang, 1997); Patrick Manning, *Migration in*

World History (New York: Routledge 2005); Wang Gungwu, *Global History and Migration: Some Patterns Revisited* (Boulder, CO: Westview Press, 1997). Exceptionally helpful in analyzing U.S. immigration policies, and the freedom to move, in global context is Ian Goldin, Geoffrey Cameron, and Meera Balarajan, *Exceptional People: How Migration Shaped Our World and Will Define Our Future* (Princeton, NJ: Princeton University Press, 2011).

Surprisingly few historians have attempted to link directly the study of international relations, diplomacy, and immigration. Of their works, the most ambitious, and the one that most influenced my own work, focuses mainly on the turn of the last century: Matthew Frye Jacobson, *Barbarian Virtues: The United States Encounters Foreign Peoples at Home and Abroad, 1876–1917* (New York: Hill and Wang, 2000). A much narrower study, but useful for its exploration of the presidential/congressional tensions of the same era, is Hans P. Vogt, *The Bully Pulpit and the Melting Pot: American Presidents and the Immigrant, 1897–1933* (Macon, GA: Mercer University Press, 2004). Roger Daniels, "Immigration," in Alexander DeConde et al., eds., *Encyclopedia of American Foreign Policy*, 2nd ed. (New York: Simon and Schuster, 2002), pp. 203–16, can provide another useful starting point, especially when supplemented for the more recent past by Sarah J. Mahler, "Constructing International Relations: The Role of Transnational Migrants and Other Non-State Actors," *Identities* 7, 2 (2000): 197–232; and James F. Hollifield, "Migration and International Relations: The Liberal Paradox," in Hans Entzinger, Marco Martiniello, and Catherine Wihtol de Wenden, eds., *Migration between Markets and States* (Burlington, VT: Ashgate, 2004), pp. 3-18. Provocative theoretical interventions by political scientists can also be found in Yossi Shain and Aharon Barth, "Diasporas and International Relations Theory," *International Organization* 57 (Summer 2003): 449–79; and Myron Weiner, "On International Migration and International Relations," *Population and Development Review* 11, 3 (1985): 441–55.

Equally surprising is how little has been written about Americans living abroad as empire-builders. Explorations of their lives are nevertheless often centrally important to interpreting key events in U.S. diplomatic history. For Mexico, see William Schell, Jr., *Integral Outsiders: The American Colony in Mexico City, 1876–1911* (Wilmington, DE: Scholarly Resources, 2001); John Mason Hart, *Empire and Revolution: The Americans in Mexico since the Civil War* (Berkeley: University of California Press, 2002). A study that focuses on contemporary Americans in Mexico is Sheila Croucher's *The Other Side of the Fence: American Migrants in Mexico* (Austin: University of Texas Press, 2009). For Canada, it is still useful to consult Marcus Lee Hansen and John Bartlet Brebner, *The Mingling of the Canadian and American Peoples*, 2 vols. (New York: Carnegie Endowment for International Peace, 1940). Nancy Green has also written recently and provocatively on the issue in "Expatriation, Expatriates, and Expats: The American in Transformation of a Concept," *American Historical Review* 114 (April 2009): 304–28. Although interested mainly in domestic politics, Aristide Zolberg's *America by Design: Immigration Policy in the Fashioning of America* (Cambridge, MA: Harvard University Press, 2006) provides the broadest introduction to the domestic implications of the changing role of the United States in the world and to the role of immigrants' domestic political mobilizations. *The*

Cambridge History of American Foreign Relations (Cambridge: Cambridge University Press, 1993) remains the best starting place for those who wish to deepen and expand the dialogue between immigration and diplomatic historians. A number of highly specialized studies suggest the many possibilities for linking immigration and the traditional study of diplomacy in creative ways. See, for example, Robbie Totten, "National Security and U.S. Immigration Policy, 1776–1790," *Journal of Interdisciplinary History* 39 (2008): 39–64; Masuda Hajimu, "Rumors of War: Immigration Disputes and the Social Construction of American-Japanese Relations, 1905–1913," *Journal of Diplomatic History* 33, 1 (January 2009): 1–37; Lorraine M. Lees, *Yugoslav-Americans and National Security During World War II* (Urbana: University of Illinois Press, 2007); Kristofer Allerfeldt, *Beyond the Huddled Masses: American Immigration and the Treaty of Versailles* (London: I. B. Tauris, 2006).

For those interested in the changing relation of trade and immigration as measures of the openness of the United States to the world, two provocative discussions come from the social sciences. See economists Timothy J. Hatton and Jeffrey G. Williamson's "A Dual Policy Paradox: Why Have Trade and Immigration Policies Always Differed in Labor-Scarce Economies?" Discussion Paper No. 2146, May 2006 (http://papers.ssrn.com/sol3/papers.cfm?abstract_id=905546) and political scientist James F. Hollifield's "Migration, Trade and the Nation-State: The Myth of Globalization," *UCLA Journal of International Law and Foreign Affairs* 3 (1998): 595–636. In considering the historically fraught relationships of the United States with Asia and with its American neighbors, two books by David Pletcher are very helpful: *The Diplomacy of Involvement: American Economic Expansion across the Pacific,*

1784–1900 (Columbia: University of Missouri Press, 2001); *The Diplomacy of Trade and Investment: American Economic Expansion in the Hemisphere, 1865–1900* (Columbia: University of Missouri Press, 1998). Finally, a highly specialized but nevertheless suggestive study is Drew Keeling, "Costs, Risks, and Migration Networks between Europe and the United States, 1900–1914," *Research in Maritime History* 33 (2007): 113–73.

A useful starting place for those interested in encouraging a broad dialogue between economic and immigration histories remains Stanley L. Engerman and Robert E. Gallman, eds., *The Cambridge Economic History of the United States* (Cambridge: Cambridge University Press, 1996–). *Historical Statistics of the United States, Millennial Edition*, ed. Susan B. Carter et al. (New York: Cambridge University Press, 2006) is an indispensable source of information for understanding the linkage of trade and immigration.

Since this book has emphasized the intertwined histories of protection through immigration and high tariffs, readers may also want to read Thomas Zeiler, "Tariff Policy" and Robert Freeman Smith, "Reciprocity," in the *Encyclopedia of American Foreign Policy* (New York: Charles Scribner's Sons, 2002), pp. 531–46 and 329–44, respectively. Although many will disagree on key points, Alfred E. Eckes provides a very useful and provocative overview in his *Opening America's Market: U.S. Foreign Trade Policy since 1776* (Chapel Hill: University of North Carolina Press, 1999). Suggestive, too, is Cecil E. Bohanon and T. Norman Van Cott, "Tariffs, Immigration, and Economic Insulation: A New View of the U.S. Post–Civil War," *Independent Review* 9, 4 (Spring 2005): 529–42.

Histories of restrictions on immigration written from both national and international perspectives have become more common in recent years, and they have been written by specialists in several disciplines. For those who first want to consider the general impact of international events on domestic politics, a good starting place is Ira Katznelson and Martin Shefter, eds., *Shaped by War and Trade: International Influences on American Political Development* (Princeton, NJ: Princeton University Press, 2003). I have been much influenced by international studies of restriction around the early Atlantic, e.g., Andreas Fahrmeir, Olivier Faron, and Patrick Weil, eds., *Migration Control in the North Atlantic World: The Evolution of State Practices in Europe and the United States from the French Revolution to the Interwar Period* (New York: Berghahn Books, 2003). For the nineteenth and twentieth centuries, Adam McKeown's *Melancholy Order: Asian Migration and the Globalization of Borders* (New York: Columbia University Press, 2008) also provides an appropriately international perspective. For the early period, readers will also find useful Gerald Neuman, "The Lost Century of American Immigration Law (1776–1875)," *Columbia Law Review* 8 (1993): 1833–1901.

For the nineteenth and twentieth centuries' politics of restriction, I often turned to Zolberg, *Nation by Design* and to Daniel Tichenor, *Dividing Lines: The Politics of Immigration Control in America* (Princeton, NJ: Princeton University Press, 2001). Tom E. Terrill's *The Tariff, Politics, and American Foreign Policy, 1874–1901* (Westport, CT: Greenwood Press, 1973) is very helpful for beginners trying to understand the complex politics of economic protectionism. Particularly useful in tracing the racialized dimensions of immigration restriction are Mae N. Ngai, *Impossible Subjects: Illegal Aliens and the Making of Modern America* (Princeton, NJ: Princeton University Press, 2004) and Erika Lee's *At America's Gates:*

Chinese Immigration during the Exclusion Era, 1882–1943 (Chapel Hill: University of North Carolina Press, 2003). Other dimensions of the politics of restriction can be found in Claudia Goldin, "The Political Economy of Immigration Restriction in the United States, 1890–1921," in Claudia Dale Goldin and Gary D. Libecap, eds., *The Regulated Economy: A Historical Approach to Political Economy*, 2nd ed. (Chicago: University of Chicago Press, 1994); Robert Zeidel, *Immigrants, Progressives, and Exclusion Politics: The Dillingham Commission, 1900–1927* (DeKalb: Northern Illinois University Press, 2004). For the years after World War II, three works were especially helpful: John David Skrentny, *The Minority Rights Revolution* (Cambridge, MA: Harvard University Press, 2002) and, for the tension between restriction and humanitarian aims in U.S. refugee policy, Gil Loescher, *Calculated Kindness: Refugees and America's Half-Open Door, 1945 to the Present* (New York: Free Press, 1986); and Carl J. Bon Tempo, *Americans at the Gate: The United States and Refugees during the Cold War* (Princeton, NJ: Princeton University Press, 2008). Finally, for a long-term perspective on the currently troubling issue of deportation, see Daniel Kanstroom's *Deportation Nation: Outsiders in American History* (Cambridge, MA: Harvard University Press, 2007). For surveys of public opinion polls on immigration, see Edwin Harwood, "American Public Opinion and U.S. Immigration Policy," *Annals of the American Academy of Political and Social Science* 487 (Sept. 1986): 201–12; and Rita J. Simon and Susan H. Alexander, *The Ambivalent Welcome: Print Media, Public Opinion, and Immigration* (Westport, CT: Praeger, 1993).

Of the many works that emphasize transnational connections between immigrants, their homelands, and their relatives in other lands, I have depended especially heavily on studies of Italians and Chinese. In addition to the works cited in individual chapters, see Sucheng Chan, *Chinese American Transnationalism: The Flow of People, Resources and Ideas between China and America during the Exclusion Era* (Philadelphia: Temple University Press, 2006); Madeline Yuan-yin Hsu, *Dreaming of Gold, Dreaming of Home: Transnationalism and Migration between the United States and South China, 1882–1943* (Stanford, CA: Stanford University Press, 2000); Donna Gabaccia, *Italy's Many Diasporas* (London and Seattle: University College of London and University of Washington Press, 2000); Adam McKeown, *Chinese Migration Networks and Cultural Change: Peru, Chicago, Hawaii, 1900–1936* (Chicago: University of Chicago Press, 2001); Guanhua Wang, *In Search of Justice: The 1905–1906 Chinese Anti-American Boycott* (Cambridge, MA: Harvard University Asia Center, 2001).

The most thorough studies of diaspora nationalism and of the complex interactions of political exiles, immigrant populations, and political mobilization aimed at change in the country of origin have dealt with Chinese and Italian immigrants. See, for example, Donna R. Gabaccia and Fraser M. Ottanelli, eds., *Italian Workers of the World: Labor Migration and the Formation of Multiethnic Societies* (Urbana: University of Illinois Press, 2001) and Him Mark Lai, *Chinese American Transnational Politics*, ed. Madeline Y. Hsu (Urbana: University of Illinois Press, 2010). Political scientist Yossi Shain takes his focus on diasporas one step further in exploring the impact on official foreign relations in "Ethnic Diasporas and U.S. Foreign Policy," *Political Science Quarterly* 109, 5 (1994–95): 811–42.

Finally, for those who wish to explore how immigrants create and maintain their foreign relations over time, there is both a rich literature on the writing of letters across borders and an emerging literature by social scientists on transnational communication in the era of new communication technologies: Richard B. Eide, *Norse Immigrant Letters: Glimpses of Norse Immigrant Life in the Northwest in the Fifties* (Minneapolis: University of Minnesota and Lutheran Free Church Publishing Co., 1925); Theodore Blegen, *The "America Letters"* (Oslo: I Kommisjon Hos Jacog Dybwad, 1928); Zempel Solveig, *In Their Own Words: Letters from Norwegian Immigrants* (Minneapolis: University of Minnesota Press, 1991); David Gerber, *Authors of Their Own Lives: Personal Correspondence in the Lives of Nineteenth Century British Immigrants to the United States* (New York: New York University Press, 2006); David Gerber, Bruce Elliott, and Suzanne Sinke, eds., *Letters across Borders: The Personal Correspondence of International Immigrants* (New York: Palgrave, 2006); Kerby Miller et al., *Irish Immigrants in the Land of Canaan: Letters and Memoirs from Colonial and Revolutionary America, 1675–1815* (New York: Oxford University Press, 2003); Nicole Constable, *Romance on a Global Stage: Pen Pals, Virtual Ethnography, and "Mail-order" Marriages* (Berkeley, CA: University of California Press, 2003); Andoni Alonso and Pedro J. Oiarzabal, eds., *Diasporas in the New Media Age: Identity, Politics, and Community* (Reno: University of Nevada Press, 2010).

NOTES

INTRODUCTION

1. Richard Peet, *Unholy Trinity: The IMF, World Bank and WTO* (London: Zed Books, 2003), 37.

2. Haiming Liu, *The Transnational History of a Chinese Family* (New Brunswick, NJ: Rutgers University Press, 2005). See also Liu, "The Trans-Pacific Family: A Case Study of Sam Chang's Family History," *Amerasia Journal* 18, 2 (1992): 1–34.

3. Jim Brown, *Riding the Line: The United States Customs Service in San Diego, 1885–1930: A Documentary History* (Washington, DC: Department of the Treasury, U.S. Customs Service, 1991), 20–21. The author sardonically describes Bowers as a "gifted and prolific writer of memoranda" to the Treasury Department, requesting funds to employ additional agents (15).

4. Liu, *The Transnational History of a Chinese Family*, 171–209.

5. Ibid., 198.

CHAPTER 1: ISOLATED OR INDEPENDENT? AMERICAN IMMIGRATION BEFORE 1850

1. See Omar Calabrese, ed., *Italia Moderna: Immagini e storia di un identità nazionale*, vol. 1, *Dall' unità al nuovo secolo* (Milan: Electa, 1982), 118.

2. "In Memory of Emma Lazarus," *New York Times*, May 6, 1903, 9.

3. Peter B. Harris, "Some Teachable Ironies about the Alfred Stieglitz Photo *The Steerage* (1907), on the Cover of *The Heath Anthology of American Literature*, 3/e, Volume 2," http://college.cengage.com/english/heath/harris.htm, accessed August 25, 2010.

4. J. Hector St. John Crèvecoeur, *Letters from an American Farmer*, reprinted from the original ed. (New York: Fox, Duffield, 1904), Letter 3, 54.

5. The *Oxford English Dictionary* points to first uses of "isolationism" only in the 1920s and 1930s.

6. Frank Thistlethwaite, "Migration from Europe Overseas in the Nineteenth and Twentieth Centuries," in Rudolph Vecoli and Suzanne Sinke, eds., *A Century of European Migrations, 1830–1930* (Urbana:

University of Illinois Press, 1991), 17–49; citation for "salt water curtain," 20.

7. Bradford Perkins, *The Creation of a Republican Empire, 1776–1865*, vol. 1, *The Cambridge History of American Foreign Relations* (Cambridge: Cambridge University Press, 1993), 200.

8. *The Interesting Narrative of the Life of Olaudah Equiano, or Gustavus Vassa, the African* (London: Printed and Sold for the Author, 1793), 30.

9. John Harrower, *The Journal of John Harrower, an Indentured Servant in the Colony of Virginia, 1773–1776* (New York: Holt, Rinehart, and Winston, 1963).

10. Elizabeth Jane Errington, *Emigrant Worlds and Transatlantic Communities: Migration to Upper Canada in the First Half of the Nineteenth Century* (Montreal and Kingston: McGill–Queens University Press, 2007), 3.

11. Joseph H. Udelson, *Dreamer of the Ghetto: The Life and Works of Israel Zangwill* (Tuscaloosa: University of Alabama Press, 1990).

12. My account is based largely on Gay Wilson Allen and Roger Asselineau, *St. John de Crèvecoeur: The Life of an American Farmer* (New York: Viking Penguin, 1987).

13. Jaime E. Rodríguez and Kathryn Vincent, *Myths, Misdeeds, and Misunderstandings: The Roots of Conflict in U.S.–Mexican Relations* (Wilmington, DE: SR Books, 1997), 25.

14. *Memoirs of William Sampson* (London: Whittaker, Treacher, and Arnot, 1832).

15. The story of the Stille and Krumme family migrations, and their letters, are in Walter D. Kamphoefner, Wolfgang Helbich, and Ulrike Sommer, eds., *News From the Land of Freedom: German Immigrants Write Home* (Ithaca, NY and London: Cornell University Press, 1988), 62–84; quoted phrase, 67.

16. Theodore C. Blegen, *Land of Their Choice: The Immigrants Write Home* (Minneapolis: The University of Minnesota Press, 1955), 266–67.

17. Kamphoefner et al., *News from the Land of Freedom*, 90.

18. Ibid., 72.

19. See discussions of debt in ibid., 107, 207, 221–22, 500–501.

20. Adolf E. Schroeder and Carla Schulz-Geisberg, *Hold Dear, As Always: Jette, a German Immigrant Life in Letters* (Columbia: University of Missouri Press, 1988).

21. John Catanzariti, ed., *The Papers of Thomas Jefferson* (Princeton, NJ: Princeton University Press, 2000), vol. 28, 507.

22. Originally published in the *American Daily Advertiser* (Philadelphia), 19 September 1796, the document is now readily available online: http://gwpapers.virginia.edu/documents/farewell/intro.html.

23. Jefferson to George Rogers Clark, December 25, 1780, in Julian P. Boyd, ed., *Papers of Thomas Jefferson*, vol. 4, (Princeton, NJ: Princeton University Press, 1951), 237–38.

24. *Journal of the House of Representatives*, 30th Cong., 1st Session, Dec. 7, 1847, 21.

25. Carl von Clausewitz, *On War*, trans. Colonel J. J. Graham, vol. 1, ch. 1., pt. 24 (electronic resource Champaign, IL: Project Gutenburg, 2006).

26. Karlyn Kohrs Campbell and Kathleen Hall Jamieson, *Deeds Done in Words: Presidential Rhetoric and the Genres of Governance* (Chicago: University of Chicago Press, 1990), 28.

27. *Journal of the House of Representatives*, 19th Cong., 1st sess., April 20, 1826, 451.

28. A full text version of *Common Sense* (Philadelphia: W. and T. Bradford, 1791) can be accessed at http://www.earlyamerica.com/early america/milestones/commonsense/text.html.

29. Cited in Drew Keeling, "The Transportation Revolution and Transatlantic Migration, 1850–1914," *Research in Economic History* 1 (1999): 41, from "Opinions of the Judges of the Supreme Court of the United States, in the case of Smith vs. Turner, and Norris vs. the City of Boston. February 17, 1849."

30. *Western Literary Messenger*, 9, 1 (August 7, 1847), 100.

31. Quoted in Aristide R. Zolberg, *A Nation by Design: Immigration Policy in the Fashioning of America* (New York: Russell Sage, 2006), 58.

32. Jonathan Elliot, *The Debates in the Several State Conventions on the Adoption of the Federal Constitution, as Recommended by the General Convention at Philadelphia, in 1787: Together with the Journal of the Federal Convention, Luther Martin's Letter, Yates's Minutes, Congressional Opinions, Virginia and Kentucky. . . .* (Philadelphia: J. B. Lippincott, 1891), vol. 5, 398.

33. Murray G. Lawson, "Research Note: The Foreign-Born in Congress, 1789–1949: A Statistical Summary," *American Political Science Review* 51, 4 (December 1957): 1183–89.

34. Alfred E. Eckes, Jr., *Opening America's Market: U.S. Foreign Trade Policy since 1776* (Chapel Hill: The University of North Carolina Press, 1995), 13–14.

35. "A Treaty of Amity and Commerce between the United States of America and His Majesty the King of Prussia," Wednesday, May 17, 1786, *Treaties and Other International Agreements* 8, 79.

36. "Treaty of Commerce and Navigation with the Kingdom of Sweden and Norway. Communicated to the Senate, December 12, 1827," *Treaties and Other International Agreements* 11, 876.

37. "Treaty of Commerce and Navigation between the United States of America and Portugal," reprinted in the *Merchants Magazine and Commercial Review* 5 (1841): 273.

38. *American State Papers, Foreign Relations* (Washington, DC: Gales and Seaton, 1858), vol. 5, 431.

39. *Journal of the House of Representatives*, 9th Cong., 1st Session, Dec. 31, 1805, 223.

40. Paine, *Common Sense* (Mineola, NY: Dover Publications, 1997), 20.

41. "Political Economy, Producers and Consumers (a review of several works by Jean Baptiste Say)," *Southern Review*, February 1832, 509.

42. Eckes, *Opening America's Market*, 17.

43. *Journal of the House of Representatives*, 27th Cong., 2nd Session, Mar. 3, 1842, 199.

44. Eckes, *Opening America's Market*, 279–80.

45. "Review of 'The Sign of the Times': A Series of Discourses Delivered in the Second Presbyterian Church, Philadelphia," *Princeton Review* 12, 1 (January 1840): 8.

46. Quoted in Adam McKeown, *Melancholy Order: Asian Migration and the Globalization of Borders* (New York: Columbia University Press, 2008), 26, from Emer de Vattel, *Le droit des gens; ou, Principes de la loi naturelle appliqués à la conduite et aux affaires des nations et des souverains* (Washington, DC: Carnegie Institution of Washington, 1916), vol. 3, trans. Charles Ghequiere Fenwick, 92.

47. See Mayor of New York v. Miln, 36 US 102 (1837).

48. Richard Weston, *A Visit to the United States and Canada in 1833* (Glasgow: R. Griffith, 1836), 52.

49. *Reports of Cases Argued and Adjudged in the Supreme Court of the United States, January Term, 1849*, vol. 7 (Boston: Charles C. Little and James Brown, 1849), 332.

50. Gibbons v. Ogden, 22 U.S. 1 (1824).

51. *Reports of Cases Argued and Adjudged*, 323.

52. Daniel J. Tichenor, *Dividing Lines: The Politics of Immigration Control in America* (Princeton, NJ: Princeton University Press, 2002), 55.

CHAPTER 2: EMPIRE AND THE DISCOVERY OF IMMIGRANT FOREIGN RELATIONS, 1850–1924

1. Baldassare D'Anna is a pseudonym for a man whose family is recorded in the *fogli di famiglia* and the registers of birth, death, and marriage held in the municipal archive of Sambuca di Sicilia. The details of this man's story are known in part because of the local political prominence of one of his children. See Donna R. Gabaccia, *Militants and*

Migrants: Rural Sicilians Become American Workers (New Brunswick, NJ: Rutgers University Press, 1988).

2. Imre Ferenczi, "Proletarian Mass Migrations, Nineteenth and Twentieth Centuries," in *International Migrations*, ed. Walter F. Willcox (New York: National Bureau of Economic Research, 1929), vol. 1.

3. The story of Rosalie Evans is from Timothy J. Henderson, *The Worm in the Wheat: Rosalie Evans and Agrarian Struggle in the Puebla-Tlaxcala Valley of Mexico, 1906–1927* (Durham, NC: Duke University Press, 1998). See also *The Rosalie Evans Letters from Mexico*, arranged with commentary by Daisy Caden Pettus (Indianapolis, IN: The Bobbs-Merrill Co., 1926).

4. Guy Stevens, "Protecting the Rights of Americans in Mexico," *Annals of the American Academy of Political and Social Science* 132 (July 1927): 164.

5. *The Works of William H. Seward*, ed. George E. Baker (Boston: Houghton, Mifflin, 1887), vol. 3, 618.

6. Edwin Atkins, *My Sixty Years in Cuba* (Cambridge, MA: Riverside Press, 1926).

7. Quoted by Andrew E. Gibson and Arthur Donovan, *The Abandoned Sea: A History of United States Maritime Policy* (Columbia: University of South Carolina Press, 2000), 4.

8. "Work not Preference," *Review of Reviews* 33 (Jan.–June 1906): 382.

9. "Message of the President," *Papers Relating to the Foreign Relations of the United States* (Washington, DC: Government Printing Office, 1894), x.

10. An English language version of the Burlingame Treaty text is available in the Online Archive of California: http://content.cdlib.org/ark:/13030/hb4m3nb03h/?order=7&brand=oac.

11. Edwin M. Borchard, *Diplomatic Protection of Citizens Abroad, or the Law of International Claims* (New York: The Banks Law Publishing Co., 1919), v.

12. "President Discusses the Monroe Doctrine," *New York Times*, April 3, 1903.

13. "Sketch of the Career of Mr. Carter: Born in Honolulu, Educated at Ann Arbor, Wedded to an American," *Chicago Daily Tribune*, January 19, 1895, 5.

14. Direct citations are from Henderson, *The Worm in the Wheat*, 12–13, 21.

15. James W. Shepp and Daniel B. Shepp, *Shepp's New York City Illustrated: Scene and Story in the Metropolis of the Western World* (Chicago: Globe Bible Publishing Co., 1894).

16. Clarence E. Edwords, *Bohemian San Francisco, Its Restaurants and Their Most Famous Recipes; The Elegant Art of Dining* (San Francisco: P. Elder and Co., 1914), 4.

17. *New York Times*, June 12, 1881, 12; *Chicago Daily Tribune*, April 21, 1905, 4.

18. *Proceedings of the National Conference of Charities and Correction* (Boston: Press of George H. Ellis, 1888), 435.

19. Bonnie C. Lew, "'I always felt out of place there': Growing up Chinese in Mississippi," in Judy Yung, Gordon H. Chang, and H. Mark Lai, eds., *Chinese American Voices* (Berkeley: University of California Press, 2006), 287.

20. "The Basic Issues as They Have Been Defined in the Campaign: The Intangible Issues of Personality and Religion Outweigh Stated Arguments," *New York Times*, Nov. 6, 1960, E3.

21. Frank Julian Warne, *The Immigrant Invasion* (New York: Dodd, Meade, 1913), 10.

22. McKeown, *Melancholy Order*, 343.

23. "Immigration Troubles of the United States," *Nineteenth Century* 30 (October 1891), 584.

24. "Emigration," *The Encyclopedia of Social Reforms: Including Political Economy, Political Science, Sociology and Statistics* (New York: Funk & Wagnalls, 1897), 556.

25. Dino Cinel, *The National Integration of Italian Return Migration, 1870–1929* (Cambridge: Cambridge University Press, 1991), ch. 6

26. Yong Chen, "Understanding Chinese American Transnationalism during the Early Twentieth Century: An Economic Perspective," in *Chinese American Transnationalism: The Flow of People, Resources, and Ideas between China and America during the Exclusion Era*, ed. Sucheng Chan (Philadelphia: Temple University Press, 2006), 171.

27. Liu, *The Transnational History of a Chinese Family*, 42–43.

28. Chen Yixi's story is in Madeline Y. Hsu, *Dreaming of Gold, Dreaming of Home: Transnationalism and Migration between the United States and China, 1882–1943* (Stanford, CA: Stanford University Press, 2000).

29. Thanks to Lisong Liu for suggesting and contextualizing possible proverbial equivalents to "*tutto il mondo è paese.*" *Si hai wei jia* ("feeling at home while being in the four corners of the world") also captures some of the same sentiments.

30. Kamphoefner, *News from the Land of Freedom*, 71.

31. Orm Overland, "Learning to Read Immigrant Letters: Reflections towards a Textual Theory," in Oyvind T. Gulliksen et. al., eds, *Norwegian-American Essays 1996* (Oslo: NAHA-Norway, 1996), 217.

32. "Letter from Anonymous Male Scottish Immigrant From Aberdeen, January 21, 1833," *Counsel for Emigrants* (Aberdeen, Scotland: J. Mathison, 1834), 57.

33. *North American Immigrant Letters, Diaries and Oral Histories* (Alexandria, VA: Alexander Street Press, 2004).

34. Wong Kai Kah, "A Menace to America's Oriental Trade," *North American Review* (January 1904): 414–24; cited in Estelle T. Lau, *Paper Families: Identity, Immigration Administration and Chinese Exclusion* (Durham, NC: Duke University Press, 2007), 205.

35. For the lives of Sambuca's returners, as well as the ties connecting this Sicilian town to various locations in the United States, see Gabaccia, *Militants and Migrants*, ch. 8.

36. The Sisters of Mercy, *Poems for Catholics & Convents: And Plays for Catholic Schools* (New York: New York Catholic Protectory, 1874), 217.

37. See the report on his funeral, *New York Times*, November 14, 1889, 8.

38. Letter from W. B. Lawrence, Tammany Society or Columbian Order, *Celebration in Honor of the Anniversary of American Independence, July 3, 1866* (New York: New York Printing, 1866), 75–76.

39. Ruth Swan and Edward A. Jerome, "Unequal Justice: The Metis in O'Donoghue's Raid of 1871," *Manitoba History* 39 (Spring/Summer 2000), n.p.

40. The best source on Bresci's life remains Arrigo Petacco, *l'Anarchico che venne dall'America: Storia di Gaetano Bresci e del complotto per uccidere Umberto I* (Milan: Mondadori, 2000).

41. English-only readers will find over fifty articles on Bresci and on Paterson's Italians in the *New York Times*, July 31–August 31, 1900.

42. Liu, *The Transnational History of a Chinese Family*, 82.

43. *Los Angeles Times*, March 7, 1906.

44. "Yellow and White: The Coming War of Races," *Contemporary Review* 92 (October 1907), 577–79.

45. "The Chinese Boycott of American Goods," *Review of Reviews* 33, February 1906, 159.

46. Hans P. Vought, *The Bully Pulpit and the Melting Pot: American Presidents and the Immigrant, 1897–1933* (Macon, GA: Mercer University Press, 2004), 47.

47. Fraser M. Ottanelli, "'If Fascism Comes to America We Will Push It Back in to the Ocean': Italian American Antifascism in the 1920s and 1930s," in Donna R. Gabaccia and Fraser M. Ottanelli, eds., *Italian Workers of the World: Labor Migration and the Formation of Multiethnic States* (Urbana: University of Illinois Press, 2001), 178.

48. Yansheng Ma Lum and Raymond Mun Kong Lum, *Sun Yat-sen in Hawaii: Activities and Supporters* (Honolulu: Hawaii Chinese History Center, 1999), ch. 1.

CHAPTER 3: IMMIGRATION AND RESTRICTION: PROTECTION IN A DANGEROUS WORLD, 1850–1965

1. Richard Bartholdt, *From Steerage to Congress: Reminiscences and Reflections* (Philadelphia: Dorrance & Co., 1930), 109.

2. Martin Gilbert, *Descent into Barbarism: The History of the Twentieth Century, 1934–1951* (New York: Harper Collins, 1999).

3. U.S. Department of State, "Papers Relating to Expatriation, Naturalization, and Change of Allegiance," # 503, in *Papers Relating to the Foreign Relations of the United States*, pt. 1, vol. 2 (Washington, DC, 1873), 1221.

4. Perry Baker et al. v. the City of Portland, 5 Sawyer 566, quoted in Elmer Sandmeyer, *The Anti-Chinese Movement in California* (Champaign: University of Illinois Press, 1973), 208.

5. Tom E. Terrill, *The Tariff, Politics, and American Foreign Policy, 1874–1901* (Westport, CT: Greenwood Press, 1973), 3.

6. Bartholdt, *From Steerage to Congress*, 153.

7. "The Democratic Review on Freedom of Trade," *American Whig Review* 76 (April 1851): 333.

8. *New York Times*, September 21, 1909, 8.

9. Warne, *The Immigrant Invasion*, 281–82.

10. Thomas W. Zeiler, "Tariff Policy," *Encyclopedia of American Foreign Policy* (New York: Charles Scribner's Sons, 2001), 531

11. Quoted in Alfred E. Eckes, Jr., *Opening America's Market: U.S. Foreign Trade Policy since 1776* (Chapel Hill, NC: The University of North Carolina Press, 1995), 69.

12. See Hoover's denial of such charges during the heated debates of the 1932 elections, "Hoover says 'Falsehoods' to Foes' Charges," *Chicago Daily Tribune*, October 6, 1932, 1.

13. Laurence Burd, "U.S. Must Lead in Cutting Tariffs: Truman," *Chicago Daily Tribune*, March 7, 1947, 1.

14. "The Chinese Must Go," *New York Times*, February 26, 1880, 4.

15. Chae Chan Ping v. U.S., 130 U.S. 581 (1889).

16. "Senator Foraker's View: Question of the Sovereign Power of the United States Settled Forever by the Court," *New York Times*, May 28, 1901, 3.

17. *New York Times*, February 1, 1909.

18. Elihu Root, "The Real Questions under the Japanese Treaty and the San Francisco School Board Resolution," *American Journal of International Law* 1 (1907): 273.

19. Immigration Restriction League, *Constitution of the Immigration Restriction League*, (Boston: Immigration Restriction League, 1894), 1.

20. "For Freedom and Civilization," *New York Times*, April 3, 1917.

21. "Lodge Punches Angry Pacifist for an Insult," *Chicago Tribune*, April 3, 1917.

22. Henry Cabot Lodge, *Treaty of Peace with Germany: Speech of Hon. Henry Cabot Lodge of Massachusetts in the Senate of the United States, Tuesday, August 12, 1919* (Washington, DC: Government Printing Office, 1919).

23. Lodge's speech to the Senate is reprinted in Henry Steele Commager, *Documents of American History,* 9th edition (Englewood Cliffs, NJ: Prentice-Hall, 1973), 160–161.

24. "Immigration Bill Enacted over Veto," *New York Times*, February 6, 1917, 12.

25. All direct quotes from "Applaud Alien Bill in D.A.R. Convention," *New York Times*, April 19, 1924, 2.

26. Franklin D. Roosevelt, "Presidential Statement of Non-Intervention in Cuba—The Good Neighbor Policy Applied," November 23, 1933, *Public Papers and Addresses of Franklin D. Roosevelt*, vol. 8 (Washington, DC: Government Printing Office, 1938), 500.

27. Aristide Zolberg, "The Archaeology of 'Remote Control,'" in Andreas Fahrmeir, Olivier Faron, and Parick Weil, eds., *Migration Control in the North Atlantic World: The Evolution of State Practices in Europe and the United States from the French Revolution to the Interwar Period* (New York: Berghahn Books, 2003).

28. All direct quotes from "Applaud Alien Bill in D.A.R. Convention," *New York Times*, April 19, 1924, 2.

29. Quoted in Tichenor, *Dividing Lines*, 160

30. Gil Loescher, *The UNHRC and World Politics: A Perilous Path* (New York: Oxford University Press, 2001), 32.

31. "Immigration Curb is Urged in Survey," *New York Times*, June 8, 1939.

32. "Senators Vote to Fingerprint, Register Aliens: Approve Measure Aimed at Fifth Column," *Chicago Tribune*, May 26, 1940, 3. First used during the Spanish Civil War, the term "fifth column" refers to resident civilian supporters of invading or threatening military forces.

33. Edward B. Marks, *Token Shipment: The Story of America's War Refugee Shelter* (Washington, DC: Government Printing Office, 1946).

34. Harry S. Truman, "Statement and Directive by the President on Immigration to the United States of Certain Displaced Persons and Refugees in Europe," *Public Papers and Addresses of the Presidents: Harry S. Truman, 1945* (Washington, DC: Government Printing Office, 1945), 574.

35. "Maria Kruk Greenstein," http://www.geocities.com/us_warbrides/AmWarBrides/KMuldoon.html; Michael J. Forrester, *Tsuchino: My Japanese War Bride* (Salt Lake City, UT: American Book Publishers, 2004).

36. "Eisenhower in Newark," *Chicago Daily Tribune*, October 20, 1952, 16.

37. United Nations Convention Relating to the Status of Refugees, Geneva, July 28th, 1951, (No. 2545) United Nations Treaty Series, vol. 189, 137.

38. "Refugees Suspected," *New York Times*, December 31, 1956, 3.

39. Him Mark Lai et al., *Island: Poetry and History of Chinese Immigrants on Angel Island, 1910–1940* (Seattle: University of Washington Press, 1991).

40. Interview of Gussie Shapiro by Dennis Cloutier, November 17, 1983, in "Ellis Island Oral History Project, Series NPS, no. 141," *North American Letters, Diaries and Oral Histories* (Alexandria, VA: Alexander Street Press, 2004).

41. Emma Goldman, *Living My Life* (New York: Dover Books, 1970), vol. 2, 711; her report differs in some details from the *New York Times*, November 8, 1919 and December 22, 1919. See also Constantine M. Panunzio, *The Deportation Cases of 1919–1920* (New York: Commission on the Church and Social Service, Federal Council of the Churches of Christ in America, 1921), 6.

42. John Cassel, "Cleaning the Nest," *Literary Digest*, January 17, 1920, orig. published in the *New York Evening World*, unknown date. http://newman.baruch.cuny.edu/digital/redscare/IMAGES_LG/Cleaning_the_Nest.gif. Accessed May 9, 2011.

43. Bartholdt, *From Steerage to Congress*, 153.

44. 54th Congress, 1st session, *Congressional Record* 28 (May 19, 1896), 5422.

45. Bartholdt, *From Steerage to Congress*, 151.

46. See, for example, "That American Tin Ore," *Chicago Daily Tribune*, September 8, 1891, 11.

47. Bartholdt, *From Steerage to Congress*, 165.

48. Ibid., 152.

49. "Certain Chicago Justices Conduct Entire Trials in Foreign Language in Disregard of the State Constitution," *Chicago Tribune*, December 9, 1900, 98.

50. 68th Congress, 1st Session, *Congressional Record* 65 (April 11, 1924), 6132.

51. Quoted in Nancy Ordover, *American Eugenics: Race, Queer Anatomy, and the Science of Nationalism* (Minneapolis: University of Minnesota Press, 2003), 34.

52. 68th Congress, 1st Session, *Congressional Record* 65 (April 5, 1924), 5650.

53. "Social Workers Will Meet Today," *Los Angeles Times*, October 22, 1931, A10; "Fares Reduced on Repatriates," *Los Angeles Times*, November 27, 1933, A14; "Mexicans Aid Repatriation," *Los Angeles Times*, November 12, 1938, 10.

54. Harold Smith, "Congress Race Given New Vigor; Sabath Target of H. G. Green in 5th District: 'Red Charge Shot at Congressman,'" *Chicago Daily Tribune*, March 10, 1940, W1. "Sabath Chides Rankin on Army Red Charges," *New York Times*, July 21, 1945, 24. See also John Fisher, "House Rebukes Rep. Sabath for Rankin Smear: Orders Insults Out of Record," *Chicago Daily Tribune*, March 25, 1947, 6. While attention focused on Sabath, it was congressman and original HUAC chairman Samuel Dickstein who was later discovered to have exchanged information for cash from the U.S.S.R., including during the years when the U.S.S.R. and the United States were wartime allies.

55. Burton A. Boxerman, "Adolph Joachim Sabath in Congress: The Early Years, 1907–1932," and "Adolph Joachim Sabath in Congress: The Roosevelt and Truman Years," *Journal of the Illinois State Historical Society* 66 (Autumn 1973): 327–40; and 66 (Winter 1973): 428–43.

56. Genevieve Forbes Herrick, "They Hold Up the Mirror; Like Results," *Chicago Daily Tribune*, June 25, 1933, E1.

57. Quoted in Robert A. Slayton, *Empire Statesman: The Rise and Redemption of Al Smith* (New York: Simon and Schuster, 2001), 310.

58. Daniel Burke, "A Catholic Wind in the White House," *Washington Post*, April 13, 2008.

59. "To Favor Immigration: A Protective League, One Million Strong, Formed to Oppose the Lodge Bill," *New York Times*, January 7, 1898, 6.

60. Charles H. Sherrill, *Do We Have a Far Eastern Policy?* (New York: Scribner's Sons 1920), 209.

61. 68th Congress, 1st Session, *Congressional Record* 65 (May 5, 1924), 8637.

62. Ibid.

63. "Refugee Aid Planned by Jewish Veterans," *New York Times*, August 30, 1938, 2.

64. Hannah Arendt, *The Origins of Totalitarianism* (New York: Harcourt Trade, 1973), 292.

65. "Roosevelt Urged to Reprove Reich," *New York Times*, March 15, 1934, 18.

66. Lorraine M. Lees, *Yugoslav-Americans and National Security During World War II* (Urbana: University of Illinois Press, 2007), 187.

67. "Assembly of Captive European Nations, Records, 1953–1972," Immigration History Research Center, University of Minnesota. http://www.ihrc.umn.edu/research/vitrage/all/am/GENassembly.htm.

68. Cited in David M. Reimers, *Still the Golden Door: The Third World Comes to America* (New York: Columbia University Press, 1992), 15.

69. Wayne Lutton and John Tanton, *The Immigration Invasion* (Petosky, MI: Social Contract Press, 1994), 3.

70. "Immigration Reformer Michael Aloysius Feighan," *New York Times*, August 25, 1965, 20.

71. Cabell Phillips, "Congress Sends Immigration Bill to the White House; Measure Abolishes National Origins System and Sets Limit for Hemisphere," *New York Times*, October 1, 1965, 1.

72. See "Text of President's Speech on Immigration," *New York Times*, October 4, 1965, SU1.

CHAPTER 4: IMMIGRATION AND GLOBALIZATION, 1965 TO THE PRESENT

1. Merriam-Webster Online Dictionary: http://www.merriam-webster.com/dictionary/globalization.

2. Don Cook, *Los Angeles Times*, November 22, 1971, E1; Soma Golden, "Grappling with Multinational Corporations; Special to The New York Times; The Problem of Coping With Global Companies," *New York Times*, December 31, 1974, 27. For the "global village," see Marshall McCluhan, *The Gutenberg Galaxy: The Making of Typographic Man* (Toronto: University of Toronto Press, 1962), 31.

3. Quoted in Daniel Tichenor, *Dividing Lines: The Politics of Immigration Control in America* (Princeton, NJ: Princeton University Press, 2001), 252.

4. 89th Congress, 1st Session, Senate Committee on Appropriations, *Departments of Commerce, Justice, and State, the Judiciary, and Related Agencies Appropriations for Fiscal Year 1984: Hearings* (Washington, DC: Government Printing Office, 1983), 1001.

5. Centre for Contemporary Cultural Studies, University of Birmingham, *The Empire Strikes Back: Race and Racism in 70s Britain* (London: Hutchinson, 1982).

6. Le Ly Hayslip with Jay Wurts, *When Heaven and Earth Changed Places: A Vietnamese Woman's Journey from War to Peace* (New York: Doubleday, 1989).

7. For her American life, see *Child of War, Woman of Peace* (New York: Doubleday, 1993).

8. The story of Don Pedro is briefly told in Robert Courtney Smith, *Mexican New York: Transnational Lives of New Immigrants* (Berkeley: University of California Press, 2006), 20–21. Others, too, have described the first Poblano arrivals in New York as two brothers named Pedro and Fermin Simon. But still others point instead to a female cook, named Maurilia Arriaga, who worked in New York for a Mexican diplomat. See Gisele Regatao, "Viva Poblanos: Mexicans from Puebla Create Mini-Version of Home State in New York," *Newsday*, May 21, 2001, C14.

9. See the interview with Arnulfo Caballero and descendents, "Chuppies," in Al Santoli, *New Americas, an Oral History: Immigrants & Refugees in the U.S. Today* (New York: Viking Penguin, 1988), 275–92.

10. Nooyi's biography can be pieced together from occasional newspaper reports in India and the U.S., including Sarah Murray, "From Poor Indian Student to Powerful U.S. Businesswoman," *Financial Times*, January 26, 2004, 3; and from the corporate PepsiCo website: http://www.pepsico.com/Company/Leadership.html#Nooyi_fb.

11. John Seabrook, "Snacks for a Fat Planet, " *New Yorker*, May 16, 2001.

12. Amy Shipley, "Simon Cho's Olympic Speedskating Opportunity Rewards his Family's Investment," *Washington Post*, January 13, 2010. See also Devin Dwyer, "Immigration: Korean Family Crosses U.S.-Canadian Border to Skirt Visa Backlog," July 30, 2010, ABCNews.com: http://abcnews.go.com/Politics/immigration-illegal-immigrant-us-olympian-korean-teens-story/story?id=10945321&page=1, accessed September 3, 2010.

13. Guillermina Jasso and Mark R. Rosenzweig, "Family Reunification and the Immigration Multiplier: U.S. Immigration Law, Origin-Country Conditions, and the Reproduction of Immigrants," *Demography* 23 (1986): 291–311.

14. Santiagos Creuheras, "The View from New York," *ReVista: Harvard Review of Latin America*, Fall 2001: http://www.drclas.harvard.edu/revista/articles/view/85.

15. "Indra Nooyi Purchases Rs.7 cr Flat at Poes Garden!" *OneIndia*, October 20, 2007.

16. "Mexicans in the U.S. Send Billions Home—And It All Comes Back," *Rocky Mountain News* (February 19, 2005).

17. Hayslip, *When Heaven and Earth Changed Places*, xv.

18. http://grunt.space.swri.edu/eastwest.htm, accessed January 23, 2009.

19. Jonathan Duffy, "Rich Friend in America," *BBC News Online*, September 26, 2001: http://news.bbc.co.uk/2/hi/americas/1563119.stm, accessed October 23, 2010.

20. Tim Weiner, "Gen. Vang Pao's Last War," *New York Times Magazine*, May 11, 2008.

21. George W. Bush, "Address to a Joint Session of Congress Following 9/11 Attacks," http://www.americanrhetoric.com/speeches/gwbush911jointsessionspeech.htm.

22. Andrea Elliott, "A Call to Jihad Answered in America," *New York Times*, July 11, 2009.

23. Susan F. Martin, *Nation of Immigrants* (Cambridge: Cambridge University Press, 2011).

24. Linna E. Bresett, "Mexicans in the United States: A Report of a Brief Survey," *National Catholic Welfare Conference* (Washington, DC: National Catholic Welfare Conference, 1929), 7.

25. http://abcnews.go.com/Politics/immigration-illegal-immigrant-us-olympian-korean-teens-story/story?id=10945321&page=1, posted on August 1, 2010.

26. *New York Times*, September 9, 1985, A15.

27. Anonymous phone caller, Spring 2007, Immigration History Research Center.

28. Robert Pear, "Immigration and the Randomness of Ethnic Mix," *New York Times*, October 2, 1984, A28.

29. Santoli, *New Americans*, 289–90.

30. Nathan Glazer, *We Are All Multiculturalists Now* (Cambridge, MA: Harvard University Press, 1997).

31. 93rd Congress, 1st session, *Congressional Record* 119 (May 8, 1973), 14610.

32. Linda Mathews, "'Green Card' Farm Labor Use Upheld," *Los Angeles Times*, November 26, 1974, A1.

33. David Binder, "Ford Asks Nation to Open Its Doors to the Refugees," *New York Times*, May 7, 1975, 8.

34. Quoted in Carl J. Bon Tempo, *Americans at the Gate: The United States and Refugees during the Cold War*, 194.

35. George de Lama, "Florida Bracing for New Wave of Cuban Immigrants," *Chicago Tribune*, April 14, 1985, 1.

36. Quoted in William J. Chambliss and Marjorie Sue Zatz, eds., *Making Law: The State, the Law, and Structural Contradictions* (Bloomington: Indiana University Press, 1992), 248.

37. "Statement on Signing the Immigration Reform and Control Act of 1986, November 6, 1986," http://www.reagan.utexas.edu/archives/speeches/1986/110686b.htm.

38. The phrase had been used for quite a number of years: see United States Congress, Joint Committee, *Joint Economic Report* (Washington, DC: Government Printing Office, 1949), 47.

39. Quoting Edward Leamer of UCLA, Eckes, *Opening America's Markets*, 286.

40. Quoted in Santoli, *New Americans*, 259, 261.

41. Ibid., 259.

42. Eric Schmitt, "Immigration Bill Debate, Divisions and Odd Alliances; Debate Over Immigration Bill Yields Deep Political Division and Unusual Alliances," *New York Times*, February 26, 1996, A1.

43. Sam Howe Verhovek, "A 2000 Mile Fence? First Get Estimates," *New York Times*, March 3, 1996.

44. Brian Bennett, "GOP Senators Signal Immigration Showdown," *Los Angeles Times*, October 29, 2010.

45. Stephen Castles and Mark J. Miller, *The Age of Migration: International Population Movements in the Modern World*, 4th ed. (New York: Guilford Press, 2009).

46. Mae Ngai, *Impossible Subjects: Illegal Aliens and the Making of Modern America* (Princeton, NJ: Princeton University Press, 2003), 249.

47. Anthony H. Richmond, *Global Apartheid: Refugees, Racism, and the New World Order* (Toronto: Oxford University Press, 1994).

48. "The Universal Declaration of Human Rights," http://www.un.org/Overview/rights.html.

49. "Convention and Protocol Relating to the Status of Refugees," http://www.unhcr.org/3b66c2aa10.html.

INDEX